The Hunger Winter

Occupied Holland 1944–1945

Henri A. van der Zee

University of Nebraska Press
Lincoln and London

Library of Congress Cataloging-in-Publication Data
Van der Zee, Henri A. (Henri Antony), 1934–
The hunger winter: occupied Holland 1944–1945 / Henri A. van der
Zee.
p. cm.
Reprint. Originally published: London: J. Norman & Hobhouse, 1982.
Includes bibliographical references and index.
ISBN 0-8032-9618-5 (pbk.: alk. paper)
1. Netherlands—History—German occupation, 1940–1945. 2. Food
supply—Netherlands—History—20th century. 3. Famines—Nether-
lands—History—20th century. I. Title.
D802.N4V28   1998
949.207′1—dc21
98-33495   CIP

Reprinted from the original 1982 edition by Jill Norman & Hobhouse,
London.

Contents

CONTENTS

List of Illustrations

b While wood was so precious, Dutch housewives struggled with their 'miracle stoves'.

14 *a* Two slices of bread, two potatoes and half a sugarbeet: a day's ration for one person.

    b When the Germans at last capitulated, Allied rescue missions often found the most appalling situations.

15 *a* and *b* Water, the eternal enemy and friend of the Dutch, made the ordeal even worse for many of them.

16 *a* When, in March 1945, Queen Wilhelmina returned for a visit, everybody knew that the end of the horror was near.

    b After five years of oppression and destruction, the Germans capitulated and the time for celebration had come.

The illustrations for this book have been gathered from many sources, principally from private individuals. The author and publisher are grateful to everyone who has helped by supplying prints or negatives.

For Barbara, Bibi and Ninka

North

Sea

Delfzyl

Leeuwarden ● Groningen

Texel

Den Helder

Westerbork
concentration
● camp

*Wieringermeer
polder*

Aikmaar

*(Zuyder
Zee)*
Ijsselmeer

Zwolle

Haarlem ● Amsterdam

Enschede

Putten

Deventer

Hilversum

Apeldoorn
Zütphen

● Amersfoort

The Hague
('s Gravenhage)

Hook of Holland

Utrecht

Arnhem

Rotterdam

R. Waal

Dordrecht

Nymegen

Heusden
Den Bosch

Tilburg

Middelburg

Flushing (Vlissingen)

Eindhoven

R. Maas

R. Rhine

Antwerp

Roermond

B E L G I U M

R. Scheldt

Cologne

| 0 | 10 | | 50 miles |
| 0 | 20 | | 80 kms |

Maastricht

G

E R M A N Y

10

THE NETHERLANDS 1944-5

The Netherlands, no larger than 12,900 square miles, was a divided country during the Hunger Winter. After the Allies lost the Battle of Arnhem in September 1944, they were compelled to leave the provinces north of the great Rhine and Waal rivers in the hands of the Germans. South of these rivers, however, fierce fighting raged on for months until this part of the country was liberated.

North of the rivers, meanwhile, $4\frac{1}{2}$ million Dutch people had to live through one of the worst winters in their history. In despairing impatience they waited for their liberators. But it was not until April 1945 that the Allied armies resumed their advance through the Netherlands, and then with amazing speed they liberated the northern and eastern parts before coming to a halt near Amersfoort.

While hunger claimed more victims every day, negotiations for relief supplies were opened between the Allies and the Nazis. The unexpected capitulation of the Germans, however, brought them to a halt on 5 May 1945. The densely populated western zone was now also freed – and none too soon. More than 18,000 people had died of starvation, and foodstocks had dwindled to zero.

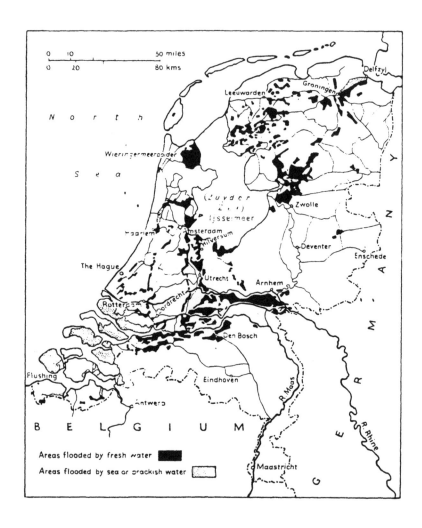

The Flooding of the Netherlands

For the Dutch people, locked up behind their dykes, flooding was their greatest dread during the Hunger Winter, together with lack of food and heating. A quarter of the Netherlands lies below sea-level, and only a complex system of dykes, canals, sluices and pumping-stations keeps the country dry.

Until the invasion of Normandy on 6 June 1944, the Germans had been expecting an Allied landing on the Dutch beaches. In the hope of halting the invaders, huge areas of western Holland had been flooded by the Nazis, and more inundations had been prepared by mining dykes and pumps. During the winter of 1944–5, the emphasis switched to defence against an Allied attack from the south-east, and it was now the turn of Holland's traditional water-lines, running through the provinces of Utrecht and Gelderland, to be destroyed.

This created serious problems not merely for the Dutch, but also for the occupying German forces, who found the defence works designed by their experts becoming ditches as soon as the water rose in rivers and canals. The Germans went ahead with their policy of inundation none the less, and the Dutch feared that Hitler's scorched-earth policy would bring about the total destruction of their canal system. When the German capitulation came it was only just in time. Without the canals, transport would have been impossible, and the number of victims of the Hunger Winter considerably higher.

Acknowledgements

The author gratefully acknowledges the assistance and encouragement he has received during the writing of this book.

In the first place I would like to thank my wife Barbara, whose influence – apart from her corrections – has been immense and whose constant love, patience and interest have been a main source of inspiration.

The assistance given to me by my parents, my two brothers and other members of the family, either in the shape of their memories or in more practical terms, has been of immense importance to the character of the book.

I would also like to express my gratitude to Alan Williams in New York, who gave the initial push, to Caroline Hobhouse in London, who maintained an encouraging enthusiasm, and to Jackie Baldick, my former agent, for her keen interest.

It would never have been possible to write this book without the invaluable help of Eduard Groeneveld and his wife Emmy, two loyal and charming friends at the State Institute of War Documentation in Amsterdam. They not only gave me all the help I needed for my research, but they were also kind enough to read and check the manuscript. My gratitude goes, of course, also to Dr Louis de Jong, until recently head of the Institute, and to Mr J. Zwaan, in charge of the picture archives. For my research in London I received important help from the ever-patient Mr I. A. Peterson. Mr Barry Gregory gave me useful advice on Operation Market Garden and the Battle of the Scheldt.

Finally, I am very grateful to my editor and colleagues of *De Telegraaf* in Amsterdam, whose understanding and indulgence during the research for, and the writing of, this book are highly appreciated.

Preface

AN AMERICAN friend, reading *A Sweet and Alien Land*, a book about Dutch New York which my wife and I published some years ago, was fascinated by a paragraph about Tulip Mania, the speculative craze that hit the Netherlands in the seventeenth century and ended in ruin for many people. I told him that the Dutch had other, worse, memories of tulip bulbs, having had to eat them to save themselves from starvation at the end of the Second World War. His reaction was one of horror and surprise, and it dawned on me that the story of Nazi-occupied Holland is almost unknown, even though, according to one American writer, of all Western democracies the Netherlands had suffered the hardest fate.

The tragedy of the hundred thousand Jews deported to Hitler's extermination-camps is well known, through Anne Frank's haunting Diary. Some have even heard of Dutch Resistance against the Nazis, and the name of Arnhem will live for ever because of the ill-fated battle. *But what happened to the Dutch after the battle was lost?*

While the war outside the Occupied Netherlands raged on, the Dutch people north of the Rhine literally starved to death, almost unnoticed by the rest of the world. They were completely cut off, and had to live through a winter that with all justification has come to be known as 'De Hongerwinter', the Hunger Winter.

Like thousands of others, I ate sugarbeets and dried tulip-bulbs; I had hardly any clothes and no shoes at all; I saw people being dragged away or hiding in fear; and I witnessed cruelty and violence at their worst. I also witnessed friendship and sacrifice at their best, and the experience gave me a perspective on life which has influenced me ever since. I was only ten years old in the autumn of 1944 but, even so, my memories are very vivid and what I had forgotten came back to me as I talked with my parents and my brother, while research in various archives and libraries provided the background information. Although my life was never in danger and although as a child my circumstances were considerably better than those of the adults – the hunted men and slaving women – writing this book has sometimes been a painful experience.

The Hunger Winter is now part of history and I would like to make it clear that I certainly have not written this book to stir up ill-feeling or old hatreds. I feel strongly, however, that we should never forget the consequences of a detestable system and an inhuman regime.

To a younger generation which was probably bored and puzzled by the stories of their parents, this book will act as proof that it all really happened. The extracts from diaries and memoirs may sound melodramatic to them, even unreal and certainly too idealistic as far as subsequent events were concerned. This was, however, the way people felt and thought during those five years of Occupation and oppression, and in that unforgettable, long, winter of 1944–5. They wrote it down in all sincerity, and I hope that this book, written thirty-five years later, will reflect their feelings, their hopes and especially their will to survive in honour.

H.A.v.d.Z.

CHAPTER ONE

Mad Tuesday

IN THE late summer of 1944, Hilversum, with its 80,000 inhabitants, was a quiet and charming garden-town, with tree-lined lanes and colourful gardens, surrounded by woods and meadows. A large part of the population commuted daily by train to Amsterdam, twenty-three kilometres away, but the place had its own claims to fame: the Hilversum radio station, the national and international voice of the Netherlands, and its Raadhuis (Town Hall), built in the early thirties by the architect William M. Dudok and featured in every book about modern architecture.

Four and a half years of German occupation, however, had left their mark. Radio Hilversum had become the unreliable and much-mocked mouthpiece of the Nazis, and the tower of the yellow-brick Raadhuis was shrouded by a green camouflage net. The Germans had feared that the bright construction would become a landmark for Allied bombers, thus endangering the nearby headquarters of the Wehrmacht, but their barbaric plan to paint the whole Raadhuis green had been given up after a furious protest by the Hilversum civic authorities.

In the town itself, many of the handsome school buildings had been requisitioned by German troops, and the only traffic now consisted of German cars and trucks, often, as petrol was very scarce, propelled by enormous gas-balloons on their roofs or by odd-looking stoves on wheels. The main shopping-streets were quiet, the shops almost empty and their windows filled with the empty wrappings of goods that had not been available for years. Only the bakers, butchers and greengrocers showed signs of activity – if only the long queues of silent people waiting for their rations.

On Monday, 4 September, the mood changed. People seemed less resigned and were more talkative. There was an air of excitement. According to the rumours – during the war the most important and often the most reliable source of news – the Allied armies, racing through Belgium after their astounding advance in France, were approaching the Dutch border. Brussels had been liberated the day before and now freedom – for the Netherlanders, too – was at hand.

The rumours became stronger during the day, and over dinner that evening in 7 Potgieterlaan, my parents' house in Hilversum, the only topic of conversation was how long it would take the Allies to reach us. Even the food – a mash of potatoes and other vegetables, without fat or meat – could not distract us, and that in itself was significant. Rations in September were still reasonable – 1500 calories a day – but they were never enough to allay that nagging feeling of hunger, and eating had therefore become the high point of the day.

The meal was completely forgotten when a neighbour rushed in. His two grown-up sons, who had spent most of the last few years hiding in an attic room to avoid deportation to labour-camps in Germany, had constructed their own radio set after all wirelesses had been confiscated, and Radio Oranje – the voice of the Free Dutch in London and named after the Dutch royal family, the House of Orange – had confirmed the rumours. The end was really in sight. Professor Pieter Sjoerds Gerbrandy, Prime Minister of the Dutch Government-in-Exile, had said so himself. 'Now that the Allied armies have crossed the Dutch border in their irresistible advance, I wish to give a warm welcome to our Allies on our native soil. . . . The hour of liberation has come.' For Gerbrandy, the leader of the Dutch in exile, it was a thrilling moment. He looked around the small studio, lent by the BBC to Radio Oranje, where the journalist Henk J. van den Broek, in Holland better known under his *nom de guerre*, 'The Rotterdammer', still looked incredulous.

A few hours before the broadcast at 8.15 p.m., Van den Broek had written the text for the Prime Minister, beginning: 'Now that the Allied armies are approaching the Dutch border. . . .' But with a determined gesture Gerbrandy had changed that to 'have crossed the Dutch border'. Noticing the surprised look on the broadcaster's face, he had asked defiantly, 'But didn't you know?' and he had told him that not only the Dutch Information Service, but the British, too, had received information that the Allied troops had reached Breda, fifty kilometres from Antwerp.

Gerbrandy's announcement was the climax to a series of amazing events, which started with the fall of Paris on 22 August. The Allied soldiers – the 21st Army Group under General Montgomery – had taken no time off to celebrate this victory, but had stormed on, steamrollering the German troops in front of them. On 1 September – 'Monty' was made a field-marshal on that day – they had liberated north-western France; on 3 September they appeared unexpectedly in Brussels; and on 4 September they took Antwerp without meeting any resistance. The result of this fast progress was not only panic amongst the Germans, but also chaos in the Allied information services. Nobody at the ever-changing front had the time to tell London exactly what the troops were up to, and official bulletins were often twenty-four hours behind the facts.

This was most obvious on Sunday, 3 September, when someone in London, 'who ought to know', told everybody that Allied units had crossed the Belgian–Dutch border near Maastricht. 'We realised that Radio Oranje had to prepare the Dutch for the arrival of their liberators,' Van den Broek wrote, and plans were made to start that evening. But another important event intervened.

Queen Wilhelmina, who three days earlier had celebrated her sixty-fourth birthday – her fifth in exile – had won an important battle of her own and wished to make it known to her people in Occupied Holland. Prince Bernhard, married to her daughter, Princess Juliana, since 1937, had been appointed Commander of the joint Dutch Resistance movement, from now on known as the Binnenlandse Strijdkrachten (BS) or the Forces of the Interior.

During all her years of exile the Dutch Queen, once pretty, but now heavy-set and severe, had followed the actions of her brave Resistance fighters with passion or – as she wrote more majestically in her memoirs, *Lonely but not Alone* – with 'interest and appreciation'. Together with her Ministers she had considered how to make those Dutchmen of better use to the Allied cause, and one evening at the end of August she had found the solution. 'I saw in the newspapers that the Maquis [the French Resistance] had been incorporated in the Allied Forces. . . . They were given the status of combatants under their own Commander, General Koenig. I realised at once that a similar arrangement would have to be made for our own Forces of the Interior.' She telephoned

Gerbrandy at once, suggesting at the same time that her son-in-law, Prince Bernhard, be made the Commander. 'Mr Gerbrandy fell in with my suggestions and spoke to the Allied Commander.'

It was not as simple as that. General Dwight D. Eisenhower at SHAEF, the Supreme Headquarters, Allied Expeditionary Force, received the Queen's suggestion with very little enthusiasm. Experience in some countries had shown that local Resistance movements often went into action prematurely – with disastrous results. It was Prince Bernhard who convinced the Supreme Command that the Dutch were different, and that a close co-operation of the different Resistance organisations under one commander would eliminate any risk of a coup after the war – if it existed at all.

On 31 August, the Queen's birthday, the Dutch Forces of the Interior were recognised by the Allies and Wilhelmina wrote elatedly and over-optimistically: 'It was a great day for us in London. . . . Our boys would be no longer shot by the enemy as *franc-tireurs*. The enemy was obliged to treat them as prisoners of war.'

The Prince was in his office in Stratton House, on the corner of Piccadilly, when his mother-in-law rang him with the news that Eisenhower had supported his appointment as Commander of the BS. 'I shall not easily forget the moment when I telephoned Bernhard about this and immediately received his surprised and enthusiastic consent,' the Queen recorded in her memoirs. 'Bernhard had at last found a task that suited his status and capacities; a fine and honourable assignment, to liberate the Fatherland as the Commander of our boys, side by side with our Allies.'

It was for the announcement of these latest developments that on Sunday, 3 September, the programme schedule of Radio Oranje was changed. The broadcast by the Dutch radio in London lasted only fourteen and a half minutes every night, which were that evening amply filled with the news of Bernhard's appointment, a speech by the Prince in which he made a personal appeal to his 'soldiers' to restrain themselves from premature action, and a stern warning by the Supreme Command not to start a general rising, even if the hour of liberation was near.

When, after this sensational broadcast, Prime Minister Gerbrandy added his own news of troops across the border the following evening, everything seemed possible. Fifteen minutes before midnight the Dutch section of the BBC revealed that Breda was liberated and a British general stated openly on the radio that German resistance was rapidly collapsing. It was a fact that every Dutchman living near the Belgian border could confirm. The withdrawal of the German troops might at first have been organised in a disciplined way, but on 4 September it turned into a rout.

'It was a flight of dirty, exhausted, silent scarecrows on foot and of sleepy men in trucks,' wrote an eyewitness. 'Hitler's drilled divisions had changed into a miserable horde ... frightened, hunted men.' They accepted their defeat without question, like the German sergeant who told the delighted onlookers near Breda to come back next day – 'It will be much better; the Tommies will be here,' he shouted.

When the Dutch went to bed that Monday evening, they indeed expected to see the British next day. The London papers on Tuesday morning were equally convinced and announced in banner headlines that Breda had been freed. In Holland the people went much farther – Dordrecht had fallen and troops were on their way to Rotterdam. With arms full of flowers thousands rushed to the city's approaches, as in Amsterdam and The Hague, and while the leaders of the Resistance prepared themselves for the take-over of power from the German authorities everybody waited impatiently for the liberators. The weather was ideal, that Tuesday: after days of rain and storm the sun was shining at last.

In some places the population decided it was the moment for more positive action. A Resistance group in Rotterdam took possession of a school, in Axel German soldiers surrendered to Dutch policemen, and in Naarden the Nazi mayor handed his pistol to his secretary. One underground newspaper in Leiden printed 10,000 'Liberation specials' and another magazine even published the names of its contributors (the editor then failed to distribute).

Nobody came, however, and as on that evening of 5 September the crowds who had thronged the streets drifted home a sense of reality returned. Even Radio Oranje was more cautious in its evening broadcast and spoke of 'no further official reports about the advance in the Netherlands'. Most Dutch people also knew better by then. One telephone call to Breda had been sufficient to discover that the town was still in German hands, not to mention Dordrecht and Rotterdam.

That London had blundered so seriously was not surprising. The advance of the Allies had been so rapidly and so insufficiently monitored, and the atmosphere in London so charged with wishful thinking, that almost everybody was fooled. It was, as someone observed, a case of 'remarkable self-intoxication'. In the end, the British troops seen in Breda turned out to be a patrol that had crossed the Belgian–Dutch border by accident. A Dutch agent had met them and had reported this to London. 'The Dutch Information Service supposed that the British censor would suppress the item if it was not true,' Louis de Jong, until recently Head of the Dutch State Institute of War Documentation, but then working for Radio Oranje, wrote, 'and the British from their side believed that the Dutch Government would never make such an important statement if the news did not come from a reliable source.' The British let it slip through after they had received the same information – from the same source.

On Wednesday, 6 September, the Dutch woke up with a hangover. The Liberation still seemed far away, and the only joy they found was in the reaction of those compatriots who had sided with the Nazi tyranny during the Occupation. Seeing many of their German protectors flee in fear and panic, they felt that for them, too, the time had come to look for safer places, far away from the approaching Allies and even farther away from the dreaded revenge of the Dutch. In one day the whole Dutch Nazi movement, the National-Socialistische Beweging or NSB evaporated. On the evening of 4 September the party leader Anton Mussert, somewhat less arrogant than usual, presided over a meeting with his most important functionaries in the NSB headquarters on the Maliebaan in Utrecht. Two months earlier – after D-Day – Mussert had sworn never to budge and had refused to prepare a contingency evacuation scheme for the wives and children of his members. The sudden Allied progress, however, had made him change his mind, and in reasonable calm the men discussed on 4 September the possibility of transporting women and children to Germany.

The false news of the liberation of Breda that brought so much joy to most Dutch people had created an atmosphere of panic on the Maliebaan. Desperately, the NSB leaders searched for a speedy solution, and it was Henk Feldmeijer, leader of the Dutch SS and a rival of the 'bourgeois' Mussert, who brought it. Like a *deus ex machina* he appeared at the meeting with an offer from the Germans of twenty-five trains for women and children. There was one condition, he told Mussert: the men had to stay and join the Landwacht, the Nazi Home Guard. Mussert had no choice but to swallow this bitter pill from his SS enemy.

Tuesday, 5 September, the 'day of shame' for the Dutch Nazis, has gone down in Dutch history as 'Mad Tuesday'. That day, in the grip of mass hysteria, thousands of NSB members fled their homes, leaving everything behind. Their leaders, with the exception of Mussert, were the first to go; NSB mayors left their posts; Nazi officials deserted their desks without even clearing them; youth leaders forgot their responsibilities; and even the most fanatical idealists, who had promised to fight to the last man, now hurried to the north-east. The ignominious flight was so massive, the NSB members lost their heads so completely, that the whole movement disintegrated for ever.

'How miserably they behave,' a Dutchman wrote in his diary. 'In all those years they have asked for the responsibility and now they run away. This fear-psychosis and flight by people who so often said they were ready to die for their ideals is – to say the least – bizarre.'

Mussert tried later to blame the fleeing German civilians for the panic amongst his followers, and it was partly true. Dr Arthur Seyss-Inquart, the ruthless Reichskommissar, the Nazi State Commissioner or Governor of the Netherlands, had set the example by sending his wife Gertrud away on 3 September, one day before he ordered the state of emergency in Holland, which made fleeing – 'also from threatened territory' – an offence. Gertrud Seyss-Inquart left The Hague with five suitcases for Salzburg in Austria, never to return. Other Germans soon followed, taking with them whatever they could lay their hands on. That was evident in front of the Amsterdam Central Station where the loot of the fugitives was piled – 'all sorts of things: furniture, desks, typewriters, stoves, even chicken-coops with or without chickens'.

The exodus continued for many days, ending temporarily at Westerbork, the notorious concentration-camp near Assen, from where almost all of Holland's 140,000 Jews had been taken to their certain death in German camps. The 850 Jews still waiting there for their final transport were charged with the administration – and delousing – of their former persecutors, before the Germans travelled on. 'It was great to have witnessed that spectacle,' one of the Jews remarked later with commendable reserve.

It was amazing and unique in the Liberation of Europe that in those first September days, fraught with tensions and disillusions, no incidents took place between the Dutch people and the NSB. The Roman Catholic bishops, who had asked their flocks to abstain from violence against the Nazis, warning that 'hate and revenge should never be the motive of human action', had emphasised the right of asylum in the churches. But nobody needed it.

The ordinary people, or 'good Dutch' as they were known, had in the meantime completely woken up to reality. 'Everything has been a dream,' one of them wrote on 6 September. And a diligent diarist, Dr H. Mees, a retired doctor in Rotterdam, added: 'We have cheered too early. The optimism has gone.' Unlike so many other Dutch, he at least understood the reason for the sudden halt of the Allied armies. 'They seem to be unable to progress farther, as they have in fact only one good port (Cherbourg) where they have to bring in all their men and military supplies.'

Most Dutchmen, however, felt deserted and let down, and Prince Bernhard, who in his new role of Commander of the Dutch Forces of the Interior had flown to Brussels on 5 September, sympathised with them. He paid a hurried visit to Montgomery and asked him for further action now that the Germans were on the run. The Field-Marshal, who had no great sympathy for the somewhat flippant Dutch Prince, answered curtly that he had no supplies and that it was too risky to push ahead. With an abrupt gesture he brushed aside reports from the Dutch Resistance about the weakness of the Germans, and there was little Bernhard could do. He left Montgomery dejected, convinced that the dour Englishman was over-cautious. 'The Germans were one hundred per cent demoralised,' he said later. In his opinion, Monty would have been able to clean up Holland in a couple of days.

Many German generals agreed with the Prince. One wrote in his memoirs that 'the possibility of ending the war several months earlier was not exploited by the Allied Command'. And another stated that in September 1944 the German front 'was so full of gaps that it didn't deserve its name'. The problem of supply, however, was not invented by Montgomery. After the race through France and Belgium, the troops, needing 18,000 tons of supplies daily, had outrun the rate at which railway and road transport could be developed. Eisenhower had not helped by ordering Monty's American 'rivals' – Patton's Third Army – to start moving again, in order to return to the original plan of a broader attack on Germany. This put an even greater strain on the chains of supply.

Although Eisenhower was convinced that the Allied armies could advance at will – 'The defeat of the German armies is complete,' he said in a memorandum of 5 September – he also felt that the British field-marshal was asking too much when he proposed to try to reach Berlin in 'one powerful and full-blooded thrust'. And he wrote to him: 'I do not agree that it should be initiated at the moment to the exclusion of all other manoeuvres.' The stubborn Englishman did not admit defeat so easily, and the Supreme Commander flew to Brussels on 10 September to try to settle the conflict.

One day later the Dutch received some genuine good news at last: the first Allied troops had crossed the border of the Netherlands at Visé and three days later they liberated Maastricht, the capital of the province of Limburg. The Germans announced that they had 'sacrificed the city for tactical reasons'.

In Hilversum on the evening of 15 September we listened with new hope – and envy – to the reports from free Maastricht broadcast over Radio Oranje by war correspondent Robert Kiek. 'Maastricht is a sea of orange,' he shouted excitedly. 'When a Dutchman celebrates something, he doesn't only wave the red, white and blue flag, but he wears orange, the colour of our royal family, and yesterday the whole town of Maastricht was covered with that colour. . . . We will never forget it. . . . The first Dutch city where we can again say what we think.'

Queen Wilhelmina learned the news while talking to some refugees from Limburg and felt 'an immense joy', shared with her daughter, Princess Juliana, who had come over from Canada, expecting the Liberation any moment. Prince Bernhard flew at once in his two-seater aeroplane to Maastricht, where an

25

enthusiastic welcome awaited him.

In the meantime Montgomery had seemingly lost his struggle with Eisenhower: the broad-front policy would be maintained, but he had achieved one thing that might have changed our fate within days. Rumours, of course, reached even Occupied Holland, and one Dutchman recorded: 'The Huns have plans to make Holland a fortress for the defence of north-west Germany and to make a stand behind the rivers [Rhine, Waal and Maas]. But Montgomery will give them a lesson.' And the confirmation that something was about to happen came from reporter Robert Kiek. On Saturday, 16 September, he warned us over Radio Oranje, now operative from Brussels, 'I can assure you that great events are at hand . . . a great battle is soon to be expected.'

CHAPTER TWO

Shattered Hopes

SUNDAY, 17 September 1944. A bright sun was shining over the gentle hills of the Veluwe forests, reflected in the silvery stream of the Rhine. On the north bank stood the spa-like town of Arnhem with a population of about a hundred thousand people, described in an English guidebook as 'a pleasant old-world city . . . the favourite residence of retired East-India merchants'. It was a quiet summer day with the smell of approaching autumn. The Rhine flowed with a fast current under the two bridges that spanned its 150 yards, and in the town most families were ready for Sunday lunch.

Suddenly the sky was filled with the ear-splitting sound of a fleet of aeroplanes, and thousands of men tumbled into the air like autumn leaves, to descend slowly under their parachutes to the heathland and browning woods around Arnhem. The 'great battle' which Radio Oranje had predicted the night before was about to start.

'I can feel it, freedom is near, no, freedom is here,' an excited Dutch girl wrote, watching the landing, and that same afternoon the Germans announced that Allied troops had landed not only at Arnhem, but also north of Eindhoven and at Nijmegen.

On 10 September, Montgomery had been able to persuade the Supreme Commander to launch a big offensive through Germany's industrial heart, the Ruhr, towards Berlin. Eisenhower's American commanders had protested, preferring to cross the Rhine near Frankfurt and to invade Germany from the south-west, but Ike had explained to them that Monty's left wing had to take precedence in order to secure adequate deep-water harbours (Antwerp or Rotterdam) and to clean out the bases of Hitler's newest weapons, the V1 and V2, which were ravaging London. He had therefore given Montgomery sufficient British and American airborne troops to lay a carpet from Eindhoven to Arnhem, over which the British Second Army could march across the three formidable obstacles, the rivers Maas, Waal and Rhine.

The whole operation, christened 'Market Garden', was, as one American general described it, the 'Sunday punch', which would end the war in 1944. Eisenhower was less optimistic and saw it as an effort to get across the rivers 'on the cheap'.

On the morning of Sunday, 17 September, Queen Wilhelmina and Princess Juliana looked up with joy to the sky from their garden at Stubbings. 'A large American air-fleet, part of which had taken off from the airfield near my house, was on its way to our Fatherland with its supplies and paratroops,' the Queen wrote. What she saw was but a small part of the enormous fleet of 3500 planes and gliders with their tugs which took off that morning, carrying at least 7000 men.

At the other side of the North Sea the spectacle was even more impressive. Like an enormous cloud the planes swept over the Low Countries to drop their loads over their different targets. 'Suddenly the sky was littered with thousands and thousands of parachutes in many colours: red, green and cream,' an eyewitness in Wageningen remembered. 'The men jumped with great speed, as if they had been swept out with a broom. . . . Overwhelmed by this great sight I raised my arms and cheered the soldiers.'

A schoolteacher, Hendrika van der Vlist, watched the same scene from Oosterbeek, but the reaction of the German soldiers who were billeted in her father's house gave her even more pleasure. 'Where are those calm soldiers who just now were smoking and chatting in the corridor?' she mocked. 'Suddenly they were running like mad. Up the stairs and down again with the baggage. It didn't take much time before the house was empty, the doors wide open. The Germans had fled.'

While the airborne landings were still going on, Gerbrandy returned to London from a weekend in the country to find in Brown's Hotel, where he was staying, the head of the Dutch Information Service, Mr C. L. W. Fock, waiting for him. With him Fock had a request from SHAEF to order the Dutch railways to halt all services. It was part of Montgomery's strategy to cut off the Germans in western Holland and to stop the transport of the dreaded V-weapons to the Dutch coast. Gerbrandy told Fock to go at once to Epsom, where the Dutch Minister of War, O. C. A. van Lidth de Jeude, was spending the weekend, and to show him the Allied request.

Van Lidth had been expecting the message since the beginning of September but hesitated, and only after the BBC news at three o'clock had confirmed the news of the landings at Arnhem did he begin to dictate a proclamation. Mr Fock returned to London only fifteen minutes before the broadcast, but after a mad race through the city he arrived at the studio just in time to announce the air-strike.

'Here is an important message from the Dutch Government,' the Radio Oranje newsreader, the well-known Dutch author A. den Doolaard, began. 'On account of a request received from Holland, and after consultation with the Supreme Command . . . the Government is of the opinion that the moment has come to give instructions for a railway strike, in order to hinder enemy transport and troop concentrations.' It was the most important act of defiance to the Nazis the Dutch were ever asked to make. More than 30,000 railway workers had to 'dive' or go into hiding, all connections in the country would be broken and not only enemy transport, but also the supply of food and coal to the crowded cities in the west and easy communication between the Resistance groups would stop.

Up till then the role of the Dutch railways had been not very impressive and certainly far from glorious. In the summer of 1940 the management had agreed with the Nazi invaders that, provided they fulfilled all German transport orders, they would continue to run their own business. Over the years, Dutch trains carried more than half a million compatriots to Germany for forced labour, more than 120,000 Jews to their extermination-camps, and some tens of thousands of political prisoners or prisoners of war to concentration-camps.

The Resistance had tried to sabotage the lines, but they were always rapidly repaired. The explosions, however, had been a warning for the management, who began to mend their fences in 1943. The first hesitant contacts were made with the Underground, and D-Day was the final push. In spite of the fact that he saw the Resistance as a 'sort of labyrinth', Dr W. Hupkes, the leading figure in the management, made it known that his men would stop working when and if 'the other side' gave the signal.

29

Railway traffic in July and August had already become very difficult. Constant air-raids by the Allies on trains and stations had made travelling a hazard. Twice in those months I had to run for my life. The first time was when, during a visit to my grandmother in Amersfoort, British planes began to drop bombs on the station there, with much noise and little effect; the second time when a plane strafed a moving train. And it was not surprising that most train drivers were discontented and 'dived', so that the Germans had to rely for most of their transport on the 5000 men they had brought in from Germany.

The situation had become unreal, and Dr Hupkes, normally a calm and quiet man, began to ask London with increasing urgency what he should do. The only advice he got was to listen to Radio Oranje, and when the message to strike came on 17 September he was as much taken by surprise as the rest of the Dutch people.

So was the Cabinet in London. Gerbrandy had only consulted his Minister of War, and another Minister protested that the decision to strike was dictated by the Allies. Gerbrandy maintained that there had been no question of 'orders' and that the strike had been decided in mutual agreement with the Allies. He believed, anyhow, that it would only be a question of a few weeks, and he remarked happily to a weary Louis de Jong of Radio Oranje: 'Don't worry. On Saturday we shall be in Amsterdam.' The radio station, in the same state of mind, assured the Dutch that evening that the Government 'intends to return as soon as possible'.

The result of the order to strike was astonishing. A Dutchman wrote in his diary: 'It has been followed by everybody from top to bottom.' He was exaggerating, but not by much. In the end only 1500 to 2000, out of the railway workforce of 30,000, disobeyed London.

At first German reaction to the strike was confused. The Commander of the Wehrmacht, Christiansen, believed that the action would have no influence at all on Germany's military activities, and the SS leader in Holland, Hanns Albin Rauter, was convinced that the strike would in the end only harm the Resistance in their communications and arms transports. But State Commissioner Seyss-Inquart felt it as a heavy blow to Nazi prestige. On 18

September a message was sent to all the papers, with the 'request' to print an editorial in which the railwaymen were criticised for their 'serious and dangerous game', which could only lead to an increasing food shortage. 'They suppose very naïvely that Holland's problems have been solved but, in the interest of us all, we hope that they'll wake up and realise that they in fact are doing everything to bring a terrible disaster on their families and compatriots.'

To Seyss-Inquart's fury hardly any of the editors, normally so co-operative, felt sufficiently 'inspired' by his message, and on 22 September he tried again. 'If the railwaymen don't return to work, a large part of the Dutch population is threatened with starvation,' ran a telex, this time more plainly. The State Commissioner even had the nerve to declare that the Dutch food authorities had given him this information, but when they hurriedly denied it most papers again kept silent. This silence had devastating results for one paper, the *Haagsche Courant*, whose presses were blown up by the Nazis on 29 September.

The patience of Seyss-Inquart began to run out. From higher German Army circles he was under pressure to put an end to the strike because it threatened the supply lines and the transport of the V-weapons. It shook Christiansen out of his apathy and nervously he asked Berlin for permission for the Wehrmacht to shoot any person 'who was not a terrorist . . . but whose passive attitude endangered fighting troops'. The advice he received was to have those people arrested by the German police. Only if circumstances made this impossible was the Army to be allowed to intervene.

In the next weeks the Germans made it all too obvious that their own food supplies were their only concern. They began to confiscate bicycles, cars and the stocks of wholesalers. At the same time they warned the Dutch food authorities not to count on them for any help as long as the strike lasted. 'On the contrary,' they told The Hague, 'we will hinder you as much as possible.'

By now the Dutch understood very well what was at stake. 'The strike will worsen the situation for our people,' a Dutchman recorded, 'but we are ready to accept that.' And it was this attitude that infuriated Seyss-Inquart most. At the end of September we, in Hilversum, saw a long convoy of German cars, preceded by a Mercedes with the well-known numberplate RK1 (Reichskom-

31

missar 1), race through the quiet lanes on its way to Army headquarters, where Seyss-Inquart conferred at length with Christiansen. It was a heated debate and the result was a plan to
evacuate the three big cities, Amsterdam, Rotterdam and The
Hague, or to isolate them completely. The only means of transport allowed were trains, which would force the Dutch to choose
between certain death or calling off the strike.

Returning to The Hague that same evening the State
Commissioner realised the impossibility of massive evacuation
and isolation, but refusing to end his 'biological war' he called for
the two most important food authorities in Holland, Dr H. M.
Hirschfeld, the Secretary-General for Trade and Agriculture,
and Dr S. L. Louwes, head of the Office for Food Supply in
Wartime. Both men, who in spite of much criticism from many
Dutch people had stayed at their posts hoping to prevent complete chaos and had had to compromise with the Germans at
times, refused point-blank this time to comply with Seyss-Inquart
and condemn the railway strike. He told them coldly that in that
case there was only one thing left to him: an embargo on all inland
shipping. For the Dutch, relying so much on their extensive
network of waterways and canals and on the barge transport
across the Ijsselmeer, it would mean famine.

That the Germans once more felt free to terrorise the Dutch was
not surprising. The Allies had lost the Battle of Arnhem and the
Rhine was again an impenetrable barrier behind which the Nazis
felt relatively safe.

Operation Market Garden had gone wrong from the start. The
narrow corridor from Eindhoven to Arnhem – correctly
described as 'Hell's Highway' – slowed down the advance of the
British tanks and infantry so much that it took them four days
longer than expected to reach the vicinity of Arnhem. Prince
Bernhard, helplessly following the operation from Château Wit-
touck near Mechelen – once the home of the painter Rubens –
had warned Montgomery that his heavy tanks and trucks would
get bogged down in Holland's soggy soil, but the Field-Marshal
had refused to listen – with costly results.

Another setback was the unexpected presence of two SS Panzer
divisions, hidden in the woods near Arnhem. One was able to bar
the approaches to the town, and only elements of 2nd Parachute
Battalion and other airborne units under Lieutenant-Colonel

John Frost reached the bridge over the Rhine. Isolated from headquarters, Frost and his 600 men had to give up after a brave fight of four days. The rest of the airborne troops, joining the army at Oosterbeek, had to follow suit and on 25 September, eight days after the triumphant landings, 2500 men of the 1st Airborne Division, under an umbrella of heavy artillery fire from newly conquered Nijmegen, were ferried back to the south bank. They left 7500 men behind – 1500 of them for ever.

'They were beaten in body, but not in spirit' – so ran an account of the famous battle in a British newspaper on Wednesday, 27 September. Some of them had wanted to go back. 'Give us a few tanks and we'll finish the job,' one of them had said, after escaping from what one London sergeant described as 'the kind of hell I never dreamed could exist on earth'. But return was impossible. Monty had lost a unique chance to end the war quickly and to liberate the Dutch. 'In years to come it will be a great thing for a man to be able to say: "I fought at Arnhem",' he wrote to them and they had certainly fought bravely, but their bravery could not make up for bad weather, poor preparation and inadequate leadership.

The optimism of the early September days disappeared completely, and Eisenhower, who on 5 September had spoken of the total disintegration of the Wehrmacht, swallowed these words on 29 September. He wrote to the Combined Chiefs of Staff in Washington that day that 'there are no signs of a collapse in morale or the will to defend Germany', adding that 'the enemy has now succeeded in establishing a relatively stable and cohesive front . . . except in the Low Countries'.

But, even if the front in the Low Countries did not strike the Allies as solid, for the Dutch north of the Rhine it seemed strong enough to close the road to freedom. A long and cold winter lay ahead of us, and Radio Oranje spelled it out: 'The weeks before us will be the most difficult in the existence of our nation.' And Dr Mees drew the right conclusion: 'Hitler will have another opportunity to take away our food stocks, to destroy our ports, inundate more land and build more defences.'

Worse even was the dread of hunger. The situation was bad enough that autumn. How would it be when winter came? A telegram sent on 27 September to London was revealing enough: 'In Amsterdam . . . we still can count on five weeks' bread, three weeks' potatoes and butter, and nil weeks' meat. . . .'

CHAPTER THREE

Public Relations

THE DEFEAT at Arnhem was an enormous personal blow to the Dutch Prime Minister in London. Gerbrandy's eager agreement with the Allied request for the railway strike and his optimistic words on Radio Oranje had given him a special responsibility – '*He* ought to know,' Queen Wilhelmina and many others had remarked – and he was now faced with the consequences. He knew all too well that the main objective of the war in Europe was the destruction of Nazi Germany and that the liberation of north-western Holland was of no direct importance militarily, now that Market Garden had failed. But could a Dutch government accept this point of view, he asked himself, especially now the reality of Germany's defeat was delayed for a long time and Holland during that period must remain occupied?

The answer to this question was a firm 'No' and it would be the key to all his actions for the rest of the war. While the sufferings of the Dutch increased, Gerbrandy began one of the most impressive exercises in public relations in the history of the Second World War. The Netherlands, till then only a small corner of Occupied Europe, was put on the map by him, helped by the impact that the Battle of Arnhem had made in the free world. The little Frieslander, who had only become Prime Minister by accident, worked tirelessly at 'shaking world opinion', so that the Allies, the United States and Britain, would at least send 'some quick relief'.

Pieter Sjoerds Gerbrandy, born on 13 April 1885 in Goengamieden in Friesland, had never been afraid of a fight. When he joined the coalition government of Dr D. J. de Geer as Minister of Justice in 1939, he rebelled against his own party, the Dutch Reformed Anti-Revolutionaries. He left Holland in May 1940 with the whole Cabinet, determined to continue the fight against

Nazi Germany, and when De Geer, dejected and discouraged, deserted the Government and returned to the Netherlands, Queen Wilhelmina automatically chose the energetic and ebullient Gerbrandy as his successor.

With his enormous moustache, which earned him the nickname 'Sea Lion', his short legs that didn't reach the floor when he sat in a big chair, his embonpoint and bullet-shaped head, he was a caricaturist's delight, but even his enemies had to admit that he saved Holland's face after the embarrassing defection of De Geer. It was due to Gerbrandy that within a few months the Dutch had shed the image of just another émigré government in London and were fully accepted. To the British he was, as one of his Ministers once said, 'the type of the stubborn Dutch peasant with a touch of the Transvaaler Boer, who doesn't budge for anyone, and whom – in secret – they always admired'.

Many of his Ministers objected to his autocratic behaviour and his whims, and Gerbrandy was indeed a man of limited outlook and capacities, but nobody denied that he was, together with Queen Wilhelmina, the soul of the Resistance. He had few pretensions and lived during the whole of the war in Brown's Hotel, just off Piccadilly, in a room described as 'chaotic and gloomy', with papers and documents all over the place.

Winston Churchill had taken a great liking to this little man with the keen eyes and the squeaky voice. The two prime ministers shared a predilection for large cigars and brandy, and Churchill appropriately and fondly called his Dutch colleague – behind his back – 'Mr Cherry Brandy', a pun Gerbrandy would have appreciated. When the Dutchman arrived in England his English was not very good, but the 'Dutch war-horse in miniature' soon learned the language with lessons and reading. His strong accent and his limited choice of words never stopped him from loudly voicing his opinion, whenever needed.

And needed it was, in the month of September 1944. The first cries for help from Holland were reaching London: food scarce, fuel not available. 'The production of gas will stop between 1 and 15 October, the supply of electricity not much later,' warned a telegram sent through Underground channels. On 28 September a special meeting of the Cabinet in London was called to discuss the railway strike, and the Minister of Roads and Waterworks, the Socialist Dr J. W. Albarda, proposed to end it now that Arnhem had failed. Gerbrandy, however, rejected the idea and enlisted the support of his Minister of War, Van Lidth de Jeude, who told his colleagues that the request for the strike had come from SHAEF. 'It is now up to them.' The answer from SHAEF came within a day: in the west the trains could roll again, but in the east, which bordered Germany, not yet. It was an impractical suggestion, and on 30 September the Government announced through Radio Oranje that 'military interests demand that the strike goes on – till the day the enemy leaves the country'.

It had been an agonising decision to take. It meant constant danger for the railwaymen and their families, and increasing hardship for the population – who deserved an explanation. On 5 October, Radio Oranje broadcast a Prime Ministerial speech. It started with a tribute to the railwaymen, whose sacrifice had helped the Allies so much by hindering the Wehrmacht. The defeat at Arnhem, the speaker admitted, had changed the picture considerably – if liberation did not come quickly, the big cities in western Holland were threatened with famine. The question is now, he went on, if this was sufficient reason to call off the strike.

From the start it was made clear in the broadcast that the Government 'on the other side' believed the strike must go on and they now wished to convince the Dutch population as well. 'Going back to work would not improve the situation at all,' the speaker reasoned. The supply of coal would not be resumed, as the coal-producing province of Limburg was now in the hands of the Allies, and food-trains would never go unmolested as Allied planes would certainly attack them. Transport would be forced to a standstill and there would not only be hunger, but also a great many victims among the civilian population.

In the hope of dispelling any impression that the Dutch in London were blackmailing those in the Occupied Netherlands, the speaker pointed to the fact that the Germans could and would use an efficient railway network to rob Holland of its last remaining stocks of food, raw materials and machines, and to transport the V-weapons to the Dutch coast. But the most important argument was saved to the last: in the eyes of the Dutch Government the railway strike was 'an act that had impressed the whole world and had given credit to the Dutch'. With that boost to their morale the Occupied Dutch were left with their problems.

Gerbrandy had meant to deliver the speech himself, but at the last minute left it to its author, Den Doolaard, because the Prime Minister had suddenly been called to 10 Downing Street to see Churchill. His visit followed a conversation that the Dutch Ambassador in London, E. F. M. J. Michiels van Verduynen, had had with the British Minister of Economic Warfare, Lord Selborne. He had revealed to the Englishman that the Dutch Government had been in touch with the neutral Swedes, who were willing to ship supplies to Holland. The Minister, who had every sympathy for the plan, approached the British Chiefs of Staff through the Foreign Office for permission to let the Swedes help the Dutch. 'Will you be so kind as to submit the matter ... most urgently, as the Swedes have informed the Netherlands Ambassador that they only await our consent before proceeding,' the Foreign Office wrote on 5 October.

It was on that same day that Gerbrandy paid his visit to Churchill, hoping to convince him of the importance of the Swedish gesture. The British Prime Minister, who, deep in his heart, still believed that the Continentals had actually eaten better than the British for the last four years, and who feared it would be the Germans who profited from the Swedish action, was not at all in favour of the idea, and it took Gerbrandy a lot of talking to win him round.

The Dutch Prime Minister began by underlining the general dangers facing his country, now that liberation seemed far away. 'He made a strong point that ... the Allied liberators might find the people of western Holland not only without food, but also without water, fuel, heat, light or sanitation,' Desmond Morton, Churchill's secretary, reported to Eisenhower's Chief of Staff, General Bedell Smith. 'According to Gerbrandy's information, the Germans want to destroy methodically Dutch towns and villages, independent of any strategic aim, and have already begun this beastly process.' The fact that the Dutchman had casually made the remark to Churchill that the Dutch people could hold out somehow till 1 December – 'after that they would starve if conditions remained the same' – had finally moved the British leader, and he promised to take up the Swedish matter with the Supreme Command. Churchill had to fly to Moscow to meet Stalin before he had the opportunity of speaking personally to Eisenhower, but Gerbrandy had done a good job – he had convinced the English also that the Allies should take a new look at the problems likely to arise after the liberation of Holland. Up till then the responsibility for the Dutch rested with SHAEF, which had created a special section, G–5, to deal with the question of food and medical stores. 'If, however, Dr Gerbrandy's forecast turns out to be correct,' a deeply impressed Morton wrote to Bedell Smith, 'it seems that something wholly outside the present experience may face SHAEF in Holland.' It would be a case of first aid, not for a few thousand people, but for a population of four million, even if 'the Germans may have killed off or driven away a large part of the population'.

The fact that so large a part of Holland lies below sea-level and is kept dry only by waterworks and pumps posed another problem. 'The destruction of the Dutch power- and pumping-stations will cause not only the flooding of certain districts ... but a complete lack of fresh water, sanitation, lighting and heating.' Morton, on behalf of Churchill, thought it therefore necessary that the case of the Dutch should be taken up in Washington – and urgently.

Gerbrandy had made his impression in high circles – now it was time to muster world opinion. And on Friday, 6 October, he met the press at the British Ministry of Information. For the first time he told the journalists of his country's ordeal. 'He spoke with great dignity and without a single complaint about the price his country has to pay,' the *Daily Telegraph* reported next day, and the press, to whom the story was new, gave it extensive coverage.

Immediately after the railway strike had started, the Germans had turned to scorched-earth and terror tactics. In Hilversum on 22 September we could hear the first explosions and soon afterwards black soot whirled down into the gardens. Amsterdam was on fire, we heard, but it turned out to be only the port. 'The old town is trembling on its foundations,' the writer Bert Voeten recorded in his diary. Through his binoculars he saw the cranes crumbling like 'constructions of reed', the warehouses collapsing. 'Under the black smoke were the ripped-up quays, the sunken docks and ships,' he noted bitterly. 'The barbarians revelled in the destruction of what has been the source of prosperity for this merchant city for centuries.'

Rotterdam was the next victim. Its heart had been bombed out by the Germans on 14 May 1940, and now it was the harbour's turn. More than 6000 German explosives experts had been sent to destroy it systematically. The Dutch Resistance ached to step in, and asked the Supreme Command for advice. Eisenhower, who could send them no help, answered that he was grateful for their offer, but did 'not wish you to hazard your lives'. And the result was that in the first days eight of the twenty-one kilometre-long quays were blown up, together with the offices and warehouses, the cranes and ships.

To us, in Occupied Holland, it was difficult to find out exactly what was going on. The railway strike had cut off almost all communications – horse-pulled barges would only later come back into fashion – there was hardly any mail, only a few telephones still worked, and the radio and newspapers, under German 'protection', wrote no word about it. But on Saturday, 7 October, Radio Oranje at last gave us all the news, when it reported on the press conference Gerbrandy had held the day before in London.

'The curtains have been pulled aside and the whole world has been able to see a tortured and bleeding Holland,' the newsreader Den Doolaard began. The introduction was somewhat melodramatic, but the facts were all too true. Apart from the ports of Amsterdam and Rotterdam, the Germans had ravaged those of Schiedam and Vlaardingen. A large part of the islands of Zeeland and Zuid-Holland had been flooded, and the sea had already swallowed a fifth of our arable land. Coastal towns and those along the Rhine around Arnhem had been evacuated. A number of railway workers had been executed, and in Apeldoorn alone the Germans had killed ten people when they refused to work for them.

These were the facts the whole world now knew, too. *The New York Times* printed the whole story on the front page and commented: 'No country has such claims on Germany after the war as the Dutch'; and *The Times* in London asked for a speedy deliverance for the Dutch people, who 'have been called on to endure sufferings probably worse than those so far inflicted on any other country in Western Europe'.

Gerbrandy's first public-relations campaign was a tremendous success, but his case had been impressive – and distressing – enough. He did not, however, leave it at that. Every Dutchman in the free world had to play his or her role, beginning with Queen

39

Wilhelmina. The Queen, who had been made a Knight of the Garter on her birthday, spoke briefly on the BBC on 9 October, thanking the British for this honour, which she saw as an 'expression of your respect for the heroic perseverance of my people against our common enemy'. She mentioned with a trembling voice the destruction, the plunder and the flooding of her country, and begged the British not to forget their Dutch friends, now threatened with famine.

The next weekend Prince Bernhard paid a visit to SHAEF at Versailles to plead for the Dutch, and Gerbrandy prepared a speech for American radio on Sunday. The day before, the Dutch Minister for Overseas Territories, Dr H. J. van Mook, had been received by President Roosevelt in the White House in Washington. Their talk lasted forty minutes and the main topic was, of course, the question of relief for Holland. Roosevelt, who never forgot his Dutch ancestry, listened carefully and promised to do his best.

Radio Oranje, who told us all this on 16 October, also revealed that the liberated part of the Netherlands had in the meantime received a visit from King George VI of England. The King had at last been able to convince Churchill that he must visit the soldiers on the Western Front and had travelled with Montgomery for five days through France, Belgium and liberated Holland. Wearing battledress for the first time, he visited the Nijmegen spearhead, three miles from Germany, where he received a tumultuous welcome from the Dutch crowd. While King George had attended a church service in Holland, his subjects in England had prayed for the Dutch in their own churches. Dr William Temple, the Archbishop of Canterbury, and his Roman Catholic confrère, Monsignor Bernard Griffin, had asked for a day of prayer on 15 October, observed by Queen Wilhelmina in a church near Stubbings, and by Gerbrandy and all his Ministers in different churches in London. One clergyman was so carried away by this wave of sympathy for the Dutch that in a letter to *The Times* he proposed abolishing the traditional sound of Big Ben before the nine o'clock news and replacing it with prayers for the poor Dutch.

Heartened by all this sympathy – and possibly by the prayers – Gerbrandy left London on Wednesday, 18 October, for the climax of his efforts to help Holland. He had received an invitation to visit Eisenhower himself at Versailles. When he arrived, however, the Supreme Commander had been held up in Brussels and his Chief of Staff, General Bedell Smith, had to take his place. Bedell Smith was taken unawares and sent an urgent message to his deputy, the Canadian Major-General Arthur E. Grasett, to study the latest reports about the Netherlands and report to him as soon as possible, 'as the Dutch Prime Minister is here'.

It was Gerbrandy's first visit to Paris since before the war, but on the way to his hotel, the Raphael, he found it little changed. 'The French capital seemed to have suffered little,' he told his Ministers later. 'Only the taxis are lacking.'

Next day there was no time for sight-seeing. Bedell Smith had done his homework well and 'it was completely unnecessary, unlike the talks with Churchill, to explain the situation', Gerbrandy noted with satisfaction. They could immediately begin with the question of aid from other countries. The American general made it clear that Eisenhower had no objections 'even if the Germans would profit from it', but in his view it was up to the governments involved to work out how to get supplies to the Dutch. Overland transport was out of the question, by air it would be difficult and the best way was therefore by ship. Another very important point was the help the Allies were going to give the Dutch immediately after Liberation. Bedell Smith was reassuring again: enormous stockpiles of food were being built up at airfields in England, three Liberty ships were ready to sail with food, and studies were being made 'as to what pumping equipment can be provided . . .'.

No word was said about the plan the Allies had for evacuating the people from western Holland to France and England after Liberation. The English were not keen on the idea and thought it impracticable, but Bedell Smith, reporting to Churchill on Gerbrandy's visit, insisted in his letter that evacuation might be necessary during the reconstruction of Holland. 'We are taking this matter up with the French and Belgian Governments, as we must prepare for the worst.' He added with understanding 'that sorely-tried England will have to take a share in the reception of these unfortunate people'.

Gerbrandy never mentioned this fantastic plan in any of his memos, and perhaps the American general – 'outspoken and realistic' though he was – felt that the Dutchman had enough to

41

swallow and did not tell him. To Churchill, Gerbrandy only wrote that the American general had given 'anything but a cheerful picture', and to his Ministers he said slightly more by telling them tactfully that 'it had not been expressly said that Occupied Holland must live another winter under the Germans, but the possibility was not excluded'.

Bedell Smith had in fact gone much farther. He had destroyed all Gerbrandy's hopes for an early liberation of Holland. When the Prime Minister had asked him straight out if the Netherlands would be free before 1 December, Smith had answered as bluntly: 'Impossible.'

It was a hard blow for Gerbrandy, and the only concrete result of his 'publicity campaign' that month was the official approval on 29 October, given by Eisenhower on 'grounds of humanity', for Swedish aid to the Dutch, 'if the German Government can be persuaded to agree'.

CHAPTER FOUR

New Terrors

THE GERMANS, in October 1944, had not the least intention of allowing the Swedes or anybody else to help the Dutch. They were still fuming about the railway strike, and their terror was spreading by the day. 'We Dutch have now entered a dark tunnel. We cannot see where we go and we don't see the end.' The young engineer who wrote this in his diary on 3 October was especially upset by news he had that day received from Putten, a small place on the Veluwe, where four Germans had been attacked and incredible reprisals had followed.

In spite of its isolation, Putten, with its orthodox Dutch Reformed and fervently pro-Orange villagers, had a bad name with the Germans. Frequent small riots had been capped in September by a skirmish between German soldiers and Resistance fighters, and ten soldiers had been wounded. The drama which shocked the engineer started when on the moonlit night of 30 September an ambush by a small group of Resistance men went wrong. The Bren gun of Keith Banwell, an English sergeant who had joined the group after escaping from Arnhem, refused to fire at the critical moment, and three of the four Germans who had been attacked escaped after a gun battle and were able to raise the alarm. The fourth man, Lieutenant Eggert, was taken hostage by the Putteners.

When the news of the assault reached Colonel Fritz Fullriede, the men's commander, he was furious. In the middle of the night he rang headquarters in Hilversum, where Christiansen's Chief of Staff, General Heinz Helmuth von Wühlisch, ordered him to surround the village and place all the inhabitants under arrest until further orders.

That Sunday morning the Putteners, going to their churches in a drizzle, heard the first rumours. Troops had been spotted searching the woods and some shots had been heard. Pastor Holland found it advisable to send the younger men home. The Germans, in the meantime, had operated smoothly and efficiently. They had rounded up some farmers on their way to milking and some innocent passers-by – a total of thirty-three men – and when the villagers left the church they watched in dread as these men were lined up in the centre of the square. Incredulously they listened to the announcement that the thirty-three hostages would be shot if the culprits of the attack of the previous night were not found.

Von Wühlisch had by now told Christiansen of the ambush at his daily briefing, and the General had burst out into one of his usual rages, shouting: 'Burn the whole place down and line the whole band up against the wall.' Telling Von Wühlisch to keep in mind that since 13 September all municipalities were responsible for local sabotage, he asked him to draft a very severe order: 'Shoot the culprits, hand the male population between seventeen and fifty over to the SS, evacuate the women and children and burn the village down.'

Fullriede, in Putten, was less than happy with this inhuman mission, but he told the police to get all the women into the church and collect the men near the school building, and to his surprise almost everybody obeyed. With some pressure from the local police, young men came out of their hiding-places and went to the school at the double, while the women walked quietly to the church, normally a place – as one of them wrote – 'with such a reassuring meaning in Putten that no one would ever think of threat and danger', and certainly not of the guns that surrounded it now.

An anxious and tense day and night followed. Nothing had yet been revealed of the Nazi decisions, but after the Germans had shot seven villagers 'in flight' early on Sunday, among them a twenty-eight-year-old girl, everybody feared for the fate of the thirty-three hostages. The Resistance group which had provoked Christiansen's fury hoped to save them and released their captive, Lieutenant Eggert, but nobody informed the Germans. When daylight returned, Fullriede climbed into the pulpit in the church and told the women to collect their things and leave the village with their children. 'It caused a lot of crying and running,' he jotted down in his journal.

Meanwhile a special detachment of SS soldiers sorted out the men. Their ages were checked and some pro-Nazis were released. Once again it was asked who were the attackers, but when a few men stepped forward the SS men refused to believe them and pushed them back into the ranks. Orders were bellowed and the procession, hostages included, shuffled through the deserted main street. The women, hearing what was happening, rushed after them and found them gathered outside the village, lying face down on the ground, while an impatient officer asked them for the last time who were the culprits. When no answer came they were ordered to get up and board a train, which had been waiting since ten o'clock.

The women at first watched in horror, then suddenly broke through the barriers the soldiers had erected and rushed up to the platform. 'They call and point and can't find their beloved,' an eyewitness wrote. 'An old gentleman throws an overcoat in a compartment in which he thinks to see his son. But the order is inexorably: "Nicht stehen bleiben. Los Mensch" ["Don't hang around. Get out of the way"]. The women are roughly pushed away, the train doors slam, soldiers stand on the footboard, an officer gives the signal, the wheels begin to turn. . . . And on the road the women stand, their parcels still in their hands, full of sorrow.'

Hardly any of them were ever to see their men again. After a short stay in the concentration-camp at Amersfoort, 589 of the 660 men arrested were sent to Germany, from where only forty-nine returned (of whom five died afterwards). The Putteners, used to being guided by their rigidly Calvinist ministers and having lived in an almost tribal isolation, were not up to Nazi ruthlessness. Only a few tried to escape and not more than thirteen jumped off the train. Spread over different camps in Germany, their morale soon collapsed. It was God's punishment, they believed, and many worked themselves to death.

The drama of Putten was responsible for the deaths of 552 people, including the seven people shot on Sunday morning. It was an act of terror which in Western Europe is only comparable with the Nazi massacre in the French village of Oradour in 1943 when 692 villagers were executed after the murder of one SS officer, and the village destroyed.

Putten was slightly more fortunate. Fullriede decided to disobey one part of the order from Hilversum and, after the women and children had left, burned 'only' 87 of the 600 houses. A young Dutchman who came to look for his parents in Putten on 4 October was one of the first to see what had happened. 'Not a person to be seen in the houses. Everywhere white flags and sheets as if the village was surrendering after a hopeless struggle. Smoking ruins and for the rest a deadly silence. . . .'

While the drama of Putten took place in the north of the Veluwe, the Germans staged another tragedy south of the forest. J. Douwenga, a schoolteacher in Wageningen, woke up on Sunday, 1 October, to hear a strange sound he could at first not identify. 'It was like the slow shuffle of thousands of feet, but there was no sound of voices.' He opened the curtains. 'We looked; we just looked. What I saw was so tragic, so terribly sad, that it over-whelmed us completely. My wife could not bear it any longer and burst out into tears. An endless stream of refugees . . . walked past in the pouring rain. . . . They were soaked to the skin, and silent. Yellow leaves were falling from the trees.'

The Germans had ordered the evacuation of a series of places which had been badly hit during the Battle of Arnhem. Their populations had for ten days lived in their cellars and had hoped that, now the fighting was over, they would have some peace and quiet. The order to depart came as a shattering blow, but dulled by recent events they began to march – with nowhere to go.

Arnhem itself had been hit by the same fate a week before. The town looked like a surrealist nightmare – it was a total ruin. On 23 September the last convulsions of the battle that had given so much hope to the Dutch were taking place on the Oosterbeek perimeter, but in Arnhem the population had surfaced and were trying to repair the roofs over their heads. Then at four o'clock that Saturday afternoon Dr J. N. van der Does, a surgeon and head of the provincial Red Cross, was summoned to SS Head-quarters. An officer, pointing to a map on the wall, told Van der Does without ceremony that everybody living south of the railway track that divided the town in half must leave before eight o'clock that evening. The rest had to follow within twenty-four hours. Van der Does's protests were cut short. 'If any man, woman or child is found in town after tomorrow night,' the officer snapped, 'it will be the worse for them. Save your breath and empty your town.'

To Van der Does, it seemed an impossible task. How to evacuate 100,000 people within thirty-six hours or less? Arnhem's Nazi mayor and police chief had disappeared on Mad Tuesday and the town elders had 'dived', fearing reprisals after a vital railway viaduct had been sabotaged. The only man who pretended to have some authority was former shoeseller A. F. Hollaar, self-styled deputy mayor, who approved the German decision. A last effort by some prominent Arnhemmers to change the mind of the Germans failed. 'No stone will be left upon another,' Major Peters, the second-in-command in the German HQ, told them, and when Van der Does received written instructions later that day the orderly warned him that a 'blanket of bombs' would be laid over Arnhem if he disobeyed.

It was too late at night to order the departure, and only next morning the horrified Arnhemmers received the fatal message, printed on a piece of grey paper and signed by Hollaar as 'Police President of Arnhem'. Van der Does advised them to carry only the barest necessities with them.

'Women cried and men cursed', but everybody started to pack obediently and to load their few possessions on prams, hand-carts and bikes. On Sunday afternoon the exodus started. Most of the evacuees went in the direction of Apeldoorn, thirty kilometres away. The hilly road was overcrowded, the rain was falling and the only sound one could hear was that of crying children 'tied on top of the luggage, cold and hungry'. The autumn nights were already cold, and no one had anywhere to go. 'It made no difference if one was rich or poor,' someone wrote. 'They all marched slowly on with the same miserable belongings, like outcasts.'

That first night, most of the refugees found a roof in one of the surrounding villages, and many of them stayed the whole winter on the Veluwe. Others travelled on to the north and passed the winter in Friesland. The few who tried to go back to Arnhem found the town sealed off by patrolling Germans, who threatened to shoot if they ever tried again to enter.

It is still a big mystery who ordered the evacuation. The local German commander never knew about it and Major Peters disappeared – seen for the last time in a car full of loot. For Van der Does it was by then too late to revoke the order. The exodus had been completed - and three thousand of the Arnhemmers would not live to see their town again.

Putten and Arnhem were but two examples of the arbitrary way the Germans acted in the autumn of 1944. Hundreds of Dutchmen became the victims of the summary justice which the Nazis had introduced with the state of emergency.

With the invading armies in May 1940 a Nazi police force had come to the Netherlands to see that new Nazi laws, creating new crimes and new punishments, were obeyed. As in the Reich, the force was known as the Sicherheitspolizei (Security Police), divided into three branches: the Secret State Police (Gestapo), the Security Service (SD) and the Criminal Police. Most Dutch people were at first confused about the different roles of the forces, but the names soon became all too familiar and spelled terror.

The incarnation of German terror was, however, the Order Police, the executive branch. The members wore green uniforms, which gave them the nickname of the 'Greens', and whenever they were seen it meant trouble. They were charged with the arrest, deportation and execution of the enemies of Nazi Germany, and that autumn they worked very hard. The month of October, for instance, began with the execution of five citizens of Wormerveer, chosen at random after a policeman had been killed. On 6 October there were three executions in Rotterdam, on the tenth twelve in Rijswijk after a railway sabotage, and on the twelfth six – because an officer had been accidentally electrocuted. On Thursday, 24 October, the 'Greens' were exceptionally busy. In Rotterdam they shot at three people who tried to pick up pamphlets in the street, killing one, and later in the day four men were executed after a group of forty-eight prisoners had been freed by a Resistance group from a police station. The biggest bloodbath perpetrated by the 'Greens', however, took place that day in Amsterdam.

It was a reprisal for the murder of one of their colleagues, SD man Herbert Oelschlägel, whose death on 23 October had infuriated the Nazis, especially since he was one of their most successful operators. 'That will put us back at least two years,' the SD chief Willy Lages complained. Oelschlägel, who had lived in Holland before the war and spoke the language, had built up an extensive network of informers, the so-called 'V-men', who had infiltrated a great number of Underground cells, with fatal consequences for many of the members.

Oelschlägel, however, had made one mistake which was to cost him his life. He insisted on keeping his contacts to himself, and the Resistance reasoned that with his disappearance his cronies, too, would fade away in the hope of saving their skins now that Liberation was so near.

The movements of the SD agent were followed for weeks and the moment for action fixed for half-past four in the afternoon, when Oelschlägel had a standing appointment with one of his V-men in the doorway of a bank in south Amsterdam. It was decided to kidnap him, as killing him might lead to severe reprisals, but on 23 October Oelschlägel for once skipped his meeting and had a drink in a bar instead. When he was discovered, the Resistance men followed him and grabbed him when he reached the Apollolaan. The terrified SD man put up a tough fight, and the bottle of chloroform fell and broke. There was but one solution − two bullets through his head.

Next day, Amsterdammers who happened to go through the Apollolaan were forced to witness the execution of twenty-nine of their compatriots, while several buildings were set on fire. 'The bodies remained in the road under the smoke of the burning houses,' one heartbroken eyewitness remembered.

That month Amsterdam looked more and more like a beleaguered city. On 18 October, Radio Oranje broadcast the story of an Amsterdammer who had been able to escape to the free south, and he had not exaggerated. 'There is no electricity. A large part of the population is hiding. Part of the surrounding country is flooded. There is hardly any food.' When he left Amsterdam there was still gas for one and a half hours a day, 'but as there is no electricity there are no longer any trams, and the telephone doesn't work, either. Most theatres and cinemas have closed down and in the evening the Amsterdammers stay in their unheated houses round a candle or oil-lamp. Thousands of them never come outdoors. Life in the once so-busy city has come to a standstill.'

For the men, in particular, it was dangerous to go outside as they ran the risk of being swept away in one of the German raids, or 'razzias' as the Dutch called them. So they stayed indoors. Poet

Bert Voeten was one of the 'divers', but he refused to be depressed. 'Even now that I watch the trees along the canal getting naked and sadder,' he wrote, 'I don't want to believe in "dying" and "withering". We have to keep the fires burning. It will get brighter.' But it was not so easy, 'preoccupied as one is with physical needs: food, fuel and fear of the "Greens", who again have taken thousands of men away'.

The situation in Rotterdam was the same. 'Our town has much changed,' the journalist Diemer wrote on 10 October in his diary. 'The trams operate for only a few hours a day, and the pedestrian is king again, now bikes have disappeared because of the lack of tyres and the confiscations by the Germans.' Car traffic had been cut down and most of the trucks, with their stinking generators, belonged to the Wehrmacht. The horse had made a comeback, Diemer noticed, adding: 'And that's an improvement, aesthetically at least.' The same could be said for walking but, as he said, 'walking uses shoes and these are unobtainable. Even repairs are impossible to get done and there is a lively trade in old car tyres.'

At the time there was at least still some electricity and gas, but the other Rotterdammer diarist, Dr Mees, reported that the town was without the latter from 25 October onwards. The lights went out at half-past nine – 'so that we go to bed at quarter-past'.

Those measures had been taken for the whole of the provinces Noord- and Zuid-Holland, but The Hague, former seat of the Government and the royal family, was hardest hit. There were almost no reserves, and when light and gas ran out the communal central kitchen, already overstretched, had to feed 350,000 persons a day.

Added to that came a new move by the Nazis. Over the years they had robbed the Dutch of whatever they needed: copper, tin, radios, church-bells, bicycles, cars and even their men. Now they wanted blankets and clothes, and The Hague was chosen for a trial run. On 26 October yellow posters appeared in the streets, which announced in German and Dutch that every family was obliged to hand in blankets and clothing to the value of 72.50 guilders. To make it easier a price-list was added: winter coat, 50 guilders; raincoat, 30; underpants, 5; and blankets, 35 guilders. In exchange, a certificate would be given as a guarantee against house searches.

This cruel measure, robbing everybody of their last protection against the coming – unheated and unlit – winter, invited a violent protest from the citizens, and the first reactions looked positive. Printers refused to handle the pamphlets, city clerks 'lost' their files, and even the Nazi-controlled press kept silent, in spite of a German appeal to help those poor soldiers who had lost everything when leaving France and Belgium. Only the pro-Nazi press agency ANP sent out a wire, arguing that an occupying force has every right to confiscate goods to fulfil its strategic needs, but the Underground press urged everybody to ignore the request.

For once even the most uncommitted Dutchman felt that the 'illegal' papers were right. To give the Germans blankets and clothing was helping them in their war effort and would lengthen the struggle. 'It was a question of principle – shall we go like sheep to sacrifice our clothes, or shall we wait until the Germans come and get it, with all the risks of searches?' The student who was wondering about this lived in his parents' house and witnessed one of the many disputes that raged all over town. 'Frightened fathers against their protesting sons, defiant wives against their prudent husbands' – and all this over one question: to give or not to give.

The Germans solved the problem for most with their usual tactics of fear. When, on the morning of Friday, 27 October, hardly anybody turned up at the school chosen for the collection, they sent a loudspeaker van through the streets and 'when the heavy voice stopped, the first people, pale and afraid, hurried to the school'. The student watched it from behind the curtains. 'Many followed. Streets, blocks, whole neighbourhoods forgot any thought of defiance and streamed in panic to the Van Heutzschool', where the Germans were waiting. 'The defeat was complete.'

Next day the Resistance hit back. With great precision they copied the certificates which the Germans had given in exchange for the goods and distributed them free in the streets. The Germans tried to alter their documents, stamps and signatures, but were unable to stop the rot, and after a few days the whole action faded out.

Another requisition, ordered a few days later in The Hague, called for another ruse. When the Germans decided to take away all the large dogs and called their owners up for 'inspection', a lively trade developed. In a street not far from the place where the 'control' took place, one could rent a small dog, which had already been rejected by the Nazis, and now at a second – or third – inspection provided the owner of a large dog with a certificate of exemption.

The destruction of Putten, the evacuation of Arnhem and the surrounding area, the frequent executions and confiscations – together with increasing hunger – had made life a hell for the Dutch in that month of October. A sinister plot hatched in Hilversum's Raadhuis was, however, to make November even worse.

CHAPTER FIVE

The Hunt for Slaves

'HERE ONE is hardly aware of the war. The quiet and peace are soothing. No guns and no planes.' After a month in the front line at Wageningen, Douwenga, with wife and children, was cycling contentedly through 't Gooi, the hilly heath region around Hilversum, on the way to their evacuation address in the old fortress town of Naarden. 'We're glad we have decided to go there.' He had hardly time to form this thought before the quiet was abruptly shattered. An old woman at the other side of the road called him. 'Don't go on. It's dangerous in 't Gooi,' she told him when he stopped. 'All the young men are arrested and taken away.' Suddenly shots sounded nearby and, while the startled Douwengas watched, a group of young men crawled like Red Indians across the road, signalling to them to turn back. Douwenga reacted fast, and the result was that they spent that night – less peacefully than he had expected – in a glasshouse, full of grapes and other 'divers'.

The raid in 't Gooi was one of the many manhunts the Germans had started at once after the railway strike had begun. Town after town had seen the soldiers marching in with orders to round up all the able-bodied young men, who were then sent eastwards to help build the German defences. Venlo was the first city, and it had been a harsh lesson to the Dutch. Twenty men were executed when nobody obeyed the orders to report. Zevenaar was next, and the people hurried to comply when the Germans threatened to flatten the place. Doetinchem, Hengelo, Enschede, they all had an unexpected visit. On 21 September Kampen dared to defy the Nazis – Arnhem was not yet lost – and paid dearly with the lives of three citizens. When the Germans returned on 7 October, 6000 men turned up. More executions took place when, on 2 October, Apeldoorn hesitated to report – the bodies of the ten men left as a warning in the streets were sufficiently convincing for 11,000 other men to register.

Hilversum's turn came on 24 October. G. J. H. Fijn, the NSB mayor, had on 17 October received a request to supply a thousand men for work near Amersfoort. Obligingly he composed a list of 1520 people, whom he thought would be acceptable to the Germans, and sent the chosen an 'invitation' to come and see him next day. Only 125 appeared, later followed by fifteen others; 680 never reacted at all and more than 700 showed him a medical certificate that exempted them from hard labour.

The Nazis couldn't accept this and on 23 October they announced that all the men between the ages of seventeen and fifty must report in the Hilversum Sportspark. My father and mother discussed that evening what to do, as my father, at forty-one years old, could still be considered an 'able-bodied man', but they decided that he would 'dive' and he made his preparations. Sensibly enough, my mother refused to tell us children where he was hiding, for fear the Germans might force us to speak.

On the morning of Tuesday, 24 October, the Potgieterlaan was silent and deserted, like all the streets in Hilversum. Curtains were drawn and no one dared even to go out in the garden. Around midday, I suddenly heard the well-known sound of heavy boots and the rattle of an armoured car. We were sitting around the table in the living-room, waiting with a curious mixture of fear and excitement. It was our first 'razzia' and for a ten-year-old boy like me it all seemed a big adventure. It was different for my mother. Cool and composed, she was changing the nappy of my one-year-old sister, when suddenly a broad face, topped by a grey helmet, peered through the window into the house, staring at us. The excitement had gone; sheer fear remained. What would happen? Stories of doors being rammed open, people being dragged out into the streets – we had heard and sometimes seen it all. But the face disappeared and the sound of the car engine faded away. An hour later, the coast was clear and my father reappeared from his hiding-place, a hole in the attic between the wall and the roof.

More than 3500 men were less fortunate than my father. They were taken to the Sportspark and led before the German officers, who, according to a satisfied Mayor Fijn, refused to look at all those documents 'one usually waves around'. All of them were transported that evening to Amersfoort and some from there to Germany.

But these raids had been no more than child's play, an introduction to a thoroughly organised hunt for bigger game. Only nine days before the raid in Hilversum, the familiar cavalcade of German military cars, with the one with number-plate RK1 in the middle, had driven into the village for another meeting between Seyss-Inquart and his military counterpart, General Christiansen. Amongst the people present was SS leader Hanns Rauter and a sinister newcomer, a high Nazi official named Hermann Liese. This mysterious figure had arrived in Holland as the representative of Dr Joseph Goebbels, whom Hitler had appointed as Minister responsible for total warfare. And Liese had come to force the Dutch to contribute more than their share to this total war.

The 'export' of Dutch foodstocks, railway material, cattle and machines to Germany was in the capable hands of other German authorities, who did all they could to promote the one-way flow, but the recruitment of young men, Liese thought, had always been rather amateurish. At the meeting in Hilversum the first foundations were laid for a plan aimed at the deportation of all Dutchmen between seventeen and fifty years old – a total of 600,000.

One of Liese's reasons for the rounding up of the 'leftovers' of Dutch manhood was the need for cheap labour to replace those German factory-workers who had been exempted from military service, but might be needed in the total war. The Third Reich also needed men to build defences – and to clear the rubble left by the Allied bombers.

Liese could count on the full support of his Nazi compatriots in the Netherlands, but for a different reason from his: the German Wehrmacht feared a rising behind the front lines. They knew that arms had been dropped over Holland and they had not forgotten the help the Maquis in France had given the Allies. The creation of the BS, the Dutch Forces of the Interior, at the beginning of September had made a deep impression on them, and with so many railwaymen out of work they expected – and dreaded – a fast growth of the Underground army.

The big question was how to carry out the order from Berlin. It seemed best to raid all large places at the same time to forestall

Dutch 'diving', but the problem was that there were not enough troops, and for such a gigantic operation they needed at least three divisions. Rauter, the only one who was unhappy with the plan, saw here a chance to spoil it. Fearing that the arrival of so many German soldiers, and the ensuing raids, would almost force the Dutch to join the Resistance and to rise, he exploited this argument in his report to Himmler, who agreed with him and decided not to send the required divisions.

When on 30 October the Nazi chiefs met again, Himmler's rejection was lying on the table. Liese, however, refused to give in and he nagged Christiansen so much that the General at last promised him every soldier he could spare. Operation Rose-branch could start, if on a somewhat smaller scale.

On Thursday evening, 9 November, the Rotterdammers found a little note in their letterboxes. In it, the Nazis advised all men to pack a few necessities that same evening and next morning to stand in front of their house. German soldiers with trucks would drive past so that the men could climb on and be taken away to one of the work-camps.

Rotterdam had been chosen as the first victim of the sweet-sounding Operation Rosebranch. That November the sea-port still shook daily to the explosions that were destroying its harbour and 50,000 Rotterdammers were already working in Germany; but Liese and General von Wühlisch, who was leading the military side of the operation, had decided that, since the population of that city was the most restless and therefore the greatest threat to Germany's western wing, they deserved another lesson.

That the Germans had little confidence in the appeal of their invitation was obvious next morning. At four o'clock all the roads to Rotterdam and all the bridges were barricaded, and traffic through the only tunnel under the Maas was forbidden. More than 8000 soldiers went into action, after first disarming the Dutch police, whom they did not trust.

'On all corners of the streets are heavily armed Germans, who stop everybody,' the indefatigable diarist Dr Mees recorded. A tram conductor, who also recorded his daily life with great care, decided to report for duty, but returned home when he found only a few clerks working, and just waited. 'At twelve o'clock a lot of soldiers in the street, in full marching kit and with rifles . . . at 12.30 everyone is told to stay inside. I hear the loudspeaker far away.' At three o'clock, still nothing had happened, 'the streets are empty and nobody goes out'. But at a quarter-past five the moment he had been waiting for came. The Germans marched into the street. 'They're calling at every door, and if nobody comes they search the house.' While he was peering through the curtain, his wife Greet quickly cooked a meal. 'God knows when I will get something to eat again,' he sighed, but when it grew dark the enthusiasm of the raiding soldiers diminished, and they disappeared, taking most of his neighbours and forgetting him.

That night the lights in Rotterdam stayed on after half-past nine, and everybody understood what it meant: the manhunt would go on for another day. Shots were heard throughout the night, and at sunrise the town was as dead as a grave. The day before, however, new ration-coupons had been issued, and the women scurried to the shops later in the morning to see what they could get. 'Everything has been reduced. Bread by thirty per cent, butter and meat by fifty per cent,' the tram conductor wrote, 'but the situation is so chaotic that nobody really worries about it, although it means hunger.'

He escaped during the following days, too, but the Germans could be more than satisfied. Liese broke all records by arresting more than 50,000 men, and on the evening of 13 November the lights went out again at half-past nine, leaving Rotterdam's 500,000 inhabitants with no more than 20,000 of the wanted men still safe in their hiding-places.

The reaction of Rotterdam to the unexpected razzia had been disappointing. The Rotterdammers had been taken offguard in spite of the invitation of 9 November, but it had surely not been necessary to flock in such masses to the collecting-points the Germans had established. 'At some moments the streets were so crowded with men going to report', one underground paper fumed, 'that it looked as if they were on their way to a football match or the cinema.' Even more humiliating for the Dutch was that some women, whose husbands had been taken away, betrayed their neighbours. 'The traitors queued at a police station, until the police chased them away,' an indignant Dr Mees heard.

Vrij Nederland, a well-known Resistance paper, revealed that even the Nazis had been astonished by the submissive attitude of the Rotterdammers. 'We heard German officers speaking with disdain about us. They considered us cowards,' the journalist H. M. van Randwijk wrote. 'Women – and not only a few – had come up to the Germans and offered themselves for sexual intercourse, if only their husbands were released. Others came with butter, chocolate and brandy to buy their men free, but the Germans were supposed to have answered that they could keep their stuff – we keep the men.'

A Nazi officer, who had to guard 600 Rotterdammers with the help of three soldiers, remarked that he had never seen such sheep. 'In Poland they would have acted differently,' he said. 'My men had one machine-gun with ten bullets and two rifles with even less bullets. I had a gun and, had they rebelled against us, we could have shot perhaps twenty of them, but the rest could have slaughtered us.'

These stories were later denied, but it was a fact that the Germans were delighted with their easy success. Liese had but one complaint: the German commander of Rotterdam, a certain Kistner, and his men, had become too pro-Dutch and had been over-generous with exemptions to men said to be indispensable to Rotterdam's economic life. 'I told these gentlemen that the Dutch will have to learn to improvise,' he reported in satisfaction to Goebbels on 18 November.

The 50,000 men had in the meantime left Rotterdam on foot in the pouring rain. 'I saw them going,' Mrs J. M. van Walsum, the wife of a mayor of Rotterdam, remembered in a television interview years later, still deeply moved. 'Suddenly I saw how the road was filling with a mass of people, who moved very slowly in my direction. They sometimes stopped and then again shuffled forward in a sort of jog-trot. It was deadly silent; you didn't hear a thing. The soldiers walked on the pavement, rifles under their arms, and suddenly there were the women. . . . You heard words of farewell and encouragement like "Long Live Orange", and the women who were following, and could not find their husbands, cried, and those who found them cried, and there were girls who pushed themselves into the mass and walked with their boyfriend, arms around his neck. And there was that woman, who had nothing to do with it at all, but she had that bag full of apples and she just threw them in the crowd until the Germans were fed up and began to shoot. . . . We had to watch this five times, that day, five times. . . .'

All along their route the sight of those long sad columns of men sent shockwaves, and the Dutch did all they could to help. Hundreds escaped, but the majority reached the east, partly by filthy and overcrowded barges across the Ijsselmeer, partly on foot, and were put to work there.

Rotterdam struggled back with difficulty to some sort of normal life, but 'the sadness was everywhere', a diarist wrote. 'And then to think that this is only a small part of the sufferings the world had to carry.'

Rotterdam had been a lesson – a very painful one – to the Dutch, and when after his victory in that town Liese tackled The Hague on 21 November most men had learned from it and 'dived'. The spoils for the Germans were much smaller – 13,000 men.

More raids followed all over the country, and only Amsterdam – rumours said that the city was infected with typhoid – was spared. In spite of Liese's hard work, however, the Nazis never achieved their aim of deporting Holland's 600,000 able men. Only a fifth of that number had fallen into their hands when, in the middle of December, the tenacious Liese developed another and even more menacing scheme.

CHAPTER SIX

The Battle of the Scheldt

NOVEMBER 8, 1944 was a special day. Not only did we celebrate my father's forty-second birthday in all sobriety, but also the illegal radio brought us two exciting news items. The Allies had made a very important conquest, which raised our hopes – they had seized control of the Scheldt estuary – and Franklin Delano Roosevelt was re-elected for a fourth term as President of the United States. No Dutchman could disagree with the comment in an Underground 'election special' that day: 'We can be grateful for the fact that the Americans have once again given power to this man at a moment when he is able to deliver the final blow to his arch-enemies.'

The production of this issue had been a very dangerous but highly successful operation. One of the editors described later how he and three colleagues had made their headquarters in a printing office in Amsterdam with a wireless to catch the latest election news from the United States. 'It was freezing cold and the radio had a lot of interference. Suddenly – at midnight – we heard running feet. We thought we had been betrayed and just waited. "A pity we still don't know if he was re-elected," one of us remarked. "And that will be difficult to find out in prison," another joked.' But nothing happened, the footsteps disappeared and, when at six o'clock the first printers arrived, the copy was ready. By ten o'clock 60,000 pamphlets had been printed to bring the Dutch the good news from America. The four men had by then discovered that the running footsteps were those of Gestapo men who had been after a couple of burglars in the factory next door.

The Dutch had always had a soft spot for the partially paralysed President, whose Dutch ancestry gave them the feeling that they had a special link with him. The fact that just three days before his re-election a Canadian armoured division had liberated the village of Oud-Vossemeer on the Zeeland island of Tholen seemed to underline that unique relationship. Vossemeer was very proud of the house from where Roosevelt's ancestors had left for the New World around 1650.

The liberation of Tholen on 4 November was part of the final stage of one of the bloodiest and longest battles in north-west Europe in the Second World War: the Battle of the Scheldt – the estuary leading to the port of Antwerp, so essential for supplying the Allied march to Berlin.

The battle, which lasted eighty-five days and cost the Allies a total of 30,000 men – the invasion in Normandy claimed 18,000 victims and was a 'picnic' in comparison – was mainly due to the blunder of Montgomery in not pressing on to open the port of Antwerp as soon as he had entered the city on 4 September. Until the twenty-second no effort had been made to occupy the entry to the port, the Scheldt, or to prevent the Germans fleeing to Walcheren, where they now had the opportunity to strengthen their defences around the estuary. The northern bank of the river mouth in particular, formed by the Zuid-Beveland peninsula and Walcheren, was turned into a formidable fortress by the Wehrmacht, which was very much aware of the importance of its position there. In an order of the day for 7 October the German commander made no secret of the fact that the defence of the Scheldt was, as he said, 'decisive for the rest of the war', explaining that with the port of Antwerp liberated the Allies would be able 'to give us the deathblow before winter comes'. The order ended with the rousing words, so often used on similar occasions: 'The eyes of the German nation are upon you.'

Eisenhower finally gave the order to advance on the Scheldt on 27 September. Arnhem had not been captured and Montgomery now gave complete priority to this campaign by the Canadian First Army. Very tough weeks followed, with hard fighting in the most depressing circumstances. Not only had the Germans flooded most of Flemish Zeeland and the islands, but it also rained almost continuously and the men saw nothing but water and mud. A military commentator once remarked that it was a battle for 'men with web feet and waterproof skins'.

By the end of October, Flemish Zeeland and Zuid-Beveland were in the hands of the Canadians, and Walcheren's turn had come. 'The Garden of Zeeland', as it was often called, had been turned into an impenetrable bulwark, with twenty-five batteries along the coast, gun-nests in the meadows and stakes planted everywhere to impede airborne landings. The German troops defending it were mainly soldiers who had been posted from other fronts on account of gastric trouble, but in spite of their nickname 'The White Bread Division' they were still perfectly able to fight.

There was only one way to break their resistance. Most of Walcheren is below sea-level, like a big bowl protected by dunes and dykes, and in the hope of flooding the Germans out, or at least inundating their defences, the Allies decided to bomb the dykes and let the sea in. The population received a warning on 2 October. But where could they go? 'We could not get off the island, and all we could do was get away from the coast,' a Zeelander remembered. 'It saved a lot of people.'

It did not save the forty-seven men, women and children who had taken refuge in a mill not far from the gigantic Westkapelse Dyke. When, on 3 October, 259 Lancasters dropped their load of bombs, one of them hit the mill. 'It collapsed completely and the people were trapped under beams and stones.' Most of them were still alive, but by the time a rescue team arrived it was too late. The first bombardment had been a success; there was a gap of about a hundred metres in the dyke and the sea was storming inland, drowning forty-four of the forty-seven.

Two more air-strikes followed and a total of 2672 tons of high explosive were dropped before most of Walcheren was flooded and the attack could be launched. On 1 November, British troops landed near Flushing and sailed through the gap in the West-kapelse Dyke, while in the east the Canadians tried to reach the island over the causeway which connected it with Zuid-Beveland. 'It was a terrible fight,' a Zeelander wrote later. 'Hundreds of Englishmen drowned before they even reached the coast and survivors told us that it had been more arduous than the invasion of Normandy.' The German soldiers fought hard and well. 'We were very disappointed because we expected them to surrender at once.'

The battle lasted till 6 November, but late that day the German commander in Middelburg, Major-General Daser, gave orders for a ceasefire. According to Radio Oranje, he then took an aspirin and went to bed. 'Hardly had he pulled his yellow sheets over his head', when the first British soldiers rowed into the capital of Zeeland.

Middelburg had once been a beautiful old town, but after suffering a bombardment in 1940 the centre was in ruins. The floodwaters made the city even more desolate. 'The houses are standing in water up to their letterboxes, and that's during ebb,' a visitor noticed. 'The swell caused by our duck-boat opens and closes the front doors in the narrow streets in a terrifying rhythm. In the living-rooms the water sloshes against the wall, the chimneys. Somewhere I see a lamp, hanging lopsided over a floating table ... and everywhere is water, which comes twice a day in millions of litres. . . .'

However ruined the city, nothing could dampen the celebrations that night. Normally the population was 20,000, but the number of refugees had doubled this and they all turned out to fête the 300 British soldiers who reached the town that first day. Less happy were the 2000 German soldiers, who with a good deal of bluffing were rounded up by the handful of British troops and assembled in the market-place. 'They made no difficulties,' Radio Oranje told us. 'They gave their arms and helmets to the British and even helped them next day by providing their own transport, by rowing-boat, to the prison-camps.' It had been one of the most bizarre liberations so far.

The capture of Walcheren made it now possible to sweep the mines in the Scheldt, a total of 267, a task that was completed on 26 November, when three coasters reached Antwerp. *The Times* in London reported triumphantly: 'The first Belgian ship to come is now being unloaded. She is a Liberty ship, and her cargo is made up largely of food for the liberated part of Holland. Next to her is another Liberty ship – a Dutch one.' It was probably the *Amstelstroom*, which made the crossing at the beginning of December with 500 tons of food. War correspondent John O'Connor had been on board and reported via Radio Oranje how shocked he had been at the sight of Flushing. 'Not a house undamaged – large parts are under water and boats are the main means of transport.' The Englishman was, however, heartened by what he called a 'typical Dutch sight': a woman on a bicycle. 'The water came up to the hubs, now and then she swayed, but keeping strictly to the right and sitting very straight, she just pedalled on' –

the symbol of the indestructibility of Zeeland and living proof of its motto, *Luctor et Emergo*, 'I struggle and rise again'.

Although the Battle of the Scheldt had had priority, the rest of the Allied armies in the Netherlands were on the move, too. By the end of October most of Limburg was free, while in Noord-Brabant important places like Eindhoven, Den Bosch and Tilburg were liberated. The conquest of Tilburg had been a glorious moment for the Dutch: it had been almost completely conquered by Dutch Commando troops, the Princess Irene Brigade.

The Brigade was formed in 1940, when the Government-in-Exile decided to call up all young Dutchmen in the free world to join the struggle for Holland's liberation. In August 1941, Queen Wilhelmina came to the Brigade's base at Wolverhampton to give the men their colours and the name of 'Royal Princess Irene Brigade', after her second granddaughter, born nine months before the Nazis had invaded her country.

Recruiting for the Brigade had been a constant problem, but turning it into a cohesive unit was almost as tricky. Though all its men were Dutch, many had never spoken the language and on one occasion two sentries passed each other the instructions in Greek, to the despair of the corporal on duty. A volunteer from Turkey had to be discharged as he could not communicate with anybody and fell ill with misery. The only common language for the troops – coming from thirty-two countries and speaking fifteen languages – was therefore English.

In August 1944, the Brigade had been transported to Normandy to take part in the campaign in Europe, under the command of Colonel A. C. de Ruyter van Steveninck. The Dutchmen landed on 8 August and had their baptism of fire under the command of the British 6th Airborne Division at the River Orne near Bréville, christened by the Canadians 'Hell-Fire Corner'. They lost one man. In pursuit of the retreating Germans the Brigade arrived in northern Belgium in mid-September, where another engagement killed fifteen men. They marched on, and on Wednesday, 20 September, exactly at midnight, they crossed the Dutch border near Valkenswaard, south of Eindhoven.

'It was more than four years ago since, in Flemish Zeeland, the last Dutch troops were forced to leave the Netherlands' territory,' a reporter wrote. 'For four dark years the Dutch have been

Sunken, grey and lifeless—as one journalist described the faces of the Dutch during that last endless winter of the German occupation, the Hunger Winter. There was no food, no gas, no light, no warmth, no transport. It was a winter of despair in which the Dutch discovered—according to one of them—that 'they only consisted of a stomach and certain instincts'.

Right Arrogant, still confident of victory, German and Dutch Nazi leaders give the Hitler salute at a rally. It was a brief moment of glory and unity, which came to an end on 'Mad Tuesday', 5 September 1944. (Behind the microphone: SS leader Hanns Albin Rauter; on his left: Reichskommissar Arthur Seyss-Inquart and Dutch Nazi leader Anton Mussert.)

Below (from left to right) Two Austrians, a German and a Dutchman: four men who represented the evil of Nazism in the Occupied Netherlands.
Arthur Seyss-Inquart, the Austrian 'traitor' who became the Nazi overlord of the Dutch.
Hanns Albin Rauter, another Austrian, whose hated SS divisions never succeeded in stamping out the Dutch Resistance.
General Johannes Blaskowitz, the Wehrmacht commander who obeyed every order, despite his dislike of the Nazis.
Anton Mussert, the engineer who failed to inspire the Dutch with his Nazi ideology.

The harshest edicts of the Germans and the confiscation of wirelesses did not deter the Dutch hunger for news—even when the home-made set had to be hidden in a telephone directory.

Left Prime Minister P. S. Gerbrandy, called in by Queen Wilhelmina, was able to command the respect of the Allies, thanks to his loyalty to their cause.

Right Prince Bernhard, son-in-law of Queen Wilhemina, faced a hard task when he was appointed Commander of the Dutch Forces of the Interior, but performed a miracle by uniting the Dutch Resistance.

During the Hunger Winter executions were frequent, and it was common
Nazi practice to leave bodies lying in the road as a warning. To many
Dutch people this was a challenge—and the Germans had hardly turned
their backs before the bodies were covered with a Dutch tricolor.

Others died less sensationally, simply from starvation. They were many—too many—and the undertakers could not cope with such numbers. As a result, corpses often rested in a church until a coffin and some form of transport could be found.

One of the evils of the war was the black market. The most famous was in the Jordaan, in the heart of the working-class district of Amsterdam.
There the girls stood, day in day out, selling cigarettes, cigars, coffee or tea for vast sums of money. Even a slice of bread with a smear of margarine seemed worth a fortune to those compelled to live on sugarbeets.

struggling and waiting before they could welcome the triumphant Dutch soldiers at the border of Brabant. It was tremendous.'

In Operation Market Garden the Dutch fought at Grave, but
the original orders to advance to Apeldoorn had to be cancelled
after the Allied failure at Arnhem. Instead, they were sent to
Tilburg on 10 October, to fight the battle that, according to Radio
Oranje, became 'the feat of arms the Brigade is most proud of'. It
was a gruelling fight – 'water to the chin and grenades to your
toes', as one soldier described it – and in the two days it lasted
little apparent progress was made. The Germans, however, gave
up at once when reinforcements arrived: a Scottish division,
which to the envy of the Brigade marched straight into the city for
which they had fought so hard. The Tilburgers made up for this
disappointment on 5 November when they gave the Brigade the
recognition it deserved with a spectacular welcome during a
parade before Prince Bernhard.*

Soon after Tilburg, Breda, too, fell into Allied hands, and when
November began the Germans held only two bridgeheads south
of the Maas, one of them at the end of what was then the longest
bridge in the Netherlands, the Moerdijkbridge across Hollands
Diep, and one of them at Heusden on the bank of the Maas,
twenty-five kilometres from the capital of Noord-Brabant, Den
Bosch.

The 2000 inhabitants of Heusden, an attractive seventeenth-
century fortress, waited in those first days of November with
increasing impatience for their liberators. They knew that Den
Bosch had been free since 27 October and did not understand
why the Allies did not advance farther. Allied guns constantly
shelled the town in preparation for an attack, but nothing more
happened and the population were hiding miserably in their
cellars.

About one hundred and fifty of them had taken shelter in the
solid basement of the elegant Gothic-styled Town Hall, with its

---

*The PIB spent the rest of the winter in Zeeland, guarding the Scheldt. At the
end of April 1945 they were sent to the front along the Maas, where during a last
battle they lost thirteen men. On 8 May they made an entry into liberated The
Hague and two months later the Brigade was disbanded. In total, forty-three men
were killed in action.

forty-metre-high tower, and they felt relatively safe. But the tower had a strategic importance as a look-out, and some citizens became suspicious when on Saturday, 4 November, the Germans carried baskets and boxes up to the top. One Heusdener warned that the whole lot was going to be blown up, but he was accused of creating panic, and when a couple of Dutchmen secretly had a look at the baskets it seemed that they contained sand. The presence of eight German telephone operators in the Town Hall was another reassurance, while the doctor of a German Red Cross team told the worried Heusdeners that there was nothing to fear.

Constant bombardments had cut off all communications, and nobody in the Town Hall knew that the Germans had paid similar visits to the two other towers in town, those of the Protestant and the Catholic churches. Again, some boxes had been carried in and upstairs, but when Father P. Manders asked one of the Germans if there was any danger the officer told him: 'You can do whatever you like, as long as you don't go into the tower.' Another, with a broad grin, sat down and played 'Silent Night'. Father Manders' feeling that this was a sinister warning was correct. That night at two o'clock his tower exploded, followed by the Protestant one.

The explosions woke the sixty-year-old Pieter Schmiehuysen, who, since the Allied bombings had started, had slept under the staircase in the courtyard of the Town Hall, keeping an eye on the building. He rushed up to the first floor to see what damage had been done and bumped into three Nazi soldiers, who were just coming down from the second floor. 'Having a walk?' he asked them, but the Germans just shrugged. Schmiehuysen explained that he was on guard and asked them if they had seen anything suspicious. 'Everything is all right,' one answered, 'nothing is the matter' – and they disappeared in a hurry.

Twenty minutes later a heavy explosion rocked the whole of Heusden. The three soldiers were explosives experts and had lit the fuses in the tower. Startled people came running from all sides to the Town Hall, but when the cloud of dust was blown away by the wind they saw only a big empty space and a shapeless mountain of rubble that covered the one hundred and fifty refugees.

In a mad fury everybody began to dig and hack away until Father Manders tried to restore some order. Lying down on the ruins, he called out, asking those down below if any fresh air was getting to them. The muffled answer was negative, and frantic digging began again. It was not fast enough, and Father Manders complained later: 'We had enough people, but not nearly enough tools.'

When, six hours later, the Allies marched into town there was for once no enthusiastic welcome. They found instead a shattered community that needed a week to count its dead – one hundred and thirty-four out of the one hundred and fifty.

The explosion was obviously meant to prevent the Allies using the tower as a look-out, but why the Germans never warned the sheltering citizens is unknown. Not even the eight German telephone operators, to their fury, had been given any warning, but they escaped unharmed. It was simply another of the many acts which that winter typified a sick and ugly regime with no respect for human life. It is sad to reflect that the Allies, who expected a strong German defence at the south end of the bridge at Heusden, could in fact have taken the place in one go as most Germans had already been withdrawn to the north bank of the Maas long before the tower was blown up.

The other German bridgehead near the destroyed Moerdijk-bridge fell on 8 November. Brabant was now completely free and, as Eisenhower had told his commanders on 2 November, it was now up to them to decide how far western Holland should be cleared. He warned them, however, that this decision must be based on 'military factors and not on political considerations'. The humanitarian aspect was not even mentioned, and for the 4.5 million Dutchmen trapped north of the rivers the misery was to continue.

Churchill, celebrating his seventieth birthday on 30 November, was by now very much aware of the suffering and felt deeply sorry. But he could do little. 'I'm trying to have Holland cleared up behind us,' he wrote on 3 December to Field-Marshal Jan Christiaan Smuts, the Prime Minister of South Africa and a great friend of the Dutch. But as Churchill confessed: 'It is not so easy as it used to be for me to get things done.'

CHAPTER SEVEN

Out to the Farms

'Life in occupied territory is like life in a prison – the guards can come into the cell whenever they want, there is no light and heating, and once a day you get a bite of food that is completely inadequate,' a Dutchman wrote at the end of November 1944. The lack of transport, gas and electricity had created an atmosphere of deadly apathy which covered the whole of western Holland like a thick grey blanket. Decay and poverty dominated. 'People degenerate, too,' he went on. 'Hunger and cold leave their mark and the drabness increases by the day.'

The weather in November made it still worse. It never stopped raining. 'The statistics tell us that we have to go back to the year 1864 to find such a wet November,' Diemer in Rotterdam wrote, and Dr Mees remarked bitterly: 'Some begin to believe that Our Dear Lord has become pro-Nazi as the weather has an unfavourable effect on the Allied progress.' Even Jan Jansen in Kampen, normally so positive in his chronicles, seemed to have lost hope and wrote on 25 November: 'The Allied winter offensive brings no decision. . . . And water, to which the enemy has sacrificed half our country, prevents the Tommies bringing effective help to our western provinces, kicked into the mud by the tyrant.' He counted the days – 'one day, one grey day out of thirty, sixty, a hundred, two hundred . . . ?'

The nights, spent in fear, brought no relief, either. 'At two o'clock we're woken up by footsteps in the street. They're coming. Heavy boots with their iron nails stamp in the streets. A car approaches with shrieking motor and whizzes past. Then, just when you dare to breathe again, you hear the brakes. Again the boots, and again they walk by. . . . Four, five seconds of silence and then not far away the shouting and banging on the doors. "Aufmachen, aufmachen" – "Open the door".'

68

The country was badly in need of immediate help. 'In the big cities in western Holland there is famine,' a telegram warned the Government in London on 24 November. 'Riots make victims. Potatoes and bread next week reduced to one kilogram. Shortly sugarbeets are to replace potatoes.'

In The Hague particularly, the situation was tragic. Amsterdam was still getting some food supplies from the tip of Noord-Holland, and Rotterdam from the islands in the south, but The Hague, the former royal residence, had no 'hinterland' and many, in despair, began to loot. 'They steal whatever they can,' a housewife in The Hague wrote, 'and all the shops have now put up their shutters as their windows have been smashed.' The Germans intervened without mercy and shot a few people. 'One young man had to hold a piece of paper in his hand on which was written "I'm a looter".' She had watched in horror. 'He had to write it himself – and then they blindfolded him and executed him.'

But Rotterdam, too, was hungry. The ration for one day had gone down to 300 grams of potatoes, 200 grams of bread – which meant five slices – 9 grams of fat, mostly rapeseed oil, 28 grams of pulses and 5 grams of meat and cheese, if any was available. There was only skimmed milk and even that was scarce. 'It is just too much to die on, but certainly too little to keep you alive,' many complained.

For an increasing number of people the central kitchen was their last hope. Secret preparations for this institution had started in 1940. When the Germans heard about it, they were furious and they told Louwes, the man responsible for food supplies, that it was a purely communist measure. People would lose the habit of eating at home and would learn to eat together as in Russia. Louwes persisted, and in the first year it was a great success: in Amsterdam alone more than 45,000 people were fed each day in 1942. When the quality of the food deteriorated, interest diminished, but when, in October 1944, gas and electricity were cut off the need for the kitchens came back. On 23 October central food distribution started throughout the whole of western Holland, and for the sum of twenty cents, and a potato-coupon per week, every citizen could get half a litre of food per day.

The Germans had by then changed their minds, and the 1400

69

'Bolshevist' kitchens were allowed to operate freely, distributing a total of two million meals every day. In Amsterdam, with a population of about 770,000 souls, no fewer than 437,000 reported for a ration that was not only inadequate in quantity, but had hardly any calorific value, either. Sometimes you queued for hours for a plate of soup made from unpeeled potatoes, or for a mash of sugarbeet and beetroot. But the hunger was so great, an inspector reported, 'that the central kitchen very often served food, approved for human consumption, but which animals would refuse'.

As the food was usually steamed, it rapidly turned sour and it was best to eat it as soon as possible. One inspector complained: 'If one consumed the food at once, it was very tasty, but it often happened that the stew soured by the evening and was inedible.'

The first central kitchen in Hilversum was opened in March 1942 and in October of that year the kitchen in the Langgewenst – for every Hilversummer a very familiar name, which very inappropriately meant 'long-wished-for' – was officially opened, but interest was small, and in June 1944 not more than 500 citizens were fed. In November, however, the daily customers had increased to 8000 and they would grow to 40,000 in March 1945, out of 80,000 inhabitants.

I tasted the food seldom, as my father had his own way of provisioning his family. 'A few times in the week I took my bike, loaded with bags, sacks and empty milk-bottles,' he remembered. 'We left at seven o'clock in the morning as soon as the curfew was over to try to find a farmer kind enough to sell us something.' Born businessman as he was, he succeeded soon enough in making some solid contacts, farmers who had taken a liking to him or pitied us, and who allowed him to come back. If they didn't want money he could offer them apple jelly or tinned fruit, leftovers from his business, which were stored in the cellar and guarded like gold bars. And it was very rarely that he didn't come home with a few bottles of milk, some eggs or a sack of potatoes that he had been allowed to glean for himself in the fields.

One day, my father had a stroke of luck. Leaving on one of his provision trips he discovered that our lane was blocked by a dead horse. The Germans had obviously shot it, after an exploding mine had wounded it that night. 'Within a few seconds I was hacking away with my pocket-knife and, when others joined me surreptitiously, I returned home with an enormous piece of meat.'

Thousands of Dutchmen made the same sort of trip – 'out to the farms', it was called – but in the middle of November a sudden change in the attitude of the Wehrmacht Command made an improvement in the food situation probable. The Government in London received news of it on 17 November. 'Wehrmacht now disapproves embargo of State Commissioner on food transport from north to west,' a telegram stated. 'Wehrmacht demands steps by Dutch food authorities to prevent famine and problems with population.'

Seyss-Inquart had in fact already decided in mid-October to lift the embargo on inland shipping, but the German Army at that time had frowned on his proposal as long as the railway strike lasted. Seyss-Inquart had given in. 'I said to myself that the Dutch people themselves were responsible for this state of emergency, and that the military interests of the Reich were, anyhow, equally important,' he explained later at his trial.

The Germans needed the Dutch barges badly for the transport of the fruits of their systematic looting of Holland, and of their own supplies. And they told Seyss-Inquart they could not spare the 450,000 tons of shipping they had confiscated. In fact they would have liked more tonnage, which forced the skippers of the one million tons that were left to keep their barges hidden.

The same fears that caused the manhunts in November made the Wehrmacht now look again at the food situation. They realised that famine would bring epidemics in its wake, provoke even greater hatred and could lead to rebellion – and that in the rear of the troops. Besides, the general misery was beginning to have a demoralising effect on the German soldiers, even if they themselves had enough to eat.

But the lifting of the embargo did not at once make the great difference they expected. There was little co-operation between the Nazi civil and military offices, and the Dutch skippers had little trust in the promise of the Germans not to confiscate the 100,000 tons of shipping needed for food transport. Rauter even promised the protection of his Ijsselmeer fleet, but on condition that the empty barges, on their way back to the north, would transport German booty, which delayed the operation again. And in the last week of November only 1988 tons of potatoes were carried to the west, 8000 tons less than was needed for one week.

It was ironic that, while the west was starving, the north had plenty of potatoes, beets and rye. Transport was the only problem, and the Nazi press took care that no Dutchman could forget that. The NSB weekly, *Volk en Vaderland*, never stopped referring to the railway strikers, who were the reason that 'millions of kilograms of foodstuff' were rotting away in the north-east. But, if it was indeed a fact that the strike considerably increased the difficulties facing the Dutch food authorities, this was not the only cause of the shortage.

When the Third Reich invaded the Netherlands in 1940, the Dutch Government had built up reserves of about 1.2 million tons of food. Immediately, measures were taken to try to feed the Dutch entirely from their own soil, but the Dutch farmers had immense problems. Not only did the Germans force them to sell a great part of their produce to them – some sources speak of sixty per cent – but there was also a great dearth of fertiliser, of weedkillers, of insecticides and of machinery. The deportation of many young farmhands to Germany did not help, either. In spite of the fact that twenty per cent of the livestock was killed off – mostly pigs and chickens because they consume much the same basic foodstuffs as humans – output went down year by year, and after the bad summer of 1944 reserves were almost nonexistent.

The authorities had calculated that under ideal circumstances the Dutch farmers could produce about 2000 calories a day per head, nearly sufficient to provide the 2400 calories a grown person needs. But the circumstances were anything but ideal, and in October 1944 a Dutchman was getting on average no more than 1300 calories, which decreased in November to 900 – an Englishman at the same time received 2500 calories.

Some cities, impatient over the delay in the transports, began to take their own measures. The pro-Nazi mayor Edward J. Voûte of Amsterdam decided to appeal to the many unemployed in his city to go and lift the potatoes in Drenthe themselves. He summoned to his office Dirk U. Stikker, director of the Heineken brewery and a representative of the Dutch employers' organisation, to enlist his support. 'The picture he drew was indeed very depressing,' Stikker wrote in his memoirs. 'The Germans had confiscated so much coal that the bakeries had only supplies for two, and the central kitchens for only three months. The bread position was even more difficult. There was so little flour that there would be bread for only two and a half weeks.'

Stikker, deeply concerned, promised his support and together with Louwes he published a proclamation asking people to help in his 'national effort'. Radio Oranje, however, intervened passionately and warned the Amsterdammers that the potatoes would go straight to the Germans. Stikker sent a sharp telegram to London, remonstrating that the authorities in Holland were better informed than London, but there was no change of heart and Dr Mees wrote sadly: 'The potato-lifting in Drenthe doesn't seem to work.'

Now that food from official sources was hardly to be expected, it was up to the individual Dutchman to go and get what he needed, and one of the most dramatic episodes of Nazi occupation in Holland began. City dwellers left their homes by hundreds of thousands to descend like locusts on the farmers. 'The urge that drove the people out of towns to the land was so great that very little stopped them reaching their so much desired goal: food,' Dr G. J. Kruijer wrote in his study of the hunger trips. Lack of money or goods to exchange was no reason to stay at home. The weather, too, had no influence. Insufficient clothing and worn-out shoes were a nuisance, but stopped few. Raids and road blocks, confiscations by the Nazis and air raids by the Allies – they were all unable to put an end to the interminable flow of people, roaming along the roads, hunting and begging for food.

There were no trains, buses or motorcars; so only the bicycle was left. Before the war the eight million Dutch owned four million bikes, but intensive use and constant raids by the Germans had halved this number. They were indispensable in the autumn and winter of 1944, because with a bicycle almost the whole of the country was within reach – 'they were the tentacles that stretched out of the cities'. Very often they had no tyres and only a rubber or wooden band around their wheels; sometimes you just rode on the rims. If you had no bike, you hired a pushcart or took a pram, or a wheelbarrow, and only two per cent of the hunger-trippers went without any transport at all, on foot.

How many people took part that winter in the mass exodus to the farms is not known, but research in Amsterdam has revealed that in sixty-two per cent of the Amsterdam families at least one member went on a hunger trip.

There they went, along the straight, open roads of the flat polders, often bent over their handlebars, struggling against wind and rain, hardly protected by the tall poplars along the seemingly endless highways, with bags and boxes on the luggage carriers. Some cycled alone, others preferred company, but very often they were too tired, too hungry and too wet to want to talk, except about food and about what they could ask the farmers in exchange for a sheet, a watch, a gold bracelet. Sometimes they travelled hundreds of kilometres for a sack of potatoes or cabbages, a dozen eggs, some milk and butter. 'Society had reverted to the primitive stage of bartering,' Kruijer wrote. 'Spoons, services, knick-knacks, tools, everything was good to exchange.'

Like almost everybody, my father joined the stream to the north. 'The farmers around Hilversum had not got enough,' he explained, 'and for pulses, butter and wheat you had to go past the Ijssel.' The Veluwe in between was useless, the farmers inhospitable and often even hostile. 'When I once, near Nijkerk, asked for a bowl of water to check a punctured tyre, the farmer's wife slammed the door in my face,' my father remembered. The only exception was the Fino soup factory in Harderwijk, where the trekkers could get a bowl of thin but hot soup, an opportunity daily grasped by 3000 people – a total of 150,000 people during the whole winter.

My father's longest trips were to Friesland, where my grandparents lived in the little hamlet of Oudega. It helped. Friends and neighbours were always willing to sell my father something, in particular meat, bacon and butter. On his way up he always stayed a night in Kampen with the same baker, Breed, who had given him hospitality the first time, but the return trip was often done in one day. On one of those journeys he was stopped near Amersfoort by the Landwacht, who confiscated almost everything. My aunt, who got away scot free by bluffing that she had already been checked, shared with my father what was left.

The homecoming was always a triumph. Even now I can remember the surprise and delight with which we stared at the pieces of greasy bacon, the yellow butter, the white eggs, the dirty potatoes, the mellow cheese or the wheat – and the joy was not spoiled by the knowledge that I would have to grind the latter for tedious hours in my mother's old coffee-mill.

It was the same in many households, where everybody had his own adventures and experiences, often not very favourable to the Dutch farmers, who many hunger-trippers found to be mean and greedy. The farmers, on the other hand, complained that the town people, who had never had much respect for them, were rude and untrustworthy. Small gestures in such a tense situation meant a lot. A glass of water refused sometimes condemned a whole village; a slice of bread for someone on the verge of collapsing turned a farmer's wife into an angel. 'Before we went to bed, they gave us a plate of porridge and eight sandwiches – we almost shouted hurrah,' someone remembered. But somebody else still talks bitterly about the one bowl of soup a woman gave him and his son, with two spoons. There were farmers who taunted the trippers by putting signs in their gardens saying 'Linen-cupboards full', or by placing a shoe on a table at the gate with the words 'To exchange for food'. A farmer near The Hague refused to sell his potatoes by the kilogram, cruelly admitting that he was waiting until he could sell them one by one.

'Very often one was treated like a beggar,' an out-of-work journalist, J. G. Raatgever, from The Hague, wrote. 'I never felt more humiliated than when I was waiting, with sixty other men, for the farmer who had said he was selling that afternoon. We, poor suckers, stood there for hours in the soaking rain, while he was doing something on the roof. He didn't even bother to look at that bunch of beggars and we stood there, just like a pack of beaten dogs, with pale faces and empty bags, until we realised that he was not going to sell. We just crept away.'

It was difficult for everybody, particularly the first time, to knock on a farm door and ask for food, but many farmers helped as much as they could, only to be treated badly by their customers in return. Some found their potato cellars emptied next morning, their chickens or the leather harnesses for their horses gone, their cows milked. And the problem was that the stream never seemed to stop. 'I could not help it,' one farmer confessed later, 'but I sometimes lost my patience when they came knocking at my door, day and night.'

The misery was heartbreaking. 'People with their feet torn,

blood in their shoes . . . some had no shoes and wrapped their feet in rags . . . children not older than ten and hardly clothed,' my father remembered. Kruijer mentioned other cases: 'a young boy with a pushcart in which he had his younger brother, dead . . . two boys who had been going from farm to farm for months . . . a dying woman in a cart'.

'The misery some suffered was terrible to watch, every push-cart, every pram was a tragedy, no smiles on their faces,' an Amsterdammer wrote, who had just returned from a trip to Waterland, north of the city. There was little left on the farms there, but many Amsterdammers had no choice – it was nearest. 'They just stumbled on, in their slippers, clogs or high-heeled shoes, insufficiently dressed, underfed, with their carts, their poverty and their worries. They had nothing to barter with and no money for some food or a bed, and they were happy when they reached Amsterdam with the few goodies they had collected, without them being confiscated.'

CHAPTER EIGHT

Dark December

'AN ARMY of amateur woodcutters has gone into action in Holland, destroying what little scenery the Germans have left,' the journalist Raatgever reported in December 1944. The Dutch had no choice. The winter was bitterly cold, there was no coal, gas or electricity and, if you wanted to cook or to warm yourself, you had to go out and get some fuel. 'Early in the morning or after sunset you can see respectable gentlemen creeping through parks and public gardens, past lanes and canals, judging everything on its burning qualities.'

The result was that tree-lined streets became bare in one night, while bridge-railings disappeared and little parks were razed to the ground. After all the seats had been stolen, Amsterdam's largest park, the Vondel-park, had to be closed when some cynics started to auction its trees, which – for a steep price – they would cut, saw up, and deliver to your home. The Woods in The Hague had for years to come a memento of that winter: a large oak tree, attacked on one side by an axeman, who had given up, the other side assaulted by two men with a saw, which got stuck and was left behind – and heavily damaged at the top by bullets from a Spitfire.

My father, my elder brother Wim, and I also had to search for wood, and the nearby Korversbos was very handy. There, we looked for a manageable tree, preferably not higher than eight metres, which was stripped of its branches, sawn in three and carried home on my father's bike, my sister's pushchair or my toboggan. The trees in front of our house had long since disappeared.

The Germans and their helpers, the Landwacht, tried to put a stop to all this and regularly confiscated the loads, but they never succeeded in halting the massive deforestation of western Holland. Amsterdam, for instance, lost 22,000 of its 42,000 trees in a few months. All the wooden paving-blocks between the tram-rails were lifted, and even the canals dredged in the hope of finding something that would burn. In the Jewish district, empty now since the inhabitants had been taken away to the extermination-camps in Germany and Poland, 1500 houses were robbed of every bit of wood, joists, beams, staircases, door- and window-frames, and most collapsed in ruins, often killing the wreckers.

Most of the wood, after hours of exhausting sawing and hack-ing, disappeared into the so-called 'miracle stoves', euphemisti-cally so christened because they were supposed to give maximum heat with minimum fuel. The stove – a little grid in a small tin placed in turn in a larger tin – was in fact a greedy monster. 'It demanded more attention than a baby,' one user complained, 'because you can leave a baby alone for ten minutes.'

In this atmosphere Holland's most homely festival was cel-ebrated – the day of St Nicholas, or Sinterklaas, on 5 December. 'We live on short commons,' Diemer wrote, 'but St Nicholas remains a national day.' The Germans had forbidden the bakers to do anything special, the shop windows were empty, and the Saint and his traditional black page-boys stayed out of the streets, but by the light of a candle or oil-lamp and around the blazing 'miracle stove' the home-made presents with accompanying witty poems were exchanged – 'forgetting for one evening the war and oppression'.

Not many had a sweet that day – I couldn't even remember the taste of chocolate or the traditional fudge – as the only delicacy which was available was a sort of mock cream, called 'klop-op', a bit of sugarbeet-foam, which, if you didn't eat it immediately, melted away into a sad little yellow puddle.

It was on days like St Nicholas that the Dutch thought more nostalgically than ever of their good cup of pre-war coffee and tea, not to speak of cigarettes. Now none of these was obtainable, except at very high prices on the black market, and most people had to make do with substitutes. The Dutch were supposed to be lucky as they had the best 'ersatz' coffee – even better than that of the Germans. The tea-substitutes were less successful. All sorts of blossoms were tried, but none of them was really satisfactory.

Tobacco was also almost nonexistent. Homegrown tobacco had

been on the market since 1943, under the name Beka, but the fact that the Dutch insisted that this was an abbreviation of 'Beslist Eerste Klas Afval' ('Certified first-class garbage') said enough. The home-made cigarettes did not fare much better. Their name, Consi, meant – according to some wits – 'Cigarettes Under National Socialist Influence'. They were, however, slightly better than the so-called Belgian cigarettes, a mixture of seaweed, peat-dust and heather.

My father grew his own tobacco in our back garden. The large leaves were picked in autumn and hung for weeks in the attic to dry. Then followed the fermentation, and finally an expert would prepare it. 'The quality was really quite reasonable,' my father assured us. What I remember is the stench.

On the black market cigarettes fetched a tremendous price. For a pre-war one the price was one guilder at the beginning of December, but by Christmas the price had rocketed to five guilders. Loose tobacco had doubled in price in the same period and cost one hundred guilders an ounce, and cigarette-paper, before the war eighteen cents for a hundred, was now fourteen guilders. The Dutch Bible Society stopped the sale of their Bibles, printed on India paper, because they discovered that the increase in sales was due not so much to the growing piety of the Dutch as to the fact that the pages made a fortune for black-marketeers, who sold them in batches of one hundred pages to cigarette-rollers.

With Christmas looming, the thought of 'something extra' crossed the mind of every Dutchman, but it was only a thought. If one had no contacts with a farmer or money to buy on the black market, one had to live on the ration for the week of 17 to 23 December which was : one kilogram of potatoes, the same weight of bread and 100 grams of meat, if available. For the children there were 210 grams of flour and an extra kilogram of potatoes. It was not much for a festive Christmas dinner.

Hopes of a slight improvement in the situation had by then disappeared completely. During the whole month of November the food officials Hirschfeld and Louwes had tried to get the shipping transport from the east going, founding on 5 December their own 'company', the Central Shipping Company for Food Supplies. They had assembled a fleet of 227 barges with a tonnage of more than 70,000 and received a guarantee from Seyss-Inquart that there was no danger of the ships being confiscated, but just when their efforts began to bear fruit and the transports started there was a severe frost. The canals and the Ijsselmeer froze over, and on 23 December one of the coldest winters in memory began, lasting until 31 January.

Never during the whole war had the situation looked so desperate to the Occupied Dutch. On 16 December the Germans had unleashed, out of the blue, a massive offensive in the Ardennes, the Battle of the Bulge. Three complete armies tried to break through to the Allied supply centres at Liège, Brussels and, of course, Antwerp. Taken off-guard – their intelligence had totally failed – the Allies reeled back. 'The weather was foggy and therefore favoured the enemy in that it hid his movements and intentions and also prevented us from using our massive air power,' a British general explained later.

German success would have meant that the American First Army, the British Second Army and the largest part of the First Canadian Army in Belgium and the southern Netherlands would have been cut off; the Germans could have strengthened their eastern front; time would have been gained to produce Germany's latest secret weapon – and the end of the war would have been delayed for months, if not years.

For the Occupied and Liberated Netherlands it looked very bad. The Ardennes offensive ended all hopes of a speedy liberation for western Holland, and filled the free provinces with dread of being reconquered. The Germans had planned to attack from the north of the Maas in the direction of Belgium, forming bridgeheads south of the river, from which the Germans could advance to Antwerp, while airborne troops were to occupy strategic positions in Limburg and Noord-Brabant. Both provinces would once again become a battlefield.

In Breda and Eindhoven the Dutch Forces of the Interior, the BS, mobilised all their men to defend their cities, and plans were made to follow the Allies if they should withdraw. 'Everybody already had terrible visions of returning Germans, who would start a reign of terror, compared with which the past would be child's play,' Henk van den Broek, transferred from Radio Oranje in London to the newly founded Radio Rising Netherlands in Eindhoven, wrote later.

The worst danger seemed over when Christmas arrived. A

sudden change in the weather had given the initiative back to the Allies and, although the battle was to last till the end of January, the Dutch in the south could breathe again. Their freedom was no longer threatened.

For the Dutch in Occupied Holland, however, it meant that the end of the war would be longer delayed – Montgomery had to postpone his planned offensive across the Rhine by a month, but it was almost worse that the Ardennes offensive had forced the Germans to intensify their search for men. Although the Wehrmacht, which in the past had been used for the raids, was now involved in the fighting in Belgium, the need for Dutchmen to build the German defence works was more urgent than ever.

During the autumn Liese had had the time to think of a more foolproof scheme which, according to this representative of Goebbels, would guarantee the co-operation of at least half a million Dutchmen. On 24 December posters signed by Liese appeared in every city and village of Occupied Holland, announcing that all men between sixteen and forty years of age would soon be called up to work for the Germans. He promised that every man who could prove himself indispensable at home would receive a certificate of exemption, a so-called 'Ausweis'. The others were promised, in exchange for their work, good food and support for their families. It was an undertaking which, in the miserable month of December 1944, might work like a magnet.

The Dutch Resistance saw the danger at once and went into action. Already, on 21 December, the underground paper *Trouw* ('Faithful') urged its readers to sabotage the German measure by all possible means. The Nazi posters were quickly covered with a proclamation from the Resistance, asking women in particular to support their husbands and sons in a 'principled rejection' of the Liese action. At the same time 'the other side' – the Government in London – was asked to appeal through Radio Oranje. The Resistance leaders warned the Government that 'the delay of the Liberation and the famine had begun to undermine the spirit of resistance in the population'; and a few firm words of warning against the new Nazi campaign were badly needed.

Torn between fear for what the Liese action might bring them and their hatred of the Nazis – and sometimes the promise of food – worried about the events in the Ardennes and in general

beaten, bullied and starved, the Dutch celebrated the unforget-
able Christmas of 1944. The churches, unheated, were full, and
in a deep silence everybody listened to the defiant joint appeal
from the Protestant and Roman Catholic Churches. 'After all our
nation has suffered from the Occupation, we are now threatened
with the biggest disaster: to perish by starvation,' it began. 'The
sufferings of 4.5 million people in the western part of our country
are unbelievable . . . never before have we realised so well what it
means to pray for "our daily bread".' But, the Churches stated,
there were still ways and means to alleviate the suffering, and they
asked in particular the farmers to fulfil their tasks and the skippers 'to brave all the risks'.

According to a German historian, the Churches in the Netherlands were, during the whole of the war, the most 'pervasive and
widely influential opposition to Nazi ideology'. From the first
year of the Occupation to its end the Churches always spoke out
'in defence of Christianity and humanitarian principles'.

The last time they had spoken out was in a letter to Seyss-
Inquart, written in November 1944. It was not a request or a
protest, it was a denunciation of a régime that – so the Churches
said – since Mad Tuesday had taken off its mask and revealed its
demonic urge for destruction. It sounded like a farewell – for the
last time the arrogant rulers were reminded of their duty to God
and mankind. 'Do you, Sir, know that the lives of innocent citizens
are being regarded as of no value; that thousands, under age, too,
are taken out of their houses to work for the Occupier; that theft
of goods is being encouraged and is in any case not stopped . . . ?'
If nobody disentangled 'the knot of all the injustices of this
terrible war', there could be only one outcome, the Churches
warned: 'The hatred and desire for revenge, fed by German
atrocities, will be so enormous' that it would be impossible ever
again to imagine 'a real living and working together of the Dutch
and German people'.

With this letter the Churches broke the last links with the Nazi
authorities, and switched from spiritual guidance to practical
assistance. The German Occupation had bridged the gap that
history and dogmas had created between the Dutch Churches,
and together they had formed a Committee for Inter-
Ecclesiastical Consultation, the IKO, where they could study
together the possibilities of working together. It had made them

much stronger against the Germans, who never dared to risk a conflict with the united clergy, although a great number of individual ministers and priests were deported and lost their lives.

When the Churches decided in December to give more concrete assistance to the hungry, the IKO was the ideal body, and under the motto 'By the Churches, for all' they founded the IKB, which in close co-operation with the Dutch food authorities would take care of the many special cases in the Netherlands. The IKB got permission to try to collect the so-called 'free stores' – those not claimed by the authorities – and to transport them to the cities in the west. They worked fast, efficiently and with success, and on 9 January they could open their first posts – twenty-two to begin with – where they at once distributed 6000 hot meals to children.

Another initiative the Churches took in December had less effect. A Dutch lawyer, Dr H. L. F. J. van Deelen in Amsterdam, who had good contacts with the Roman Catholic authorities and with the Nazi Military Commander in Amsterdam, put a proposal before the latter to make the Occupied Dutch provinces neutral territory. The German had at first shown no interest, but when the persistent Dutchman told him he wanted to enlist the help of Pope Pius XII himself the Commander changed his mind. On 21 December a meeting took place in Utrecht between Van Deelen and the highest Roman Catholic authority in Holland, Archbishop Dr Johannes de Jong, who enthusiastically promised all the help he could give. The plans were sent to Rome, accompanied by a letter from De Jong, but nothing was ever heard of the scheme again.

By coincidence, the subject of neutralisation had also been discussed when a week earlier Dr Hirschfeld had been invited by Seyss-Inquart. Hirschfeld was astonished, because up till then the State Commissioner had tried to avoid any direct contact with him, but very soon it became clear what Seyss-Inquart's intentions were. Left alone for three hours, the two men talked about the food problems and the railway strike first, and then the German suddenly pointed to a map on the wall of his office. There were, he said, in the future only two options for the Netherlands: being flooded by the Wehrmacht to stop the Allies, or being declared a neutral zone. Hirschfeld, taken by surprise but on his guard, discussed with Seyss-Inquart for a while the pros and cons of the

latter, but the Dutchman believed the Allies would never accept it.
'They will probably say that Germany wishes to save its right
wing,' he told the State Commissioner, who put an abrupt end to
the conversation with the words: 'We have been fantasising pleasantly.'

Another German fantasy – for the starving Dutch, at least – was
the sumptuous dinner the usually frugal-living Seyss-Inquart
gave on Christmas Eve for his staff in his house, Clingendael,
outside The Hague. The hall was decorated with greenery, and
an enormous Christmas tree stood in a corner. During the meal
the State Commissioner read Hitler's Christmas message in which
the Führer wished the Germans in Holland strength and good
health. For the State Commissioner's guests there was little anxiety about the latter: on the menu, decorated with Nazi symbols,
were three different meats, five vegetables and two sorts of ice.

The 4.5 million Dutch outside had to make do with only one
sort of ice. The canals and lakes had been frozen over since 23
December, and every morning I would wake up to see frost-
flowers on my window. The streets that Christmas were very
quiet, and the tram conductor in Rotterdam who had escaped the
raids in November muttered: 'No Christmas atmosphere at all;
here and there a little branch of a Christmas tree, but they ask
four guilders for it. A joint is completely out of the question and
one meagre rabbit costs 40 to 50 guilders.' That week black-
market prices had gone through the ceiling. 'A loaf of bread that
normally costs 18 cents went in November for 4.50 guilders and
around Christmas for 18.'

Another Dutchman recorded in his diary: 'This is the most
terrible Christmas ever. There is not a thing in the house, nothing
to eat and of course no tree and no candlelight.' Of course babies
were born on Christmas Eve, and one father, Jan van Gemonden,
remembered how he went out in the freezing night to seek help.
'No one was in the streets when I took my bike – without tyres – to
get a doctor. It was ten o'clock, and my wife had felt the first birth
pangs.' He did not get very far before he was stopped by a
German soldier, rifle ready to shoot. 'It's curfew,' the man told
Van Gemonden, who, shivering with cold and nerves, explained
that his wife expected a baby any moment. Twice more he was
stopped, but every time the soldiers relented – for them, too, it
was Christmas – and at eleven o'clock he returned at last with a

midwife, and young Jan was born at midnight. 'In spite of all the misery I felt intensely happy,' his mother remembered later. When the news reached neighbours next day they all came with gifts: a bucket of hot water, two spoonfuls of tea, a lump of butter. In the week between Christmas and New Year, life became even more unreal. The weather was colder, and clear, but hardly anybody was skating. The Dutch, of whom it is said that they are born on their skates, were too weak to enjoy themselves on the ice. They had other things to do – the need for firewood was more urgent than ever. The Korversbos near us had disappeared in a few weeks, and now we had to go all the way to the Spanderswoud, an older and richer forest. But the police and the Landwacht were much stricter now and confiscated wood without mercy.

And of course you had to queue, for bread and for potatoes, even to get some wheat milled. My mother's coffee-mill was slow and agonising to operate, but fortunately the Van Wijngaarden mill near Hilversum's little port worked a few hours a day, and they were even willing to help the citizens. Waiting outside that week was so cold, and my hands and feet so frozen – my shoes were nothing more than wooden soles with a cotton strap – that I still remember the tears of pain and misery turning into icicles on my cheeks.

In Hilversum and any village it was bad, but in the bigger cities it was worse. While the Amsterdammers were destroying the Jewish district, the Rotterdammers had discovered that most of the town squares were laid on a foundation of slag in which one could still find real coal, and the squares were turned into mines. Even the air-raid shelters collapsed when people started to take out the supporting beams.

Amsterdam was a desolate city. The evacuee Douwenga from Wageningen, arriving there from Naarden with his family on the bike to celebrate New Year's Eve with friends, could not believe his eyes. 'How can one of the world's greatest cities decay so rapidly?' he wondered. The entry roads were barricaded with heavy concrete walls, everywhere in the gardens there were shelters, barbed wire, trenches, and the streets were full of German street-signs and Nazi slogans. The city was filthy, with enormous mountains of rubbish in which children were digging, and dirt floated in the canals. There was no street-sweeping any more and

– as in Hilversum – the rubbish-collector now came only once a week, swinging his rattle so that one could carry the bin outside and empty it into his cart.

Strangely enough, even in this exhausted and decaying city, some restaurants were still open and in use. There was of course only coffee- and tea-substitutes, and no milk or sugar, and if you wanted to eat you had to bring your own knife and fork. One chain of cheap cafeterias lost 46,655 utensils that winter, and from the more elegant American hotel 400 spoons and forks were stolen.

The food in most restaurants was not all that bad – the black market helped – but many served only their regular customers and at specific times. Alcohol was not available before five o'clock and then most bars had only one 'borrel' a head – a glass of old or young Dutch gin.

Amsterdam even offered some amusement still to those who had time and energy for it. In an unheated theatre the Dutch could listen to 'one hour of music' and later to 'one hour of drama'. (In spite of the fact that everybody kept his coat on, the cold was so penetrating that one hour was all anyone could take.) In the Concertgebouw the names of Jewish composers, painted along the balconies, had been blacked out.

All performances were matinées, because night life was impossible. Not only was there a curfew at six, seven or eight – that varied depending on the mood of the Nazis – but the city was pitch dark, too. There were no street lights and all windows were so heavily covered with black-out paper that not a glimmer of light was to be seen. Even torches were reduced to mere cat's-eyes, and in Amsterdam particularly, with all its canals, it was dangerous to go out after dark. In 1940, 450 people fell into the water at night, of whom 55 drowned. Dr Willem Drees, later the Dutch Prime Minister but during the war an important Resistance leader, almost lost his life in the autumn of 1944, before the canals froze. Returning from a meeting in Amsterdam he walked straight into the water. 'I thought that I was drowning, and worried about my wife,' he wrote later in his memoirs. 'Her nerves had already suffered so much. I called for help and waved with my torch, a bridge guard heard me and pulled me out.' The polluted water, however, gave him diphtheria, but while recuperating at home he used his time to write a programme of action for after the war.

The end of the war, however, still seemed far away when New Year's Eve came. The German offensive in the Ardennes had completely lost its impetus and the Wehrmacht divisions were being slowly pushed back, but according to the Nazi papers the Germans were still full of zip and optimism. Seyss-Inquart could see that for himself when he made his traditional New Year's Eve visit to a Wehrmacht bunker somewhere along the front line. Together with the soldiers, he listened to the Führer's speech on the radio, 'and again they felt their indestructible loyalty to their Leader', one paper rambled on. Afterwards they sang, 'and were making jokes with the Reichskommissar', who stayed till very late.

Most of the Dutch, however, were not in the mood to stay up till midnight. 'For the first time in my life I went to bed before twelve o'clock . . . glad that this black, disastrous year was over,' one of them wrote. The streets were deserted, and police and Gestapo cars had disappeared for once. 'Even the Huns are celebrating,' a Dutchman reported, adding with envy: 'They have drinks and cigarettes and girls, who sell their honour for one night of light and warmth.' But the silence in the town was almost frightening, he thought, and he wondered: 'Is it because a New Year starts? The year of Liberation or the year of our death?'

CHAPTER NINE

Mother of Her Country

QUEEN WILHELMINA, in exile in London, had a miserable December, too. 'We sat together round a tiny Christmas tree with but a single candle and imagined all this happening at home,' she wrote in her memoirs. Alone with her daughter Juliana at Laneswood – Bernhard was at the Front, and the two granddaughters still in Canada – she suffered deeply. 'In those days and in the months that followed I asked myself every morning when I opened my eyes: How am I to get through this day? What news will I receive today, once again worse than yesterday? Why should there be another of those terrible days? And yet – I knew I had to persevere till the bitter end.'

In her Christmas broadcast for Radio Oranje, she tried to encourage her Occupied subjects, pointing out that 'Christmas was a feast of promise' and that 'the unfathomable and consoling love of Christ exists because of that suffering', but she felt helpless. 'In our mind's eye we saw the hunger trips, those caravans of starving people who went into the country to obtain something for their families,' she wrote. And when her aide, Erik Hazelhoff Roelfzema, walked into her room one day she burst out: 'Have you heard it? They're dropping dead in the streets.' Taken by surprise he simply looked at her, and with an impatient gesture the Queen explained: 'The people, they're dropping dead in the streets.'

'She was utterly moved,' Roelfzema noticed, and when he left the room she was just sitting there, staring out of the window into the grey afternoon, 'like a wounded bird crouched under her blanket'.

The Queen was perhaps one of the few Dutch people in London who really understood how much her people suffered. Most of the exiles were, as Mr Fock once wrote, 'afraid of the hunger, but unable to imagine what it was like'. It was an 'unknown, which one could approach in one's imagination, but not with experience'. For Wilhelmina it was different. 'She identified so intensely with her people that the terrible suffering in the Netherlands became hers. She suffered for everybody, she suffered most,' Roelfzema wrote later.

It drove her to constant action. 'We considered it our imperative duty to inform people in Europe and abroad of the distress of the Netherlands,' she later recalled and she readily joined Gerbrandy in his propaganda campaign that winter. She used the return of Juliana to her children in Canada via Washington for an urgent personal plea to Roosevelt.

Queen Wilhelmina had met the American President for the first time in 1942, when he invited her to come and stay in his country house, Hyde Park, in the Hudson River Valley. 'I felt as if I was addressing an old friend, so cordial were his feelings for the Netherlands,' she wrote about this visit, which had included an address to Congress, the first ever by a woman. Now she explained her own feelings to him in a letter, copies of which she sent to King George and Churchill; 'profoundly disturbed by the terrible news of affairs in our home country', she felt that something drastic must be done 'if a major catastrophe, the like of which has not been seen in Western Europe since the Middle Ages, is to be avoided in Holland'.

'Hunger, cold, darkness, dirt, disease and floods' – that was her definition of the situation in the Netherlands, adding: 'We have before us the picture of an industrious and cultured people with a long and not inglorious history going to their doom.' It was therefore now 'the duty of the Dutch Government to ask for urgent military action for the purpose of driving out the Germans' and, if that was impossible, to urge for 'immediate relief in the form of either mass evacuation or in food, clothing, fuel and medical supplies . . .'.

Queen Wilhelmina certainly never minced her words when the interests of her country were at stake – Churchill once remarked: 'I fear no man in the world, except Queen Wilhelmina' – and from the moment that Hitler came to power in 1933 she had tried to awaken her countrymen to the threat of Nazism. She had no illusions about the mentality of the German National Socialists and no confidence in the defence policy of her own Ministers. Her constitutional position, however, made it impossible for her to intervene in practice, apart from giving frequent and sensible advice. When at the beginning of 1939, after much political bickering, she asked Mr D. J. de Geer to form a Cabinet, she did so without conviction, and he proved to her his lack of vision by refusing in August 1939 to mobilise the Army. Under pressure from her, mobilisation was decided on in De Geer's absence and three days later confirmed by him, just six days before war was declared on 3 September 1939, and eight months before the Nazis invaded Holland on 10 May 1940.

'After all these months, during which our country has scrupulously observed a strict neutrality, and while its only intention was to maintain this attitude firmly and consistently, a surprise attack without the slightest warning was launched by the German armed forces last night,' Wilhelmina told her people that day in May. 'I raise a fierce protest against this unexampled violation of good faith and outrage against all that is decent between civilised states.'

She followed the struggle with deep concern. How could the ill-prepared army of her small country defend itself against the ultra-modern Wehrmacht? One night she even called King George VI out of his bed to ask for more help, but it was in vain. On 13 May her Commander-in-Chief, General H. G. Winkelman, advised her to leave The Hague and try to reach Flushing or Flemish Zeeland. The Residence was seriously in danger and airborne troops had landed with the task of arresting the Queen if she refused to co-operate with the Nazis.

'Hurriedly I packed a few belongings, and I left The Hague that morning at half-past nine, preceded by a car with police troops.' The region through which she had to travel was infiltrated by the German paratroops, and the police took no risks. 'We frequently heard a challenge to halt from the police car in front of us. Occasionally, when it was not obeyed, a shot was fired.'

At the Hook of Holland she boarded a British destroyer, but when it sailed and she asked the British captain to warn the Dutch in Zeeland that she was on her way he told her that his instructions did not allow him to make contact with the shore. 'It put an end to our plan of going to Zeeland,' she realised. 'It would have been completely irresponsible to arrive there without previously notifying the Rear-Admiral, who would have been responsible for the conduct of the war, as well as my personal security.' And after a miniature 'War Council in life-jackets' she decided to go to England, to see there when and how she could return.

She was heartbroken. During her whole life she had been a great admirer of two of her ancestors, William the Silent, who led the Dutch rebellion against the Spanish in the sixteenth century, and William III, the Stadtholder-King, who had defended Holland against the French a century later. It had been her dream to join her soldiers on the battlefield and – as William III had put it – 'to be the last man to fall in the last ditch'. But she wrote later, sadly: 'I knew this was not granted to me.'

Just as painful for her was 'the shattering impression' she knew her departure would make at home, but she considered herself obliged, for the sake of Holland, to accept that risk of 'appearing to have resorted to ignominious flight' in order to continue her fight against Nazi evil from London.

Her departure had taken place without consulting her Cabinet, and it was a coincidence that Queen and Government met again in London – 'in the same city, but not with the same feelings and convictions'. De Geer wanted to make peace with Nazi Germany, and had even tried to approach Berlin behind the back of the British. The Queen, on the other hand, refused to consider any peace initiative with Hitler, and enlisted the support of her Minister of Justice, Professor Gerbrandy, and others.

In August her patience with De Geer ran out and she sacked him unceremoniously, rejecting a proposal to make him Minister of Finance with the words: 'Gentle doctors make stinking wounds.' She asked Gerbrandy, for whom she always had a great respect, to take De Geer's place. While the little Frieslander was repairing the damage his predecessor had done in London, De Geer was sent to the East Indies for a reconnaissance trip, but via Portugal he returned to Holland.

Wilhelmina, in the meantime, had said farewell to her daughter Juliana and her granddaughters, Beatrix and Irene, who sailed for the safety of Canada, and she now began five years of

wandering in and around London. While her Government settled down in Stratton House off Piccadilly, and after a short stay
at Buckingham Palace, she found a large dark house in Eaton
Square, which she shared with Prince Bernhard and what was left
of her court. A year later she moved to 77 Chester Square, not far
from the Palace, once a very elegant part of town, but since the
outbreak of war almost deserted. Some of the early-Victorian
houses had been destroyed, others badly damaged. The iron
railings had disappeared and the whole place looked dilapidated.
Number 77 had been hit by a bomb but repaired, and she used it
mainly as a pied-à-terre after finding a cottage in Roehampton. It
was only very small – and that was her deliberate choice. Gerbrandy later explained: 'The Queen always had the idea that she
did not belong in a palace while her people were in such a
miserable condition.'

Roehampton was not, however, considered safe enough during the frequent air raids on London, and at the end of 1941 the
Queen moved again, now to Stubbings near Maidenhead. She did
not like the house at all, found it depressing, and decided in 1943
to rent a simple property in South Mimms, nearer London. The
little place had up to then never been bombed, but on 20 February 1944 her house was hit. One policeman was killed and the
Queen had a narrow escape. She had just got out of bed to put a
bracelet in a chest of drawers when a large piece of the ceiling fell
on her bed. For a while her entourage feared that it had been an
attack on Wilhelmina, but it was later discovered that a German
pilot, chased by the RAF, had simply dropped his load by accident
over South Mimms.

After a short return to Stubbings she lived through the hectic
September days of 1944 with Juliana at Laneswood, a country
house in Mortimer, not far from Reading. Although she liked the
view there – 'it reminded her of the typical Veluwe landscape',
Gerbrandy remembered later – she always preferred her house
in Chester Square.

There she had a large living-room, on the first floor at the
front, which overlooked the trees in the square. The room was
full of pictures of her grandchildren, and a painting of a horse in
a silver frame hung on the wall. In the corner was her desk, on
which figured prominently a piece of paper with a few lines of the
poem 'Not in Vain' by the Jewish poet Maurits Mok:

But if I live to see the Liberation
And cheer the victory parade,
God, tell me that this suffering,
The sorrow shall not be betrayed.

In this room she received her guests for tea – she very often brought the milk from her own cow at Stubbings – and for those Dutch people who had fled to England she was particularly careful to make time.

During the first months of the war she and her government had been completely cut off from Occupied Holland. Very slowly communications were built up, but it was still very difficult to get a clear picture of what was going on. The 'Englandvaarders' – men and women who fled from Holland and crossed to England to help liberate their country – brought the first news, and from then on Queen Wilhelmina received them all. These meetings were never easy. Her guests were often nervous at meeting this woman who had become such a symbol of the free Netherlands, and waited in tense anticipation. After a few minutes the door would slowly open and the Queen appeared with a shy smile.

Her aide, Roelfzema, himself an Englandvaarder, wrote later: 'She always made a little bow, looking over our heads, which gave us the impression that her solemn greeting was not so much for us as for the people behind us, sunk in the dark, out of which we had come as representatives.' After this greeting the introductions followed, and Wilhelmina, with her cool voice, would anxiously enquire about the latest developments 'at home'. She did everything possible to make her guests feel at ease, while her lady-in-waiting was pouring the tea, but she could not help bringing with her always 'that air of fairy-tale-like unreality'.

Queen Wilhelmina had not had a happy life. As the only daughter of a very old father, King Willem III, and a very young mother, Emma von Waldeck Pyrmont, she grew up in the strict and formal atmosphere of a Victorian court to become Queen at the age of ten. 'Etiquette required us to lead a life that was permanently semi-official,' she wrote in her memoirs, which she titled very significantly *Lonely but not Alone*. Her marriage to the German princeling Hendrick von Mecklenburg was not a great success, and her responsibilities as constitutional Queen were too

93

limited for her taste. Her whole life she longed for more influence and more freedom – she wanted to escape from what she always called 'the cage' – and her exile in London gave her the opportunity.

Here she could mingle with her people, and here she could be a source of inspiration and encouragement. Thanks to her gift of speechmaking she was able to bridge the distance that existed between her and her subjects at 'the other side'. In July 1940 she made her first speech from abroad for Radio Oranje, and thirty-six more were to follow. All of them were written by herself and only read by Gerbrandy, who gave her complete freedom even if the content was sometimes political. He understood the value of her words, stating later that they had been 'a formidable support for our people and an excellent weapon in the struggle for life and death'. It was as near to the 'great deed' she had always dreamed of as she could get.

But, however hard she tried to behave 'normally', her background and her position in the first sixty years of her life had put an indelible stamp on her personality, and it was this which made the tea-parties somewhat uneasy. In spite of the fact that she was small and pear-shaped, without a trace of her former beauty, and very simply dressed, she had 'majesty'. One of her aides, another Englandvaarder, Gerard Rutten, described it as a 'sort of vacuum that surrounded her'. Although she lived in London almost without protocol, 'one always had the impression of an unbridgeable gap between her and the ordinary citizen'.

Whoever met her was deeply impressed. 'Very controlled and collected, but at the same time understanding and patient,' one Resistance fighter called her. Another was struck by her efficient and direct way of asking questions, a third by her beautiful grey eyes, but a fourth was amazed by the handshake, limp and fleeting. She did not laugh often, and those who knew her better found her a little ponderous and without much sense of humour. 'She sometimes forgot that one should laugh now and then,' a member of her entourage remarked once. 'And you thought twice before you told her something: she was very straightforward and uncompromising.'

This uncompromising attitude was in fact the cause of a split in the Dutch community in London. For the Queen there was only one good Dutchman, the Englandvaarder, the man who had risked his life to come and fight for freedom. As to the other Dutch in London, she always wondered if they would not have collaborated with the Nazis if they hadn't happened to be in England at the right moment. And she was not always able to hide those doubts, even from her Ministers.

No such reserve was obvious when she met 'her' Englandvaarders. 'For her they were the clear picture of a patriotic reality,' one of her biographers wrote. 'They, from their side, did not only see her as a Queen, but more as the "Mother of Patria", Mother of her country. She knew this and never grew tired of listening to them. Never before had she felt so much the warmth of real contact.'

Her enthusiasm for them, and her insistence on meeting them all, gave concern to many in London, as most of the young Englandvaarders were, according to some, 'unsettled by their experiences and the tensions' – even the strongest character needed three months to come down to earth – and were liable to give the Queen a distorted picture of what was happening in the Netherlands.

This worry was not completely groundless. Many of those who crossed the North Sea were brave, but simple, unpretentious characters, often adventurers who saw everything in black and white and who, a Minister later remarked, 'would have marched behind the NSB leader, Mussert, ten years earlier, if they had been old enough'. This was certainly not true of them all, but a great number came to tell the Queen that the Dutch were disillusioned with the pre-war party system, the political intrigues of a crumbling democracy, and wished for drastic changes after the war, in which the Queen was to play an important role.

For Wilhelmina it was proof that she had been right. She had always believed that the quick defeat of 1940 had been a 'judgment on pre-war democracy' and that things would have been different if she had had more say. Now her nation was behind her, purified by the ordeal of war and united in a longing for a better future. At last she could leave her 'cage', and she told more than one Dutchman in London that she was going to sell her palaces to live in a farmhouse, somewhere near Utrecht.

Many in her entourage knew that the picture the young men painted was not an accurate one, and the Queen's obstinate belief in this new society and a chastened nation pained them. 'She would talk for hours about Holland after the war,' one member of her staff remembered. 'And she was so full of idealism that I often had the feeling that it would end in a great disappointment. I never had the nerve, however, to argue with the Queen.'

CHAPTER TEN

The Wrong Side

THE QUEEN's heartening and sympathetic Christmas speech had been listened to by those of us who could in Occupied Holland with emotion and great attention, and by many as if it was the Gospel. The dumpy little monarch with the funny hats and the baggy coats, for whom the Dutch before the war had felt a certain respect and awe, had indeed become the symbol of freedom and a national figurehead, almost a sort of protective mother-figure. Her speeches for Radio Oranje were highlights in our lives, especially when she attacked the Germans and the Dutch Nazis. A joke went round that the little princesses Beatrix and Irene were never allowed to listen to their grandmother's speeches 'because she uses such foul language when she talks about the Nazis'. And, ironically, her enormous popularity was partly due to the State Commissioner Seyss-Inquart and his men.

The sudden departure of Wilhelmina in May 1940 had at first surprised, shocked and completely demoralised the Dutch. They felt betrayed and abandoned, but amazingly fast they digested the reality and began to understand. Already in the first summer of the Occupation a series of events demonstrated that patriotic feelings had revived, and a respect for the royal family had returned. Many people wore a *dubbeltje* (a ten-cent piece) with the Queen's head on it as a brooch, and on the birthday of Prince Bernhard on 29 June thousands, watched by the outraged Nazis, came to sign an address of congratulation in The Hague. Orange was abundant that day in spite of a decree that forbade the national colours or the orange flag.

Shortly afterwards, Queen Wilhelmina made her opening speech for Radio Oranje, calling upon the Dutch to resist collaboration with the Nazis and assuring them that freedom would win. Seyss-Inquart was furious and on 16 September confiscated all her possessions with the justification that 'she encourages the Dutch from afar to commit acts of violence against the occupying forces, which will only lead to the harshest reprisals'. Streets named after the royal family were given new names, portraits of the Queen were removed from offices and schools, stamps were altered, while the title 'Royal' for institutions and departments was abolished.

All this made Wilhelmina, more than ever, the rallying-point of resistance. Seyss-Inquart had succeeded in making her, in the words of an official report published after the war, 'the personification of the enslaved and struggling Netherlands'.

If Seyss-Inquart hated the royal family, he never had much feeling for the Dutch, either, and he never made a secret of the fact that he had come to Holland to exploit it for the benefit of the Third Reich. The Dutch had, understandably, taken an instant dislike to this rather dull, balding and bespectacled man, whose slight limp had earned him the punning nickname of 'Zes en een kwart' ('Six and a Quarter'). From the start they saw this lawyer from Vienna not only as the representative of a detested régime and a despicable system, but also as a traitor to his own country, Austria, having played a major role in the *Anschluss*, the unification of Germany with Austria in 1938.

Arthur Seyss-Inquart was born on 22 July 1892 as the youngest son of a German family living in the little Bohemian town of Stannern near Iglau, a German enclave in the Czech part of the Austrian Empire. In his early years the family moved to Iglau, where Arthur's father taught classical languages. He was a precise and quiet boy who entered Vienna University in 1910 to study law. He fought as a volunteer in the Austrian Army during the First World War, married Gertrud Maschka in 1916 and when the war was over founded a law firm, which soon prospered. Gradually he became involved in the ideas which Adolf Hitler launched in the twenties, and after he had been made Austrian Minister of the Interior in 1938 he followed the consequences of his conviction that Hitler's ideology offered the solution for the economic disintegration of central Europe – he welcomed the Führer on 12 March 1938 in Austria, to hand him his country's independence. Shortly after he received a high rank in the SS as a reward, and was made second in command in Occupied Poland.

Seven days after Germany had invaded the Netherlands in

1940, Seyss-Inquart received the message that Hitler had chosen him as his Reichskommissar, or State Commissioner, in the newly conquered country. 'The Führer wishes me to plant tulips,' he joked to his wife Gertrud over the telephone, and on Saturday, 25 May, Seyss-Inquart went to see Hitler. With him were his main assistants, three Austrians – amongst whom SS and police leader Hanns Albin Rauter was the most important – and his military counterpart, the former General of the Air Force, Friedrich C. Christiansen, now Commander of the Wehrmacht in Holland. During the meal the Führer spoke with great sympathy of Holland and its people, according to him so closely related to the Germans. He was convinced, he told Seyss-Inquart, that the Dutch had never lost their good qualities and that with a little persuasion they would soon discover that their future was in a strong Europe – his Europe.

Four days later the Dutch met the man who was to govern them for the coming years. Exactly at midday Seyss-Inquart appeared in the historic Ridderzaal (Knight's Hall) in the heart of The Hague, where in peacetime the Dutch monarchs came to open the parliamentary session. The hall was discreetly decorated with plants and flowers; most of the Dutch authorities who had not fled were present, and the whole ceremony was kept very low-key.

Seyss-Inquart's speech was almost apologetic. He explained that the Germans had been forced to invade Holland in order to prevent it becoming an Allied base. He emphasised the communal Germanic blood that made the Dutch such good sailors and the Germans such good soldiers, and he finally assured the Dutch that Germany had not come 'to enslave a nation or to destroy it, nor take away its liberty'.

The Dutch, listening to the speech with very mixed feelings, still had not grasped the fact that they had lost the war and were occupied. Their country had been at peace since the Battle of Waterloo in 1815, where they fought with the English against Napoleon. The only interruption had been in 1830, when the Belgians rose against the rule of the Orange family and achieved independence. During the First World War the Netherlands had remained neutral, and even after Hitler's rise in the thirties nothing seemed to change for them. Trade with Germany was important and what the Nazis did in their own country was their own affair. The man in the street worried more about unemployment than about the possibility of war, and only after the German annexation of the Sudetenland in 1938 did the Dutch Government begin to prepare itself for possible war. The then Prime Minister, Dr H. Colijn, was convinced that the Dutch were able to defend themselves thanks to their impenetrable Grebbe Line, a system of blockhouses, trenches and defensive waterwalls east of Utrecht. But the waterline was no match for German aeroplanes and airborne troops in May 1940, and the Dutch had to give up the fight after five days.

The Dutch were not in the least prepared for Occupation, and in the beginning did not even realise what it meant. The Germans were at first polite and helpful, and the Dutch went on living their quiet, contented and somewhat self-satisfied life as before the war. Even when things began to change, the majority preferred not to think too much about it.

The Government had gone abroad, but had left the secretary-generals of the different departments in charge, and initially they all decided that they were justified in working with the Nazis. So did most of the civil service, the police and other institutions and, although it made civilian life in Holland relatively normal until late in the war, while a lot of patriotic officials were able covertly to help the Resistance and others, it gave Seyss-Inquart the opportunity of exploiting Holland with a minimum of German administrative manpower.

In spite of the soothing words in his first speech, Seyss-Inquart was sent to Holland with only two main tasks: keeping order so that Germany's war effort was not hindered, and making sure that the Dutch delivered the goods Germany needed. The 'conversion' of the Dutch to National Socialism which Hitler had talked about would certainly be a good thing, but it could wait.

Conversion and exploitation anyhow soon clashed, and if there had ever been a honeymoon between the Dutch and the Moffen (Huns) it was over within a few months, and by 1941 the relationship had already reached a low point from which it was never to recover. Berlin was disappointed, and Himmler, who had counted on at least 600,000 young Dutchmen for his SS, was furious. It was obvious, he once burst out, that the Dutch had been corrupted by 'Jewish capitalist influences'.

While opinions of the Dutch dropped in Berlin, those of Seyss-

Inquart were rising. 'I have the impression that the treatment of the people in occupied territory is organised best of all in the Netherlands,' Joseph Goebbels, the Minister for Propaganda, wrote in September 1943. 'Seyss-Inquart knows exactly how to do it, mixing honey with the whip. He is able to introduce tough measures in a subtle way.' Hitler agreed wholeheartedly and, although he sometimes found Seyss-Inquart a little weak, he looked for someone just like him when he needed a Reichskommissar for Belgium 'as slippery as an eel, charming and at the same time thick-skinned'.

He had given the State Commissioner at parting the advice 'to live in grand style and entertain the Dutch'. But the Dutch, who found nothing subtle or charming in Arthur and his wife Gertrud, refused to come, and the Seyss-Inquarts lived very modestly in their house, Clingendael, near The Hague. With them was the youngest of their three children, their daughter Do.

The intelligent and successful lawyer from Vienna had become a sharp, sometimes ironic, man who worked methodically and who liked punctuality and simplicity. He normally got up at seven o'clock, arriving at his office at ten, where he often worked till late at night. His only relaxations were a film show at home, a long walk, a ride on horseback, a game of tennis, but his passion was music. Once a month he gave dinner parties, which were not very sought after on account of their sobriety, and only Germans were invited.

Those Dutch who would have liked to be received at Clingendael were never asked. Seyss-Inquart had from the start little appreciation and sympathy for the Dutch Nazi movement, the NSB, and even less admiration for its leader, Anton Mussert.

The Dutch Nationaal Socialistisch Beweging, the National Socialist Movement, had been formed on 14 December 1931 by a former specialist water engineer Anton Adriaan Mussert, born on 11 May 1894 in the little town of Werkendam. Mussert, who had married his aunt eighteen years older than he, and had no children, was pompous, arrogant and less intelligent than he thought he was. He based his party completely on Hitler's ideology. It made little impact and at the general election in 1937 it collected only 4.2 per cent of the votes, which gave the movement four seats in the Second Chamber. By 1939 the membership had dwindled

101

from 50,000 in the mid-thirties to 30,000, and it was obvious that the Netherlanders had stayed immune to all the propaganda, and were certainly not impressed by the 'Leader' himself.

The only hope for the NSB was the 'liberation' of Holland by its giant Nazi neighbour, but when it happened in May 1940, and Mussert reappeared from his hiding-place, very little changed. He was not even invited to Seyss-Inquart's solemn installation in the Ridderzaal and had to wait till 5 June before the State Commissioner invited him to come to his office. Mussert wrote in his diary: 'A noble and honest man, with a gentle character, who has been told by the Führer to make things as good as possible for our people.' Seyss-Inquart, on his side, was less impressed and reported to Berlin that Holland's NSB leader was 'a liberal nationalist' who was afraid of the Germans and whose political qualities were not above those of a provincial leader in Germany. The two never hit it off together, and Mussert admitted later that their relationship had remained formal to the end. 'We had nothing in common,' he added.

Mussert was indeed a nationalist and had no plans for integration with the German Reich. It would spoil all his chances of becoming the leader of the whole Dutch nation, something he often talked about with Seyss-Inquart, and even on four occasions with Hitler himself. In December 1942 he got what he wanted: the Führer made him officially 'Leader of the Dutch nation'. The title, however, gave him little real influence, and after 1943 his chances were finished. Hanns Rauter, the SS leader in Holland, who had always been an advocate of the integration of the Netherlands, got rid of the few Germans who supported Mussert. For a while the NSB leader even thought that he was in danger. When one day some Germans came to his door, he expected to be arrested. Deciding to make the best of it, he stretched his hands out to them with the words: 'I'll make no trouble and will go with you.' The Germans had come with another message and left Mussert at home.

The NSB leader had hoped that his arrest would make him a martyr and even popular with the Dutch people. But it was a vain hope. They despised the cocky little man who resembled Mussolini, and they detested his party of people who had betrayed their country and Queen and collaborated with the hated Germans. When it disintegrated on Mad Tuesday, 5 September 1944, nobody mourned.

Mussert, however, decided to struggle on, even if most of his top functionaries had left for safer places. After he had organised the panic evacuation of NSB women and children on Mad Tuesday, he drove around ostentatiously in Utrecht – 'the best manner to refute all lies about his flight', his paper *Volk en Vaderland* wrote – and whatever he did in the following weeks was much publicised in the hope of impressing the readers with Mussert's courage and detachment. Those who had the opportunity to see behind the scenes knew that the 'Leader' was less composed than he seemed. During a visit to a press club in The Hague, five days after Mad Tuesday, he even threatened to shoot two Dutchmen – one of them a Nazi – because they had criticised his officials and were therefore 'the leaders of an Underground action against his party'. It took a long time to calm the distraught Mussert, and to make it clear that the two journalists had only attacked those members of his staff who had fled.

The Sunday after this scene Mussert at last realised that he had to give the Dutch some explanation of his members' behaviour on Mad Tuesday, and on Radio Hilversum he told the few who bothered to listen that he had ordered the departure of women and children simply because these felt threatened. He added at once: 'Do not conclude, compatriots, that I ever thought our nation might murder those innocents.' But, he pointed out, 'You know as well as I do that the rabble is waiting to give rein to its evil instincts.' The threats of a day of revenge, Hatchet Day, from the Resistance had made a deep impression.

In October, Mussert, who in the meantime had moved to Almelo, farther to the east, and lived there in a house called Bellinckhof, decided that his party must be cleansed of those members who had fled so ignominiously in September. He installed a special tribunal, but the Dutch had other worries than the last convulsions of the abhorred NSB, and nobody paid any attention to Mussert as he drove around that part of Occupied Holland to encourage the men who helped the Germans in the Landwacht or the Dutch SS. Much of his time was taken up by trying to help and hearten those Dutch women who were now in Germany and beginning to feel homesick.

About 65,000 NSB members and collaborators had fled to Germany, where they were looked after by a Nazi welfare organisation, which found it hard to cope with this mass of frightened people. In October alone, eight children died in one camp, while in others the inhabitants felt more like prisoners than refugees. There were tensions because the Germans tried to force those 'lousy Dutch' to work for their keep and the German cause, and letter after letter reached Mussert from the comrades pleading for help. He could do even less for them than for his people at home, admitting later that after September 'I had nothing more to say'. His Christmas message did not bring his supporters any consolation. Pointing out that all over Europe families were torn apart, he begged them to remain loyal and believe in the Führer's victory. 'If he loses the war, you will never have a home again,' he added.

To Mussert the defeat of Hitler was an impossibility. He was convinced that the Führer was held prisoner by Himmler, but certain that he would make a comeback. 'I felt that I had to stay on, so that if Hitler ever wished an independent Dutch nation I could help make it possible,' he later explained at his trial. 'I had the movement to which he could give that task.'

Since September he had made desperate efforts to contact the German dictator, but Seyss-Inquart had prevented him. 'I wanted to ask the Führer's intervention to halt the terror and raids in Holland,' Mussert stated, and in November he produced another plan to get through to Berlin. He knew that Seyss-Inquart had aspirations to become Germany's next Foreign Minister and Mussert now suggested to him a new 'Grand Design' – his fifth – for a Nazi Europe that would unite Germany, Poland, Holland, Belgium, Denmark, half of Norway and Sweden, some of France and the Balkans. The solemnisation of this united Europe could take place in the Peace Palace in The Hague, where Hitler would be made its Führer.

It was an unrealistic idea, considering the situation, and Seyss-Inquart sent it on without comment to Berlin, where it was soon lost, and the last thing Mussert heard from the Führer was the 'warm regards' the State Commissioner brought back for him after a visit to Berlin in February 1945.

By that time Mussert, at any rate, was deep in other problems. Around the New Year he believed it time to have a thorough purge of the NSB leadership, and he sacked a few men at the top. One of them was forty-three-year-old Cornelis van Geelkerken, the man who had been Mussert's first supporter in 1931, but who was also one of the first to flee thirteen years later. When he returned in October, Mussert made it clear that he had no need for him, and sacked him as deputy leader. He would have liked to expel him completely from the party, but Van Geelkerken was in a strong position: he was Inspector-General of the Landwacht.

This Nazi Home Guard had been officially recognised in January 1944, when it received the grey uniforms which the Dutch learned to detest even more than those of the 'Greens'. In September 1944 about fifty per cent of the Landwachters fled, but most of them returned, and together with the newcomers, who were obliged to join after women and children had been evacuated, the Guard numbered 5700 full-time members and 2000 helpers at the end of 1944. They were a menace to the Dutch and even one of their own commanders called them 'an insult to Nazi Holland'. They not only robbed hunger-trippers of their precious foodstuff, but they also helped the Germans with their razzias, the deportation of Dutch people and the search for 'divers'. For Rauter, always eager for more men for his SS, they were ideal material, and when Van Geelkerken asked him for help against Mussert he welcomed him with open arms.

With most of Holland starving, a petty squabble over some 8000 uncouth Landwachters began. Mussert made desperate efforts to expel Van Geelkerken, reasoning that in that case it would be impossible for him to remain Inspector-General of an NSB force, and Rauter tussled at the other side, asking Himmler to intervene, and complaining to him on 2 January that it was 'impossible to have any political dealings with that tedious Anton'. But Mussert was within his rights and, expelling Van Geelkerken, he took his command of the Landwacht from him. To his dismay, Seyss-Inquart reinstated Van Geelkerken four weeks later, without any explanation.

While the Dutch were engaged in the struggle for survival, Mussert persisted with his ludicrous purge. Another victim was Meinoud M. Rost van Tonningen, the fifty-year-old President of the Netherlands State Bank. Rost had been one of the most fanatical members of the movement, but also an advocate of integration with the Reich. He had good contacts with Himmler, whom he asked for support when Mussert wanted to get rid of him despite the fact that Rost had not fled in September. 'I'm speechless,' Rost cabled. 'How is it possible that he dares at this moment to remove me, one of the first exponents of the Great German thought in this country, while almost all his friends had failed him in the September days?' Help came. Himmler sent Seyss-Inquart a message: 'I find this step of Mussert impossible. I know that Rost has a lot of failings . . . but he has always followed the line of Great Germany and the Reich.'

This time, nevertheless, Mussert won: Rost was expelled, and Seyss-Inquart could only persuade Mussert not to print Rost's name along with the September cowards in *Volk en Vaderland*. A few weeks later Rost joined the SS division 'Landstorm Nederland' to take part in the defence of western Holland against the Allies.

The Allies had in the meantime unwittingly removed a third enemy of Mussert in the NSB. Henk Feldmeijer, who on Mad Tuesday had organised the trains for the women and children, was hit by bullets from a British plane on his way to the front on 22 February. 'The leader, getting ready to take cover, lifted his face to the beaming sun and as a glance of surprise flashed through his eyes he was hit . . . ,' the SS paper *Storm* lamented.

Feldmeijer's funeral service, held in the woods near Apeldoorn, was the last occasion on which Dutch and German Nazis were united. Mussert exerted himself, speaking in moving terms of the young hero, 'now reunited with thousands of our comrades who knew their duty', but in fact Feldmeijer's death had come at a timely moment for the NSB leader.

As leader of the Dutch SS, Feldmeijer had great influence, was a staunch supporter of integration with the Third Reich and had constantly wrecked all Mussert's hopes of forming an independent Dutch Army (it would of course fight for Nazi Germany) by helping Rauter to swallow it up in his SS. Feldmeijer, who had joined the NSB movement as a charming twenty-two-year-old student, had become one of the worst criminals of the Nazi Party, organising the death of a great number of well-known Dutchmen in retaliation for Resistance sabotage. Mussert was relieved to have got rid of this bullying rival.

The Dutch, by that time, couldn't care less. Forgotten and ignored, deserted by his followers, Anton Mussert watched helplessly and hopelessly from Bellinckhof as his party fell to pieces and the Third Reich gradually disintegrated.

CHAPTER ELEVEN

The Prince's Men

APPROXIMATELY 25,000 Dutchmen fought for the Germans, and 10,000 of them were killed. Exactly how many fought on the other side is not known, but it is a fact that more Dutchmen fought in the field-grey of the enemy than in the khaki of the Allies. And it was one of the war's tragic ironies that, while Dutch 'Shocktroopers', drawn from the Forces of the Interior, patrolled south of the rivers for the Allies, on the north banks Dutch soldiers of the SS division 'Landstorm Nederland' did the same for the Germans.

The 'Shocktroopers' were a creation of Prince Bernhard, who on 22 September 1944, in consultation with the Americans and British, appointed J. J. F. Borghouts, alias Peter Zuid, as commander of the 'Shocktroops of the Forces of the Interior South of the Rivers'. It was an impressive name for what was in reality a rather motley-looking bunch of Resistance fighters. Most of them were in clogs, had insufficient clothing and were only distinguishable by a white band with 'Stoottroepen' on it. They were warmly welcomed by the Americans and Canadians, who were glad of their enthusiastic support, but less keenly by the British. As most of the work of these amateurs had to be done in the British Sector, the Dutch Shocktroopers had a hard life. Food and ordinary clothing were scarce, let alone uniforms, and that during the coldest and wettest winter anyone could remember.

'We were standing in the rain for hours on end, and our coats would be soaked through,' one of the officers remembered. 'The food was appalling and never enough, and our only heat came from a little peat-burning stove.' Making a tour of the barracks at Christmas, he discovered that things had gone from bad to worse. 'The boys have made some beds of straw in a stone-cold, draughty hall – no stove, no fuel, not even a cup of coffee-substitute.'

Prince Bernhard was constantly on the road to inspect his men, and to do what he could to help them. They were responsible for fifty per cent of the patrolling along the river banks and, he told the Allies, they had many duties but no rights. At a meeting shortly before Christmas in London he asked the startled Allied leaders if they had any objections if he gave his boys a few days' leave, adding that he was under the impression that the authorities hardly knew of their existence, and would therefore not miss them. His irony did not help matters.

Despite all these problems, this was perhaps the happiest time Prince Bernhard had ever known in his life. Married in 1937 to Juliana, Crown Princess of the Netherlands, Bernhard von Lippe-Biesterfeld, a former employee of I. G. Farben, had not had much opportunity to show what he was capable of. Queen Wilhelmina, who had always been the dominant partner in her own marriage, at first expected little else in her daughter's. In May 1940 she ordered Bernhard to take Juliana and the two children to England and she refused him permission to return to the battle-front. The Prince, however, was not so easily bossed around and managed, with the help of his wife, to reach Zeeland. There he discovered that the last Dutch troops had surrendered to the Germans, and in June he returned to London, where he spent most of the war, while Juliana and her two daughters were in Canada.

Initially, there was little for him to do, and his German birth was a major handicap. Slowly he made his mark after his mother-in-law appointed him liaison officer between the Dutch and the British. He was created colonel in the Dutch Army, a captain in the Dutch Navy, and the RAF gave him a passion for flying, making him 'Honorary Air-Commodore'. Between Wilhelmina and him, in the meantime, a close relationship of mutual respect had grown up, and his great chance came when in September 1944 she gave him command of the Dutch forces, consisting of the Princess Irene Brigade and the Forces of the Interior. He once said that without that role he could never have accomplished what he wanted – 'I would have been just another royal figure-head, lashed to the bow of the Ship of State'.

The Nazis in Holland treated his appointment with contempt. *Volk en Vaderland* sneered that 'Der Von Biesterveld' had to be careful if and when he came to the Continent. 'They may think he is a disguised Hun, because in spite of all his shouting against Germany he still does it with a German accent.' A certain lack of enthusiasm also existed in Dutch Cabinet circles. Some Ministers feared the growing influence of the Orange family, others were afraid because the Prince's life would be constantly in danger. But in the end everybody agreed that the Prince was the man the Dutch Resistance needed.

The Underground movement in the Netherlands was as old as the Occupation, but active resistance was, at first, rare. Most Dutch people felt ill at ease with the methods of sabotage and terrorism; the flat and featureless countryside made hiding much more difficult than the wooded hills and mountains of the French Maquis, and the menacing Nazi police, the Gestapo, was more powerful than the Army, since Holland, unlike France and Belgium, had a civilian administration. Only as Liberation approached was there a sudden rush to join the Resistance, but even then not on the scale the Germans feared and the Allies hoped. Some British officials even doubted the usefulness of the movement, and hesitated for a while to drop arms as they believed that the number of freedom fighters was not more than 12,000.

The Dutch Institute for War Documentation has made an estimate of the number of 'resisters' – part-time and full-time – and worked it out at about 76,000. About 5000 of these belonged to the fighting units, while 4000 worked as spies. More than 25,000 were involved in the illegal press, or helped Allied pilots escaping and forged official Nazi documents, while 40,000, finally, gave help to 'divers'.

Apart from lack of recruits, the Dutch Resistance had to struggle with the problem of fragmentation. There were dozens of small local groups, preoccupied with all sorts of activities like helping concealed Jews, the forging of identity papers and ration-cards, the publishing of newspapers, sabotage, spying on troop movements, the escape of prisoners, and even murder. And, if they sometimes co-operated, more often they refused to work together – sometimes for personal, but often for political or religious reasons. London recognised only the three largest groups: the Ordedienst, OD (Order Service), the Raad van Verzet, RVV (Council of Resistance), and the Knokploegen, KP, the so-called 'Fist-fighters'. Of the three the OD was the most tricky to handle. Formed in 1940, mainly by ex-servicemen, the members were conservative and rather passive, preparing themselves thoughtfully to take over after the war. They saw the members of other movements as 'little Red Indians', who risked their lives by foolish attacks on Germans, the liberation of prisoners or bank robberies. It was a highly prejudiced view that many Dutch shared. But, looking at an incomplete list of some of the KP activities in December 1944, it is impossible to doubt that, for all their mistakes, the 'Fist-fighters' saved many lives. On 11 December they freed twenty-nine people from the prison in Assen, on 28 December eight men in Meppel, and in early January eighty in Dordrecht. Their most daring and spectacular coup took place on Friday, 8 December, at the impenetrable, old-fashioned, dome-shaped prison in Leeuwarden.

The local KP group had been preparing itself for weeks when two of them, dressed in police uniforms, knocked at 4.30 p.m. that Friday at the doors of the prison. They had three 'prisoners' between them and were let in after a cursory check. Within seconds the porter and other clerks were tied up, and fourteen other men let in. Together they surprised the guards and forced them to open the cells of the thirty-nine men and eleven women, selected beforehand because of their importance to the Resistance. Just as the whole group was ready to leave the building, two German policemen entered with two more prisoners and everything seemed to have gone wrong. But, before they knew what had happened, they joined the other guards, and exactly one hour after the attack had started the released prisoners left the prison in their stockinged feet. Some of them had difficulty in walking after the tortures they had gone through, and a little boy who saw them disappearing said later that they looked 'like a bunch of drunkards'. The rest of the escape was as perfectly organised, and within a few hours everybody was in his hiding-place. Dogs set on their trail were put off the scent by pepper strewn on the bridges of canal-rich Leeuwarden.

These were the sort of men Prince Bernhard had to unite with the more cautious OD men, and the task seemed impossible. There were jealousies, intrigues and misunderstandings, and the only aim they had in common was a free Holland. But the Prince had tact, patience and endurance, and was – most important of all

– politically neutral. 'The men adored him and listened to him,' the Prince's chief of staff, Charles van Houten, said later, 'and by bringing the brave, but jealous, idealistic, but egotistical, men to unity and discipline Prince Bernhard performed a near-miracle.'

Efforts to form a more cohesive Dutch Resistance had started in June 1944 – after D-Day – when Queen Wilhelmina had sent a telegram to Holland asking that all the groups should be co-ordinated and should appoint a number of 'foremen' who in an eventual 'vacuum' would act on behalf of the Government. The events of September overtook all calm considerations, and in a hurry the Forces of the Interior, the BS, was formed, under the joint command of the three large organisations. To prevent rivalry at the top it was decided to appoint one man as national commander in Occupied territory.

The choice fell on the sixty-one-year-old Henri Koot, a reserve colonel of mixed Indonesian, Chinese and Dutch blood, who was approached on 20 September. Although the Germans had twice arrested him for short periods, he wavered for only half an hour before he 'packed his suitcase, wrote a letter to his wife and travelled to Amsterdam', so the Prince was told. Koot, who had told his wife that 'the Fatherland comes before you', called the events of that day 'a sort of kidnap', but he soon settled down in his headquarters in the Nes, significantly choosing as his *nom de guerre* the name of 'Mr Clerk'. And on 20 October Bernhard, having first made careful enquiries, confirmed him in his post.

The delayed Liberation created new conflicts, mainly about the old question of active or passive resistance. The OD was still averse to sabotage, but the other groups reasoned that the Allies did not drop their loads of weapons 'to save them for the hour on which they themselves will be hawking at. For wasp-stings and pinpricks,' a Resistance fighter wrote, 'that's why we get them.'

The quarrel became so violent, and such a threat to the efficiency of the Dutch Resistance, that the British decided to intervene. On 4 November they sent a very sharp telegram to all Resistance forces in Holland:

With great misgivings we have followed the exchange of messages relating to disunity which apparently exists between certain Underground organisations. We, the British, have been doing our best to supply you with arms with the object of helping us kick the Germans out of your country, when the right time comes. By their present attitude Underground organisations are doing exactly what the Germans would like them to do. They are wasting valuable time. Please get together and long live your Queen. From your British Allies.

An embarrassed Koot at once circulated the rebuke and added: 'This serious and urgent admonition from our British allies will fill you, like me, with feelings of shame and regret that it has come to this, that we, who are expected to give our lives for Queen and Fatherland, should have to receive such a solemn and well-deserved reproach.' And he wrote gratefully to the British that their 'authoritative appeal would be the redeeming words to bring forth the indispensable unity in our midst'.

The Dutch Government, also concerned about the problems of the Resistance, had asked advice from another body in Holland, the Vertrouwensmannen, the Confidential Councillors. This committee had been formed in August 1944 with the task of bridging the period between German rule and the return of the Government after an Allied victory. Four of the seven members had been prominent Dutch officials, one a politician, and the other two were representatives of the Resistance. The Chairman was L. H. N. Bosch van Rosenthal, a former Queen's Commissioner in Utrecht.

The appointment of the seven, chosen by the Queen and Gerbrandy, had hardly arrived on a microdot hidden in an agent's cufflink before the Allies approached the Dutch border and the moment of a possible power vacuum seemed near, while no preparations had been made to take over power from the Nazi officials. Expecting an advance of the Allied troops on two fronts, three of the Councillors met at Bosch's house in Leiden on 5 September to compose two proclamations, one for The Hague, the other for Amsterdam, intended to appeal to the Dutch to stay calm and maintain law and order. 'The atmosphere was highly emotional,' one of the men, the socialist Dr Willem Drees, wrote later. 'We believed already that we might be too late.' The ink was hardly dry when two of them rushed to take the tram from Leiden to The Hague which, as they thought, might be the last for some time. Not knowing Leiden very well they waited on the wrong platform, only realising this when the tram for The Hague was leaving. The astonished Leideners saw two very respectable gentlemen run after the tram and jump on it, only to discover in The Hague that all their hurry had been in vain.

During the rest of the war the Councillors remained very active and even opened an 'office' at 17 Javastraat in The Hague. They met frequently and secretly in the head office of the Dutch Reformed Church in Amsterdam and, being in close contact with the Resistance, could advise the Government on its activities. When London asked anxiously about the rift in the Underground, they were able to reassure the Ministers. 'Conflicts are on limited scale,' they cabled, 'and mainly caused by the actions of some high-handed elements, who . . . damage the authority of generally highly appreciated commander.'

It was not all that simple. The Resistance movement remained restless, and the fact that so many had joined only recently – disdainfully christened 'September Warriors' by the old hands – did not improve the atmosphere. Queen Wilhelmina added, quite unwittingly, another source of conflict. She sent a telegram to Holland asking that a deputation from the Resistance be sent, who, she thought, 'would be able to inform me of their work, of the feelings of the population and the general condition of the country'. She waited for them in vain and wrote sadly: 'This invitation could not be accepted as the men were indispensable.' They were in fact too busy quarrelling, not only about who should go, but also about if they should go at all, and on 3 October they sent the Queen a message, admitting that they had had a difference of opinion. The debate revolved around the question of whether the Underground movement should give advice over future problems of Government. While the Left wing believed in political involvement, the Centre and the Right of the Resistance felt that this should be left to the parties and that a democratically elected parliament should tackle possible constitutional changes. The discussion went on for six months, and in the end it was too late to send a delegation at all.

If these tribulations were not sufficient warning for Wilhelmina, the Underground press should have made it clear to her that Holland was still as divided as before the war. The papers were not only sources of information, but very often also a platform for lengthy discussions about the future, and each had its own ideas.

The first Underground or 'illegal' paper had appeared on 15 May 1940, one day after the Dutch had capitulated, and was soon followed by a stream of others. Over the years they developed from little ill-printed pamphlets into almost sophisticated magazines, concentrating more and more on news from the fronts after the Germans confiscated all radio sets in 1943. The most important role for the press came after the failure of Operation Market Garden. With German terror on the increase, the starving and frightened population was badly in need of every scrap of encouraging news, and at the end of 1944 more than 500 news bulletins had emerged under the most difficult circumstances. The old illegal papers became almost national, and the one with the largest circulation, *Trouw* ('Faithful'), brought out sixty issues. It paid dearly for its efforts: 120 people who worked for it were killed by the Germans, who detested the illegal press so much that they constantly intensified the hunt for the men responsible. The Underground journalists hid in churches, attics, caves and even haystacks, as long as there was a radio set and a duplicating machine. Printing-paper was obtained by stealing it from the Germans or buying it from sympathetic wholesalers; distribution was mostly done by girls on their bicycles.

The disappearance of electricity in the autumn of 1944 made the work even more difficult. Lack of food, heating and gas, and the fierce cold all added to the problems. As Ton Koot, editor of the *Vrij Nederland* bulletin in Amsterdam, described: 'We were faced with the stern reality of an unheated room, a plate of watery soup and a sugarbeet, danger, constant danger surrounding the house, air armadas thundering across us and anti-aircraft guns – the roaring and crashing of bombs around.' In January 1945 warnings appeared in the daily papers that the use of current was equal to sabotage, and in February a campaign was started in the 'legal' press to the effect that the tapping of electricity was a capital offence. 'We once added up that we could be liable for the death penalty four times over,' Koot recorded. 'A little more or less could not harm us much and made us indifferent to these threats.'

When the current was cut off they had to,work with batteries. 'People were not always willing to help charge the empty batteries. Hunger heightened suspicion.' A propeller on the roof was unreliable as there was not always sufficient wind, and one of the staff members slaved day and night to get new batteries, 'plucked from the air, as it were'. But, in spite of these difficulties, the bulletins were almost always published on time.

During the whole war 1193 different underground papers were published – and avidly read. Lydia Winkel, in her study of the 'illegal' press, gave number 1191 to a nameless pamphlet produced in the small village of Breukelerveen. It was the work of a young student from Middelburg, L. Polak, who lived in a houseboat, hiding from the Nazis. He worked entirely alone but when he was arrested on 14 April 1945 – a few weeks before the Liberation – the Gestapo refused to believe this, and tortured him so savagely that he died seven days later.

Although in the Hunger Winter the numbers and the quality of the 'illegal' press grew and flourished against all oppression, the 'legal' press had a very difficult time. Undisguised Nazi papers like *Volk en Vaderland* and *Het Nationale Dagblad* numbered no more than two small pages and, after March, were simply stencilled sheets. The last issue of *Volk en Vaderland* appeared on 4 May – a most appropriate farewell issue as it contained only one article, an obituary of Hitler.

The ordinary Dutch press was completely under German influence. Most editors were NSB members or sympathisers, who printed what the Germans dictated, or what the pro-German press agency, ANP, fed them over its wires. After Mad Tuesday they all had a slight change of heart and attacked, among others, the fleeing NSB. Only one paper, the *Nieuws van den Dag*, got into trouble for doing so as it wrote too explicitly of the 'people, who in word and writing and behind the safe microphone, always spoke so bravely about the New Society, but who, now they are in danger of having to defend that ideal, take to their heels'. The railway strike showed that the 'legal' editors had become a degree more defiant when they refused to print Seyss-Inquart's fulminations against the strikers but they were never taken very seriously by the Dutch readers, who bought the papers mainly for the list of ration-coupons announced for the coming week.

Just as insignificant was the official Dutch radio. Most people had no sets anyway, and the news broadcasts were as biased as the newspapers. Airtime was mainly filled with music, often of the German *schlager* genre, and now and then a programme of

American songs, of which the lyrics were subtly changed into German propaganda. It could in no way compete in popularity with the BBC, in English and Dutch, Radio Oranje in London and, since October 1944, Radio Rising Netherlands in Eindhoven. The four first notes of Beethoven's Fifth Symphony, which introduced Radio Oranje – the Morse code for V for Victory – were the sweetest sound for every Dutchman who had a hidden set somewhere under the floorboards. Both Dutch radio-stations-in-exile worked with a very limited staff and in primitive circumstances. The first was in the BBC's Bush House in the Aldwych, the second was in the Philips factories in Eindhoven, where the transmitter had been built under the eyes of the German occupiers, ready to be installed as soon as they had left.

Though their normal broadcasts were important for the morale of the Dutch in Occupied Holland, the stations served another purpose, too, by passing coded messages to 'the other side'. 'Louis has to see the pastor; the milk is boiling over; Jan, you have to cut your moustache.' No German could decipher it, but someone somewhere in Holland knew what the message was – an arms drop, the safe arrival of an agent, a warning against an infiltrator. The composers of these messages needed imagination. Henk van den Broek described in his book *Radio Oranje* how, for instance, they were faced with the case of two important Resistance fighters, Karel and Harry, who were expected in the Liberated south with important documents. If they arrived safely, the message would be 'The pear is ripe'. Only Harry came through, so Radio Rising Netherlands broadcast 'Half the pear is ripe'. After a few days they began to fear that Karel had been arrested and that the discovery of the documents could endanger the lives of other patriots. These had to be warned, and a third message was invented: 'Take care of half the pear; it's not Karel's.'

How essential those coded messages were was proved by the fact that between September 1944 and April 1945 six hundred parachute drops were announced over the radio. Bad weather prevented 400 of them but, despite that, more than 20,000 weapons were delivered, together with many tons of explosives and sabotage material. Allied Special Forces (the British SOE and the American OSS) dropped at least a hundred agents in the same period.

*

Another way to get an agent or arms into Occupied northern territory from the south was the river 'crossings', and valuable military information came back the same way. In particular, the Biesbos, a watery labyrinth near Dordrecht with treacherous morasses, was excellent for 'crossings' as it was very difficult to patrol. One group which specialised in this aspect of underground work was Group Albrecht, who had two secret routes mapped out, and during the winter of 1944–5 made almost daily trips across.

The rush of people who wanted to get out of Occupied territory was in the end so great that the organisers in Holland could not cope any longer. They sent a telegram to London asking them to categorise people according to their importance: 'This is necessary because of queues at this side.' Amongst the candidates were politicians and Resistance leaders, Allied pilots whose planes had crashed behind the lines, and British airborne troops who had been left behind after the Battle of Arnhem, in hiding with the Dutch. One of the most sensational crossings was that of a group of German soldiers who had been taken prisoner by the Resistance. They were at first kept in two houseboats in the Biesbos, but handed over in November 1944 to a Polish general. A request to occupy the Biesbos was politely rejected by the Pole as it did not fit into the Allied plans.

Finally the crossings were a blessing for thousands of diabetics. The stock of insulin in western Holland had dwindled almost to nil, and the Allies had tried dropping supplies. The 'crossers', however, succeeded in bringing forty times as much, together with other medicines.

In total, more than 370 crossings between Liberated and Occupied Holland were made between October 1944 and May 1945, and only two of the hundred men who took part in this dangerous operation were killed: one of them on his fifty-third trip.

Another means of daily contact between north and south was the Resistance's own telephone network, in operation since 1942. Two engineers of the Dutch mail and postal services had made numerous extra connections, which could be used with complicated code signals and with numbers that ran into twenty figures. It was a great surprise for the Americans when, as they entered Limburg in September 1944, the former police inspector, W. E.

Sanders, welcomed the first American officer on Dutch soil, Edward Maithe, over the telephone from Utrecht and gave him the first military information from Occupied Holland. Other telephone contacts were made through a network from the provincial electricity company in the south, the PNEM. The Underground had perfected a method of attaching a telephone to the major transmission wires at a convenient power sub-station and were thus able to talk to their comrades in the south. A radio scoop by the Dutch war correspondent Robert Kiek put an end to this ingenious system. On 16 November, Kiek had been allowed to talk to a colleague in Occupied Holland through the PNEM system and subsequently described it all in a broadcast, heard also by the Germans. Kiek was sacked, but his blunder cost a number of Resistance fighters in the north their lives. 'May God forgive the stupidity of the Allied military censor who let it through,' Prince Bernhard exclaimed when he heard of it.

The Prince had moved from his castle near Mechelen to Breda in September. His staff, grown from seventeen to fifty, was housed in the post office of this garrison town, where all the telephone connections converged. Bernhard had settled in a tower room, simply furnished with an ink-stained table and some chairs. There he dealt with the problems of the Forces of the Interior in northern Holland and the 'Shocktroopers' in the south. Commuting constantly between Breda and Brussels in his personal bright-blue Beechcraft four-seater, a gift from the Dutch in America, he battled for better equipment and uniforms for his men. But Montgomery had little time for the Prince, who in January 1945 decided to look for justice at the top. He flew to Versailles where Eisenhower and Bernhard's personal friend, Bedell Smith, listened with sympathy – but only gave vague promises.

It was good enough for the Prince, who flew back to Brussels and told Monty's quartermaster that he needed 6000 coats – 'and Ike has given me the OK', he added. The surprised man gave him 2400 coats, to the immense anger of Montgomery when he later heard of it. Relations between the Prince and the Field-Marshal were from that moment chillier than ever, but Bernhard did not mind being called 'a highway robber' as long as his men were provided for and the 'PB Grocery Store' in Breda – as it was called – well filled.

CHAPTER TWELVE

'Actions Horribles'

FOR THE Dutch in the Liberated provinces the Queen, Prince
Bernhard and the Government-in-Exile were able – thanks to
constant nagging – to do something. After great supply difficulties rations, which at first had dropped down below the Occupation level, rose in January to 1600 calories a day. They had to
stand by helplessly, however, while the Dutch north of the rivers
Rhine and Maas were driven to the limits of their endurance. The
bitter cold meant that food transports across the Ijsselmeer were
still impossible in January, and the daily ration had decreased to
460 calories, not even a fifth of normal needs. The Resistance felt
it was time to tell the world once again what Nazi Germany was
doing to the Netherlands, and through secret channels one of the
most moving appeals reached London on 13 February:

> The people of the Netherlands for four, nearly five, years
> fought among the United Nations [it began]. Hundreds and
> thousands have sacrificed their lives. Tens of thousands have
> been sent to German concentration-camps. A still greater
> number have lost all their possessions. . . . Many of our towns
> are ruined, but we shall build them again, many of our fac-
> tories have been destroyed, but we will build better ones.
> Water has flooded our fields, we shall drain them again. The
> German tyrants are trying to make us submit by starvation, but
> we will overcome this trial, too, thinking of those fighting at the
> fronts and the grief endured by other nations. But [the tele-
> gram was coming to its point] now the Germans have thought
> up another scheme which, if successfully carried out, would be
> fatal to our nation: deportation. Nine-tenths of our men have
> resisted it. Our country is thickly populated, it possesses no
> great forests or mountains, nevertheless some hundreds of
> thousands of men have been able to go underground. Should
> the German plan succeed, one and a half million men, includ-

119

ing those who have already been deported, will have been taken away from the Fatherland. Their fate would not only be that of forced labour, but they would also be doomed to death through exhaustion, lack of clothes . . . they will become victims of hunger and disease.

The writers of the telegram didn't ask for pity – 'We know what we are fighting for, [but] we call out to the free world: an old, civilised, nation is threatened with destruction by the German barbarians. Let the free world raise their voices. . . . We shall hold out.'

The cry for support created an enormous stir outside the Netherlands, but by the time it was published the Liese action, to which it mainly referred, had already become a failure, thanks to the Resistance and the opposition of the man in the street. Instead of the half-million men the Germans wanted, not even a tenth of that number had reported, with the excuse that they were compelled by hunger.

From the start the Underground had campaigned fanatically against any co-operation. Posters and bulletins had been distributed with such messages as: 'If you think the Huns won't cheat you, you're fools, they damn well beat you.' Another rhyme went: 'You may think this is a disaster, but the Hun will kill you faster.' One poster showed a donkey in a labour exchange with the subtitle: 'I'm going to Germany; they say the grass is greener there.' But more was done. 'We have destroyed or stolen our population registers, confused the national administration, stolen and forged ration-cards . . . all in order to make the manhunt impossible' – and it was no bluff. In the first months of 1945 in Noord-Holland alone, fifty-three registrars were attacked and robbed. Nor was the Resistance afraid to kill. In Amsterdam the Germans had appointed eight NSB-ers to do the dirty work of registration, but before they could start five of them were shot. The Germans hit back by executing five hostages the next day.

While the Resistance followed one line, there was more confusion in the higher ranks of Dutch authority. The more cautious ones there, like Dr Hirschfeld, reasoned that, without the exemptions Liese had promised, the so-called 'Ausweis', nobody would be able to work and food production, such as it was, and transport would come to a complete halt. On 6 January the Dutch food authorities sent a telegram to London to point this out. 'Within two weeks there will be no more food, no water,' they warned, and Louwes called it 'a choice between famine or starvation'.

The Government, however, had on 2 January already forbidden any form of co-operation, and for the BS commander Koot that was sufficient. He listened to the arguments of the others, but when they lasted too long he gave orders to kidnap them or give them a good going over with a black-jack or bludgeon. The Heineken director, Dirk U. Stikker, who had agreed with Hirschfeld and Louwes, received on 4 January a message from an Underground friend telling him to stay at home as his life could be in danger. 'I told my friend to inform the group that I would take a walk between 11.30 and 12 that morning on the left side of the De Lairessestraat . . . ,' Stikker wrote in his memoirs, 'but he begged me not to do it.' Stikker went ahead and nothing happened.

The Underground were by now getting moral support from the Churches, who gave a stern warning against registration. 'The best sabotage is that our whole nation, as one man, ignores the summons,' Archbishop Johannes de Jong wrote, and the Bishop of Haarlem ordered his priests to hide all necessary documents – 'otherwise you will soon be rid both of the books and your male parishioners'.

On 9 January, Gerbrandy himself appeared in the studios of Radio Oranje to put an end to the uncertainty in the Netherlands and to explain the Government's attitude. He told the Dutch that the decision to order nonco-operation in this case was taken with full consideration of the difficulties in Holland, especially now that the Germans seemed stronger than had been expected, but he remained convinced that only in unity – with the Allied effort – could the enemy be defeated. One Minister underlined Gerbrandy's words next day in stronger terms: 'In this crusade from oppression to liberation no man should report, no employer co-operate and no civil servant assist. This is the order, this way it has to be, it can be and it shall be.'

The inevitable 'razzias', in the meantime, had started. Not happy with the reporting of only 50,000 men, the Germans once more began raids upon one town after another. The first one was Dordrecht, where the inhabitants were woken up on 13 January by the usual banging on their doors, and volleys in the air, and 3500 men were arrested. The Resistance did all it could to alert towns and villages before a raid took place, but could sometimes only report what had happened. 'Leiden, 14 January – yesterday all bridges were opened and all passers-by (women, children and old people included) driven to schools, where their identity-cards were confiscated.' From the schools the miserable groups were pushed to the station, but on the way a row broke out among the patrolling soldiers, 'so that most people just went home'. Gouda, Delft, The Hague and Amsterdam followed; and at the end of January my father, on one of his 'milk rounds' to the farmers outside Hilversum, saw the first signs of a raid. He hurried home, alerted the neighbours and disappeared into his hiding-place in the attic. A few hours later we did indeed see the dreaded grey helmets appearing in the street, but the 'razzia' was less thorough and the Germans arrested only those whom they surprised in the streets. The results were negligible.

During the preparation of the Liese action, Seyss-Inquart had stayed in the background, but once it had started he made his contribution with a speech on 7 January. In it he not only stressed the fact that it was 'total war', so that everything was permitted to help the German war effort, but he also accused the Resistance of 'creating trouble'. According to him, nothing would have happened if the Dutch had been allowed to register for work in a normal and orderly manner, and he added in all seriousness that the Germans hated these raids, since they were 'more sentimental' than the Dutch.

Dr Mees in Rotterdam had listened with increasing fury to the speech and commented bitterly: 'The Dutch nation can look to the future with confidence, he said, but in the meantime there is no fuel, food and clothes. . . . He says that they will leave the Dutch undisturbed in their private lives . . . but what about the concentration-camps, the prisons, the executions, the deportations, the raids?' And the biggest affront, he felt, was Seyss-Inquart's assurance: 'The Germans fight for the equality and freedom of all nations.' How dared he to say this? 'Once again, everything was twisted lies and hypocrisies.'

The speech was a particular disappointment for Dr Hirschfeld as after a second conversation with Seyss-Inquart that same morning he had expected more. There had been some general discussion at first, but then Hirschfeld suddenly reminded the State Commissioner of their conversation of 14 December about a possible neutralisation of northern Holland, and he asked him if he had been serious. Seyss-Inquart froze for a second, then answered: 'I only called it a fantasy at that time because you did not react very favourably.' He insisted that he had meant it. Hirschfeld nodded and told the German that in that case he would like to discuss it with other Dutch leaders. Seyss-Inquart agreed, and as they parted he asked Hirschfeld to listen carefully to his speech that night, since it would contain something that would be of interest to him.

Hirschfeld listened carefully, but the only phrase that struck him came when the State Commissioner began to talk about a war on Dutch soil. Seyss-Inquart called it an impossibility: 'Either one takes it [Holland] in four days as the Germans did in 1940 or if this fails – as in September 1944 – one will see an unimaginable disaster.' It was not much to go on, but enough to encourage Hirschfeld to call together some of his contacts and go to the chairman of the Confidential Councillors, Bosch van Rosenthal, to discuss Seyss-Inquart's ideas. Bosch hesitated, but in the end informed Gerbrandy by cable. The Dutch Prime Minister recorded later that he received such a cool reception from Churchill, when he went to see him about it, that he quickly changed the subject – and the men in Holland waited in vain for a comment.

Seyss-Inquart made one last effort to induce the Dutch to co-operate, and on 2 February advertised the most attractive conditions yet for those who registered and were deported. They would receive at least 3.5 kilograms of potatoes, 70 grams of oil, 2 kilograms of vegetables, 3.5 kilograms of bread, 500 grams of cheese, while their families would be allowed to keep the men's ration-cards, a very welcome addition to the meagre rations. It was too good to be true, and the reaction was almost nil. By now the Dutch had heard about conditions in the work-camps and preferred to die at home, rather than in Rees or Oud-Leusden.

The employment of the hundreds of thousands of men who had been rounded up or had reported was never a problem for the Germans. They worked in Germany in the factories, cleared the rubble in bombed cities or dug defences in eastern Holland.

123

Housing them, however, was something else, and so was feeding them. In most places the men were put into barracks, factory buildings or brickyards. Their beds were normally just layers of straw, and coats had to serve as blankets. As most of the men had been taken unawares, they seldom had sufficient clothing or a decent pair of shoes.

The worst conditions were in the work-camp at Rees, just over the Dutch–German border, near Emmerich. The Reverend W. A. Zeydner from Rotterdam, who went on an inspection tour in February, was more than upset. The 3000 men in the camp were housed in a circus tent and in a barracks. 'The chinks in the walls are stuffed with straw,' he reported. 'There was one blanket for each man and during the frost they were covered with snow.' Those who fell ill were sent to another barracks, which was much too small to contain them all, and where untrained amateurs looked after them. 'Some of the men go barefoot in clogs and I've seen cases of frozen and amputated feet.' A visit to the nearby 'lazaret' in Holland was even more shocking. The 250 men there were a 'pitiable sight – covered with lice and almost without clothes. . . . They all complain of maltreatment and beatings. . . . At the beginning of February seventy-three men had already died.' Later reports revealed that of the 3000 men who worked at Rees one-third had perished or were mutilated for life. 'The worst camp my eyes have ever seen,' a German with experience in Poland called it, but it took months of protest before Seyss-Inquart intervened and had it closed down.

In the Waterloo camp at Oud-Leusden near Amersfoort the situation was almost as bad. The 1500 men locked up there laboured at the defence works at Hamersveld, which meant a daily walk of two hours on hardly any food at all. 'It completely reflects the Nazi ideals,' Radio Oranje sneered, 'the sort of boxes, full of straw, in which in peacetime the pigs sleep. No blankets and no food, just half a loaf of bread and at night a bowl of soup.' Most men suffered from colds and bronchitis, and when the lights were turned off 'a two-hour concert begins – a constant and heart-rending coughing'.

If the fate of the men in the work-camps was bad, still worse was life in the Dutch concentration-camps. Names like Amersfoort, Ommen, Vught and Westerbork instilled instant fear into every Dutchman.

Amersfoort had initially been a transit camp for political prisoners, but later it also became a camp for those who tried to desert their jobs in Germany, and for arrested Resistance fighters. Its commandant, Kotälla, was a notorious sadist, and knew how to destroy any man's dignity and energy within a few weeks.

They had to labour on the defence works, like the others, and an aunt of mine who lived in Amersfoort often watched as they straggled slowly through the town, forced to sing as they went. 'They had to cross a railway line and after a while the men who worked there took care that the crossing was closed as soon as the sad procession approached. Families were waiting there, and sometimes when the German guards turned their backs for a second they were able to give the men something. Once or twice someone even succeeded in escaping there,' she remembered. 'It was so terribly sad that it always made me cry.'

Kotälla used Christmas 1944 for another one of his persecutions, as a Resistance fighter, B. W. Stomps from Heemstede, arrested in June, recalled. On 23 December, Kotälla announced a ban on parcels for three weeks, which meant no Red Cross presents for Christmas or New Year. He further cancelled breakfast, lunch and dinner on Christmas Day itself, using the discovery of a smuggled letter as a pretext. And as an extra punishment on Christmas morning he kept the men standing on the parade ground, which was covered with thick snow, from their roll-call at seven till half-past midday. A few days before, the geese for the guards' Christmas dinner had been on show, hanging on the barbed wire.

Camp Erica at Ommen was another creation of the Nazis, where, amongst others, many of Holland's gypsies – considered by the Germans as 'anti-socials' – were locked up. But the worst and most lethal camp was in Vught, near Den Bosch. It was the only purpose-built concentration-camp in Holland, constructed in 1943 after Rauter had complained to Himmler about the overflow from the Dutch prisons. Rauter, fearing adverse publicity, tried to make it different from the SS camps in Germany, but it got off to a bad start. The Commandant, Karl Chmielewski, came straight from the extermination-camp at Mauthausen, and of the 2500 Dutch prisoners involved in constructing Vught 170 died, followed by 140 others in the first half-year. Some improvement followed when Chmielewski was

replaced by Adam Grünewald, but not for long as his régime
came to an abrupt end when he punished seventy-four women by
cramming them together into one cell that measured 2.24 metres
by 4. After an indescribable night, ten of them were dead and
Grünewald was sacked by an incensed Rauter.

A total of 17,500 victims went through Vught, and those
remaining – 4000 men and 700 women – were hurriedly
deported to Germany when the Allies approached in 1944. (Most
of them ended up in Ravensbrück, where hundreds died.) Entering Vught, the Allies found the bodies of four hundred men, shot
at the last minute.

Although many of Vught's prisoners died, there was still a chance
of survival for some. No hope, however, existed for the 12,000
Jews who came to that camp. Most of them knew that the
extermination-camps in the east awaited them. The last group,
consisting only of women and children, left Vught in June 1944
for Sobibor – 'the worst transport I ever witnessed', confessed a
hardened guard later.

The number of Jews in Vught was only a small percentage of
the Jews that found their way to certain death through the camp
at Westerbork in Drenthe, from which the last transports left for
Germany on 2 September 1944. Among the thousands who
travelled that day in the cattle-trucks to Auschwitz, Bergen-
Belsen, Ravensbrück and others was Anne Frank, the fourteen-
year-old girl whose diary has become the most moving testimony
against Nazi terror, 'outlasting for ever the shouts of the murderers'. She was sent to Auschwitz, and from there in October to
Belsen, where she died in the arms of a fellow-prisoner sometime
in February.

Anne and her family had, for more than two years, lived
hidden in a 'backhouse' on the Prinsengracht in Amsterdam,
before they were betrayed and taken away on Friday, 4 August
1944. They were just one family among the thousands of Jews in
Holland who tried to avoid the German clutches by 'diving' and,
like so many, they failed.

In 1941, after one year of Occupation and uncertainty in Holland, the first steps towards the extermination of the Jews had
been taken. Jews were removed from public life and excluded
from restaurants and hotels. The Germans ordered the compul-

sory sale of Jewish businesses and agricultural property, and the first 400 young Jews were deported, after putting up a fight.

It led to a two-day strike in February by the dockers of Amsterdam, broken up by harsh German measures, and to the creation of a Jewish Council. Two very respectable Jews, Professor D. Cohen and Mr A. Asscher, walked straight into a German trap by accepting the joint chairmanship of this new council, which obliged them to arrange the registration of all Jews. They cooperated in blind innocence, convinced they would be able to save their people.

The isolation of the Jews became total when, late in 1942, the Star of David, which every Jew had to wear publicly, was introduced. The Dutch, who apart from the February strike had only made weak protests from time to time, now began to show more loyalty to their Jewish compatriots. But after a few non-Jews, defiantly wearing the Star, had been arrested and taken to the Amersfoort concentration-camp the protest fizzled out.

Two months after the Star was introduced, no Jew was any longer allowed to cycle, take a tram, taxi or train, and he had to stay indoors between eight o'clock at night and six next morning. Most of the Jews had to move to Amsterdam, where the lively Jewish district became a ghetto, surrounded by barbed wire and warning signs. In July the first deportations started, and there were few exemptions. One Jew, who had lost a leg in the fighting of 1940 and asked General Christiansen for mercy, was refused with the words: 'Jew is Jew, with or without legs.' And, in October 1943, the last Jew disappeared behind the fences around Westerbork, the last stop before Germany.

Ironically, the Dutch Government had built the camp before the war for German Jewish refugees from Germany. It was in a desolate region, sandy and at times very muddy, and was surrounded by towers manned by the SS. Just outside the barbed wire was the villa of the SS Commandant Gemmeker, who, with his mistress, the dreaded Frau Hassel, lived there like a prince, spoilt by Jewish servants and entertained by the best artists Holland once had, all of them hoping that he would allow them to stay. Gemmeker made no exception for anyone, and even the leaders of the Jewish Council, Asscher and Cohen, contrary to all undertakings, were arrested by the Nazis and were sent on from Westerbork – in their case to Hitler's 'show-place', Theresienstadt, from where they both returned after the war.

The real horror of Westerbork was that, as in many other camps, most of the dirty work against the Jews was carried out by members of their own race. The guards were Jewish inmates who were picked as members of the order service, had some privileges and were bitterly hated. In the end even they did not escape the transport to the east and the gas-oven, and many of them were on the trains that left the camp on 2 September 1944. These were the last of the total of 91 trains that had departed from the little station near the camp. Most of them had gone to Auschwitz, where of the 60,000 Jews from Holland 500 survived, or to Sobibor, from where nineteen of the 34,000 returned.

Of the more than 120,000 Jews who were deported to the east, only 5500 came back to Holland. Two thousand Jews survived by fleeing abroad, 10,000 were exempted because they were married to non-Jews, and the 850 Jews who survived to delouse their frightened NSB enemies on Mad Tuesday in Westerbork were still alive when Liberation came.

Between 8000 and 10,000 Jews lived in hiding through the war, protected by friends or with their whereabouts unknown to anyone. They were forced to stay inside for years and were often not even allowed to go near the windows as neighbours could never be completely trusted. Most of the Dutch were too frightened to hide a Jew – and some chose not to because of a certain anti-semitism – since you could share his fate if you were found out. The Jews were ruthlessly hunted down by a special command, the Henneicke group, whose members worked on piece-rates – 7.50 guilders a head to begin with, which was later increased to 37.50 guilders. In consequence those rescue organisations which sought out hiding-places for Jews had enormous problems, and one of their leaders, frustrated and angry, remarked later: 'Could get ten British pilots into one house, but not even one Jew into ten houses.' Many were betrayed or starved to death during the Hunger Winter, and of the 25,000 Jews who were still alive in June 1944 more than 15,000 disappeared before the end of the war.

One survivor was Henriette Davids, one of the most popular cabaret stars in Holland and better known as Heintje. She and her husband, journalist Philip Pinkhof, in hiding since 1943, were moved on 2 September 1944 to the Pathological Institute in

Utrecht, where they settled down happily. 'They had devised the most ingenious precautions,' Heintje recorded in her memoirs. 'The Institute has a morgue in the cellar, where there were always a few corpses, lying on little trolleys. In the event of a raid, my husband and I were to lie down between the corpses, covered by a sheet and, like the others, with a little label tied to our toe.' This sinister charade was never needed as a German medical team moved into the Institute – ignorant of the couple's identity – and the Gestapo never raided the place. Heintje made herself useful by now and then pressing a German uniform, or by mopping the kitchen floor.

Henriette Davids and Pinkhof shared their lot as 'divers' in 1944 with 300,000 other Dutch people – a number that was doubled in the Hunger Winter during the Liese action and the raids. The 'divers' led an unnatural life, isolated, hungry and constantly in fear of being found out. The diarist Adriaan van Boven, alias Jan Jansen, wrote of 'healthy men, spending their time in idleness and in that way serving their country'. Most of them tried to make themselves useful, like the author Maurits Deker, who was exploited by his 'landlady' as a man of all trades. Others knitted or sat behind a spinning-wheel, and one student in Rotterdam disappeared to his attic room in December 1944 with a Russian grammar, an atlas, a red pencil and a stack of French books on nineteenth-century literature. He failed to record how his Russian was after all those months, but he never forgot one passage from Victor Hugo's *Lucrèce Borgia*: 'Nous vivons dans une époque où les gens accomplissent tant d'actions horribles qu'on n'en parle plus de celle-la' – 'We live in a time where people commit such horrible acts that we no longer talk of hers.' Nothing could have been more fitting.

CHAPTER THIRTEEN

The Great Escape

WHILE 300,000 Dutch 'divers' waited helplessly in their some-times very uncomfortable hiding-places for Liberation, another, smaller, group of young men made effort after effort to cross to the free provinces of the south. They were the soldiers of 1st Airborne Division left behind after Arnhem who had managed to avoid imprisonment by the Germans. The group was no larger than about 250 men.

The most important was British Brigadier John W. Hackett, who after a distinguished war career in Syria, the Western Desert and Italy had landed near Arnhem as the commander of the 4th Parachute Brigade. He had been severely wounded in the abdomen and had had to be taken into hospital. At the beginning of October, when the Germans began to transport the British wounded to Germany, the Dutch Resistance had smuggled him out to hide him in the little market-town of Ede. There, three elderly spinsters, Mien, Cor and Rie de Nooy, nursed him back to health in their best room, knowing very well that they would be arrested and almost certainly executed if they were found out.

Hackett was deeply moved by their courage and dedication, and he wrote later: 'Words could not express the gratitude I felt for the way they housed, fed and looked after me. A fighting soldier in wartime takes the dangers and tensions that bear upon himself for granted. It is quite a different thing to contemplate the actions of other people, to observe their bravery, contrivance and self-sacrifice, in protecting and looking after someone thrown by hazard into their care. There is nothing to be taken for granted here.'

In hiding not far away was the man who had saved his life, Captain Lipmann Kessel, RAMC, a young surgeon from South Africa who had been dropped at Arnhem with 1st Airborne

Division. Together with his colleagues he had worked in the enormous red-brick St Elisabeth Hospital on the outskirts of the town, performing with them up to 200 operations a day, one of which was on Hackett. When the Germans closed the hospital on 11 October, he had joined his commanding officer, Colonel Graeme Warrack, RAMC, at the Willem III barracks in Apeldoorn until the moment came to disappear in order to avoid being sent to prison-camp in Germany.

He had been less lucky than the Brigadier in finding a comfortable hiding-place, and had to make do with a dug-out shelter on a farm. 'The entrance ... was in the form of a narrow tunnel perhaps ten feet in length,' he remembered later, 'this sloped acutely for the first few feet and, before reaching the hideout itself, there was a sharp bend, so that to enter you had to slide in head first and wriggle on your belly.' The chamber itself was underneath the barn floor and it was impossible to stand erect, but 'it was surprising how quickly we became accustomed to crawling on all fours in the deep carpet of straw'.

Warrack had found the same kind of accommodation after one of the most bizarre escapes. Reckoning that it would take the Allied armies no more than three weeks to return, he decided to wait for them in the Willem III barracks. He had noticed that there was a hollow space above the wardrobe in his bedroom, behind a panel. 'It couldn't have been more than eighteen inches across, but I squeezed in fairly comfortably,' he told later. He equipped his hide-away with half a dozen blankets, three loaves of German bread, eight bottles of water and several other items.

On 17 October, when he was ordered to evacuate the barracks with his patients, he disappeared into his wardrobe. The Germans, furious that their most important prisoner had vanished, turned the building almost inside out, but finally concluded that he had left. Ten days later, the last patients departed, to be replaced by a German detachment. An officer took Warrack's room, and an anxious time followed. 'I could even hear the bastard breathing,' Warrack recalled and he was so afraid of making a noise in his sleep that he stayed awake all night.

After two weeks the Allies still had not turned up, and the doctor realised that the only way to join them was to go and look for them. He stealthily left his wardrobe, climbed out of a window and a few hours later knocked on the door of a Dutchman, who found refuge for him in a cave in the woods near Otterloo, just big enough for one man.

The problem now was how to get back to the Allied front south of the rivers. Had he been able to escape a few days earlier he could have joined the first group who had tried to cross, but he was too late.

The Veluwe, the dense forest region north of Arnhem, was ideal for the airborne troops who had escaped the Germans. With its isolated villages, its hidden paths and shrubs, it was made for hiding in. Most of the Dutch who lived there were willing to help the men whose failure to liberate them from German oppression had brought disappointment, but no resentment. The Underground movement, always in need of fighters, was very happy with the experienced support they were now getting and hoped to play a more active part when the Allies made another effort to cross the rivers.

The commander of one group of the British soldiers was Major Digby Tatham-Warter, young, energetic and very tall. He had been slightly wounded at Arnhem, but had almost at once escaped from the St Elisabeth Hospital, and after some wandering found refuge in the house of Bill Wildeboer, the leader of Ede's Resistance. From there he organised the ranks, cycling casually from hiding-place to hiding-place, and established contact with the 'other side' through a secret telephone connection that ran along the power cables of the provincial electricity company. It was his intention, he told Gilbert Sadi-Kirschen of the Belgian Company of the Special Air Service (SAS) – known to him as Captain Fabian King – to integrate his men with the Dutch Resistance in readiness for the Big Day. He, like Warrack, was convinced that the Second Army would soon begin a new offensive and cross the Rhine.

A few days later, however, he had changed his mind. It became increasingly difficult to hide so many young men and, while the Second Army failed to appear, the Germans became more active in hunting down the airborne men. Tatham-Warter himself was daily confronted with danger, as the Wehrmacht billeted four soldiers in Wildeboer's house. The Major was supposed to be an evacuee from The Hague, and the Germans were perfectly polite, but it was obvious that his activities could not go unnoticed for ever. And when the Germans began to show some astonishment at the great number of 'evacuees' that regularly visited Wildeboer he decided to try to leave the country – with as many men as possible.

It was 16 October when the vague plans to cross took shape. That day Lieutenant-Colonel David Dobie, commanding officer of the 1st Parachute Battalion, walked into Wildeboer's house after a few weeks of wandering in the Veluwe. He was warmly welcomed and at once appointed as the man who would cross first to Liberated Holland to prepare the escape from the other side. That same day, he left on a bicycle and guided by Dutch Resistance fighters reached the little village of Maurik, from where he was rowed by night across the Waall to the village of Wamel and was taken to the commander of the Second Army, General Sir Miles Dempsey. The General received them in his luxurious caravan, parked near Eindhoven, and listened carefully to Dobie's story and his proposal to smuggle the men out. 'When Dobie was finished there was a silence that seemed interminable,' an eyewitness remembered, 'but it could not have lasted more than several seconds.' At last Dempsey opened his mouth. 'Get them out,' was his only comment. Operation Pegasus could begin.

The General's order reached Kirschen soon afterwards in the chicken-run near Barneveld where he had made his headquarters with his two assistants and a wireless set. He hurried to Tatham-Warter, and the two men sat down to plan the final details of the evacuation. The Dutch Resistance were also told, and it was a hard blow for them. Not only would they lose precious support, but they also understood that the departure of their friends and allies meant that SHAEF had given up all plans to try to liberate the rest of the Netherlands – at least for the moment.

Nevertheless they offered all possible help to the troops, guided the British officers sent out to reconnoitre the route, and organised transport for the soldiers, who were scattered all over the Veluwe, to a central point of departure. From there, Bill Wildeboer told Hackett on his sick-bed, they would be conducted to the Rhine, where, if all went well, boats would pick them up. The day chosen for the operation was Sunday, 22 October, and the crossing was planned for one hour after midnight.

The chances of success looked good. The positions of the

German posts along the river were known, the bank was still only lightly guarded, and a mass escape was such a novelty that the Germans would not expect it. Moreover, the men were well trained and fit after only a few weeks of hiding. 'With reasonable luck,' Hackett thought, 'most, if not all, of them would get across.'

On Saturday morning, 21 October, the signal was given. All over the Veluwe from that moment onwards little groups of soldiers left their sheepfolds, barns, chicken-runs, farmhouses and even a cemetery to follow their Dutch guides. The Germans had ordered the evacuation of the village of Bennekom and, while it was a tragedy for the villagers, it was a stroke of luck for the escapers. Dressed in their borrowed overalls, coats and old jackets they passed unnoticed amidst the stream of civilians with their goods piled on carts and bikes who had to leave their homes.

One of the airborne officers travelling to the rendezvous was a signals officer, Major Anthony Deane-Drummond. He had managed to escape after having been made prisoner by the Germans, and had been forced to stay hidden in a cupboard in a German guardroom, from which he staggered out after thirteen days. Like many of the other escapers he roamed the Veluwe for days before he managed to get in touch with the Resistance, and was taken in by a local schoolmaster in Velp. After a merry party the night before, he was picked up on Saturday morning by a wheezing old Red Cross lorry driven on charcoal gas, and taken to a hut somewhere in the woods between Ede and Arnhem, where Tatham-Warter waited. With him was another important escaper, Brigadier Gerald Lathbury of 1st Parachute Brigade, recovered from a spinal wound while hiding with Menno de Nooy, the nephew of Hackett's spinsters, in Ede, and now dressed in a black clerical suit that made him look like a 'rather seedy don'. He had played an important role in the planning of the crossing and shared the responsibilities with Tatham-Warter. Both officers, towering over their men, welcomed the groups and divided them into three parties for the three lorries that would take them to the woods near Renkum, from where they had to walk the last five kilometres to the riverbank.

The whole group was 120 men strong, and when the lorries arrived Deane-Drummond wondered how they all would fit in. But without any hesitation Tatham-Warter ordered them to get in. 'The fifty of us were piled in quickly and laid on the floor,'

Deane-Drummond described later, 'while the Dutch drivers covered us with empty sacks so that we looked like lorries full of potatoes.' They were told that if a German checkpoint stopped them they were to try bluff. 'If that failed we would have to jump out and overpower the post.'

Bumping over the roads and waved through by two German posts, they reached the Renkum woods safely and got out. Only the last walk was left and Deane-Drummond, who had already escaped once, from an Italian prison-camp at Sulmona, worried how such a large group would be able to reach the Rhine undetected. But the weather was with them. Lying in the woods, dressed again in uniform, the men saw a fine mist rising and when at nine o'clock at night the signal for the march was given it was so dark that one could hardly see a hand before one's face.

The Dutch guides had departed and there was only one of them left to take the column through the dense forest. 'Sometimes the trees closed over us like a tunnel,' Deane-Drummond wrote in his book *Return Ticket*. A rope was passed along the stumbling men, but it could not prevent them from slipping and falling, and the march of the 120 men sounded, as Tatham-Warter later remembered, like 'a stampeding herd of wild elephants'.

Without incident, however, the column reached the edge of the wood, two kilometres away from the river. Open fields waited now, with two German positions, each containing a mortar battery and some infantry. The Dutch guide left them here, and they had to find their own way. During the reconnaissance Tatham-Warter had found a drainage ditch one metre deep that ran straight to the riverbank, and crawling through this the soldiers reached the river. This time they did not go completely unnoticed. A German patrol saw them going, but was so intimidated that they only interfered with the last men and, as Hackett learned later, arrested one of the two Russians who had joined the escape.

Standing on the shore Deane-Drummond looked at the river. 'We could now see the other side through a layer of swirling mist that clung to the surface,' he recalled, but no sign of movement could be seen anywhere.

At the other side Dobie, in charge of the rescue operation with twenty-four assault-boats, was looking at the same river. As promised, they had given a signal at midnight – a burst of Bofors tracers – but there had been no answer. The prearranged 'V' signal that Tatham-Warter gave with his red torch had been too weak to be seen across the wide stream, and everybody feared that something had gone wrong. About half an hour after midnight, however, they saw a tiny light flicker on and off followed a few minutes later by a faint red pinpoint of light signalling 'V' for Victory.

The men hurriedly pushed the boats into the river and after a rapid crossing landed at the other side. One of the rescuers jumped overboard and ran in the direction he had seen the red light. 'After a little time I heard a strange sound like wind rustling through the meadows,' he recorded, 'but I saw no one. . . . The sound started and stopped several times and then gradually became louder. The origin was now unmistakable. A grey, amorphous column took shape in the dark, shuffling slowly over the meadow.' He soon discovered the leaders, Tatham-Warter and Lathbury, and pointed breathlessly to the boats, not far off. Half an hour later the last of the airborne soldiers was on board to arrive safely in Liberated Holland.

At eleven o'clock on Monday morning a phone call from the south brought news to the Resistance in Ede that the operation had been successful. Kirschen received that day a signal from London telling him the same, and on 28 October the BBC confirmed it with a 'message from Bill. Everything is well. All our thanks.'

Warrack, Kessel and many other 'latecomers' had to wait for almost a month before they received an alert that the success of Pegasus justified another attempt at escape. Hackett, still too weak to join, had misgivings this time. The secret telephone communication between north and south had broken down, and the candidates for this crossing – they expected 160 men – were much less fit and, since they were a mixed bunch of British, Americans and Dutch, had no cohesion or joint discipline. More ominously, the Germans had evacuated the zone north of the river, no traffic was allowed within ten kilometres, and they were much more on their guard than in October.

'The difference between this plan and the last was what most distinguished good plans in war from bad ones,' Hackett later wrote. 'The other had a high probability of success if it did not run into really bad luck, this one would need very good luck indeed to have even a sporting chance.'

It had been decided that Major Hugh Maguire, an intelligence officer of 1st Airborne Division, in hiding since the defeat at Arnhem, would be the commander of this operation, christened Pegasus II. Though the men would follow more or less the same route as the first escapers, the important difference was that because of the no-man's-zone they had to march at least twenty-three kilometres before reaching the shores of the Rhine, instead of the five kilometres of a month earlier.

Unaware of all these problems, Kessel and his companions left their low-ceilinged dug-out in good spirits. 'With luck, within twenty-four hours you'll be drinking pink gins behind the British lines,' the guide told Kessel, admitting at the same time that he had his doubts. But even the rain, dribbling down his collar, could not destroy Kessel's high spirits, and when he discovered his friend Warrack at the farm, where the expedition was to start, he believed that nothing could go wrong. They told each other their latest adventures, while Maguire tried to get some order into the mixture of airborne troops, RAF and American airmen, and Dutch civilians leaving the country to avoid arrest by the Germans. While they waited for the moment to leave, the party practised an exact drill for crossing the main obstacle to the escape: the motorway between Arnhem and Utrecht was certain to be heavily guarded. 'At least it helped to keep us warm,' Kessel remembered.

When they left, the wind had dropped and the torrential rain of the last days had stopped. 'The wood was assertively silent, and whispered voices and the crackling sound of footfalls ricocheted alarmingly among the tree trunks. It was now dark, too dark.' And chaos was inevitable. The column soon split up, shots sounded, people started running, but the main body moved steadily on the motorway. It was a frightening sight, Warrack thought. 'In front of us the road stretched right and left, broad, white and horribly exposed.' The men started to cross it, and he was in the middle when he heard 'Halt'. Rapidly, he almost jumped across, escaping German bullets by flinging himself in the bushes.

Kessel, who had crossed at the same time, threw himself on the

137

grass bank at the other side. 'Bullets were tearing the air and whining as they streaked the metalled surface.' In the trees ahead, he saw several figures running frantically and he followed them. For him it was the end of Pegasus II. Warrack managed to reach the riverbank with three others and planned to swim across, but had to give up this idea and returned to his 'old lair', while Kessel found refuge on a farm run by Willem Donck.

For Hackett the news of the failure came as no surprise. 'Before daylight on the morning fixed for the crossing, the 18th of November, I heard distant shooting from my bed.' He knew too well what it meant. Only five men managed to reach the south.

For the Resistance group in Ede, the operation was disastrous. Most of the Dutch guides had been arrested or wounded, and everybody felt very badly about the outcome. 'Every sort of rumour circulated,' Hackett was told. 'That every man had run like a rabbit at the first shot, for instance, and that most of the men had been drunk anyway.' He did his best to calm things down. 'No one should be blamed. For the very best of reasons they had tried to do too much.'

For those airborne soldiers who had to remain hidden in Occupied Holland the months that followed were very long. The Hunger Winter started for them as well, and for the Dutchmen – who ran the risk of being shot if they were found out – it became increasingly difficult to feed their Allied guests. Kessel and his four companions were forced to stay inside by their unwilling and rather mean host, as the Germans were never very far away. Both Willem Donck and his farmhand were constantly on their guard. 'At the slightest sniff of danger one of them would come rushing into the room: "De Moffen, de Moffen" and instantly a well-rehearsed drill would go into operation,' Kessel wrote in his book *Surgeon at Arms*. 'Without a word books, playing cards, shaving tackle would be piled into a box always kept at hand; the chairs round the stove would be rearranged; and we would scamper up into the haystack.' Thanks to regular practice they could do it in twenty-seven seconds.

The five men were hungry, too. In spite of the hundred guilders Donck received for hiding them, plus the extra coupons and a weekly piece of an illegally slaughtered pig, he never gave them more than a single slice of potato-meal bread for breakfast, some boiled potatoes and sometimes a piece of meat for lunch, and for supper another slice of potato-meal bread with a two-inch cube of raw pork fat. Warrack, hiding with an American OSS man in a house not far from Kessel, had a better life, like Hackett, but they, too, felt the pinch.

'Things in their domestic aspect got harder now,' the Brigadier wrote. 'The bread ration was cut. The meagre allowance of gas for cooking ceased entirely and there was no coal.' His doctor told him that the official ration for the Dutch amounted to about 600 calories a day. He listened that winter to stories about the hunger trips and saw every day the sad files of 'dispirited Dutchmen, shepherded by grave looking old men' on their way to or from the defence works. He watched from behind the curtains the men and women pulling their sledges or carts out to the woodlands to fell a tree and drag it back. 'It was a grim struggle.'

Even the SAS operator Kirschen, whose chicken-run had burned down and who had found shelter in the house of Vera Hoogewegen in Maarn, was hungry in spite of the containers London dropped now and then at his request. On 1 February he wrote in his diary: 'It is no use pretending that we are not hungry. We're starving. It is not a terrible, violent hunger, but a gnawing constant hunger which makes you dream of frying chickens. . . .' As in any Dutch household, the conversation in Vera's house revolved around food, and when he proposed to make a shopping-list to signal to SAS Headquarters at Moor Park, Hertfordshire, everybody eagerly made a contribution. Chocolate, candles, coffee. . . .

The telegram was sent, and two days later HQ answered. 'Six friends are calling tonight.' Kirschen knew what it meant: six containers from the sky. Lying on the heath that night, he waited, however, in vain and two nights later he was back. 'How many men somewhere in Europe are doing the same,' he wondered, 'flattened against the soil, shivering with cold and with beating heart, waiting for a large black plane from England?' This time it arrived. 'The plane is over our heads now . . . it circles and comes straight to us and while we salute it with our torches, six solemn parachutes open. The six friends.'

As promised, the boxes were full of coffee, pâté, ham, chocolate, tobacco, even two shirts and some letters, the first in five months. It was an incredible treasure and worth a celebration.

But, while Kirschen was lucky enough to be able to help his Dutch hosts with some extra provisions, Kessel, Warrack and all the others had to live on their meagre rations and were delighted when at Christmas Donck agreed to kill a chicken. 'It was scraggy,' Kessel remembered, 'but we had it boiled with potatoes and, as an extra treat, there was cabbage.'

John Hackett had rabbit on Christmas Eve, but he ate it without much attention. His health had improved considerably and it had been planned that he should leave next day for the south. All his Dutch friends came that evening to say goodbye, but next day the expedition had to be cancelled as the moon was too bright. The Brigadier was disappointed, but took it philosophically. 'Again we had done all we could. In the end everything would work out as it was meant to be.'

It was not until 30 January that Hackett finally set out for his escape. After a stay of four months with the De Nooy sisters there were sad farewells. 'I hugged and kissed each one,' the normally so-reserved officer remembered. Jan Snoek, a young friend from Ede, accompanied him when he cycled away on his high Dutch bike with the massive tyres. He was dressed in a thin Gestapo coat on which the sisters had pinned a deaf-button, so that he could pretend not to understand what was said to him. Now the farewells were over, and he was on his way, he felt elated in spite of the pain of his stomach wound. 'It was like leaving school. There was the expectation of excitement and change, of freedom and a new life and the delight of setting out to go home.'

It was a tortuous trip through a snowstorm, which gave them, however, one advantage: all the German roadblocks were unmanned. Late in the afternoon he reached the first destination, Doorn, where Jan and he would stay at Huis te Maarn, once a stately home but now an institution for old people. He was deathly tired, but cheered up when he discovered that Kessel was another guest in the house.

'The Brigadier looked fit, though much thinner,' Kessel recalled. The two men greeted each other warmly and a little later were joined by Warrack, who thought the Brigadier in spite of his weakness 'in good spirits and very enthusiastic about his escape plan'.

Kessel and Warrack had arrived four days earlier at the Huis te

Maarn after another failure to cross, and they told Hackett the whole story. This time their escape had been organised by Kirschen, but from the start the expedition seemed jinxed. Kessel, 'crazily overdressed', fainted twice to begin with and fell from his bike. He was taken back to Barneveld while the others went on, but pleaded so convincingly with his Dutch helpers that in the end they agreed to let him go and join his friends in Scherpenzeel. The rest of the trip was as bad as the start. Boats were not where they should have been, guides had just been arrested, farmers refused them shelter, and all the time there were blizzards and tempests. Roelof van Valkenburg, their Dutch companion, made every effort to get them to Tiel, where the Allies would be waiting to send a boat across, but they could not get through, and on 19 January Kirschen received the message that it was no longer possible to come and collect the men. 'The moon is too high.'

Kirschen returned to Barneveld, while the doctors found a hiding-place at the Huis te Maarn, waiting for another opportunity to escape. Meeting the Brigadier on his way to the south seemed to offer them this next chance, and it was Warrack who cautiously approached Hackett with the idea that they should perhaps travel together. The Brigadier reacted hesitantly, afraid that so large a party would jeopardise the trip, but before his guide Jan Snoek left to reconnoitre the route he asked him to try to persuade the people in the south to fit in at least two more on this crossing.

During the next two days the little group of escapers spent their time playing chess, chopping wood and walking through the park around the house. Kessel could not resist looking at Hackett's stomach wound and was disappointed to see that it was still festering. With the help of the Underground he got hold of a set of instruments, and tidied the wound up.

The men followed the activities in the house where they were staying with great interest. It was the cottage next to the big house and it was obviously a centre of the Resistance. Isolated in the woods, Cornelis Idenburg, the caretaker of the Huis te Maarn, his wife and two sons not only sheltered a large number of Dutch 'divers', but also had a press in the cellar on which a daily newssheet was printed. Hackett was slightly worried to have to wait in such a dangerous beehive and was relieved when Jan at last returned with good news. He had made his contacts and the crossing could take place. He had even received permission for Hackett to bring his two friends, and on 3 February the journey began.

While Kessel and Warrack travelled by night, the Brigadier, protected by his false papers and his deaf-button, was, together with Jan, travelling by day. The weather was much better, a hesitant winter sun had melted part of the snow and the trip was considerably easier. There were no incidents for Hackett, but the two doctors were less lucky. When they stopped at a house to ask for some water, the two men standing in the door stared at Kessel's shoes, 'a handsome brown military pair'. While one of the men told them to go to the kitchen, the other cycled away in great haste, and when the woman of the house offered them tea they felt it was time to leave rapidly. 'You seem in a hurry . . . ,' their host remarked slyly. 'Going far?' Warrack and Kessel just smiled, and their Dutch guide mumbled something like 'Beyond Rotterdam'. When they were out of earshot, back on their bikes, their guide told them that he suspected it was an NSB household, 'and that the man who had gone off was by now reporting our presence to the German police'. They raced down the road, crossed a river in a ferry and reached Groot Ammers, the village where they were to spend the night.

Hackett arrived a little later, to hear with disappointment that a crossing was not possible, as the wind was too violent. After two days the gale abated and the three men were taken to Schiedam, where the last stage of the journey would begin. The Brigadier felt strange. 'Something was over and something else was about to begin,' he wrote later. 'I was a sleeper about to awake, not suddenly but slowly.' In a house overlooking the windswept Merwede he changed into the battered remnants of his own uniform, the torn battledress blouse with its faded parachute wings and medal ribbons, and its dull bloodstains. Over this he wore his Gestapo coat, and in this rather inadequate outfit he set out that night for a long cold trip across the water. It was an unreal journey, full of drama. Dark figures in swirling fog, whispered passwords, flashing light signals, long walks through marshland and finally the crossing, past German posts on the bank. The storm had returned, and for Hackett in his canoe the world was 'all plunging darkness, wild movement and crashing noise'. He held on to what he could find, his face whipped by the spray, shivering in his thin coat.

There was one moment of fright when the Germans sent up a white flare, but the little boat remained unseen and at two o'clock he reached his destination, the small port of Lage Zwaluwe. 'I was helped out of the canoe and up the steps, very stiff and awkward,' Hackett remembered. A cheerful voice greeted him with the words 'Hullo, Shan,' and a bottle of brandy was handed to him. 'We've been expecting you. Have a drop.' The man who loomed up in the dark was Major Tony Crankshaw, commander of B Squadron 11th Hussars, whom Hackett had last met in the Western Desert two years earlier.

At the nearby farmhouse another surprise waited for him. Warrack, who had made the trip in another canoe, had arrived a few minutes earlier, but he was very worried about Kessel, whose canoe had leaked and who had had to stay behind in the Biesbos while Warrack went to look for help.

'Don't move from here. Whatever you do, hold on.' These were the last words Kessel heard from Warrack. Then his friend had disappeared into the fog, leaving him with his Dutch guide Hans on an island that was more like a lump of mud, on which three willow seedlings tried to grow. Exhausted by the struggle with the sinking canoe, and wet through, the two men jumped up and down to get warm and dry. They calculated that it would take at least two hours for their rescuers to find them, but when daylight came no one had appeared. 'It was a grey sadistic morning,' Kessel wrote, 'and our mud island was caked with frost.' About a hundred metres from them was a German post, and they could easily see the guards, pacing up and down. The only way to remain unnoticed was to crawl behind the reeds that surrounded their island.

To keep themselves warm and busy they tried to plug the leaking seams of their canoe. It was useless; when they tried the boat that evening, it stayed afloat for only four minutes. Another long wait began in the hope that someone would turn up, but at one o'clock they decided to try to row to the nearest bank. The canoe made it just in time, and turned turtle as they jumped on to land, and drifted away.

Dizzy with hunger and fatigue they waded through the marshes, falling over half-sunken tree-trunks until they reached a road and found a farmhouse. 'From then on we were engulfed in a familiar warm-hearted pattern,' Kessel recorded. Their clothes were soon drying before the stove and the farmer's wife fed them with Dutch biscuits while the husband went to contact the local Underground. Hidden in a cart full of hay they were taken next day to Sliedrecht, where Kessel stayed only two days before another crossing took place.

'The thought of the Biesbos sickened me,' he confessed, but when his guide appeared he felt reassured. It was the same Dutchman who had taken Warrack across and who told him now that he had come back to look for him, but had not been able to trace him.

The journey this time was much easier, and after a crossing of a few hours Kessel reached the port of Lage Zwaluwe. 'Gazing down at us through the gloom was a lounging, steel-helmeted figure with a rifle. It was watching us coming ashore. It didn't move. It didn't speak, let alone call out a challenge.' It was the British lines, and in spite of this cold reception Kessel could have kissed the guard. He was free.

That winter, another thirty-seven men followed Hackett, Kessel and Warrack along the same route. One of them was Kirschen, who on 12 February suddenly received a mysterious phone call in his hiding-place at Barneveld, telling him to come to Rotterdam. From there his crossing to the south would be organised. Cycling through Holland he quickly reached the great port, but he had to wait four weeks before a young man came to see him with the message that he was taking him across that same evening. It was a moonless night full of stars when Kirschen, alias Fabian King, left the country where he had arrived for a few weeks seven months ago. His main task had been to report about the launching-sites of the V1 and V2, but much of his time had been taken up by organising the return of the airborne men, and now that there were only a few left his mission was at an end.

Sitting in the canoe that took him back to freedom, Kirschen listened to the song of the water and his thoughts went back to the period he had spent in Holland and to the friends he had made and who had helped him. Would he ever see them alive? 'There are already so many who have disappeared. . . . All those who waited for us on the heath, that first night . . . rich and poor, people from different backgrounds. . . . They have shared their meagre rations, their hopes, their disappointments, their warm friendship with us, at the same time keeping us out of the hands of the enemy. One after the other has fallen. . . .'

CHAPTER FOURTEEN

The Lowest Point

'THE GERMAN children of 1918 are so grateful for the good food they got in Holland that, in 1945, they give every Dutch child two slices of bread and one potato a day.' This bitter allusion to the flood of German and Austrian children who came to Holland after the First World War and enjoyed Dutch hospitality and kindness was one of the jokes that circulated in the Hunger Winter. But just how deep the resentment was Captain Lipmann Kessel discovered when, shortly before his escape to the south, he was staying with a doctor in Sliedrecht. A visiting nurse remarked that some of those same German children 'are now helping to starve out and destroy the provinces in which they were once guests'.

Earlier, the doctor had told Kessel about the Resistance among his colleagues. 'It had been begun by three doctors who'd met secretly in a station waiting-room. Their plan was to get members to resign from the Medical Association that had fallen under Nazi influence, and to enrol them in a new secret one soon to become known as the "Medical Front".' They had been successful and only a short while ago had sent a strong protest to Seyss-Inquart, in which they referred to the gesture of the Dutch towards the German children in 1918. 'We cannot resist asking you if you have forgotten that, at the time when German and Austrian children were suffering, they received hospitality, food and clothing in this same country that is now looted by your compatriots and driven to starvation,' ran their letter of 22 January.

It left Seyss-Inquart cold, like every other protest, but he did make a gesture. Hirschfeld, whose shipping operations were still paralysed by the frost, had asked him to let some trains through with German personnel, and on 26 January three trains arrived in Amsterdam, Rotterdam and The Hague with just enough potatoes to keep the central kitchens going for a few days more.

The State Commissioner now offered more, and proposed to send ten trains a week with 500 tons of potatoes, and four grain-trains with 600 tons each, from the north-east to the west. Hirschfeld informed London, adding: 'but he demands Dutch personnel'. On 6 February the answer from London arrived: 'Ask Confidential Councillors and BS Commander. . . .' Their re-action was a firm 'No Dutch personnel'. The decision was taken in spite of the fact that there were absolutely no stocks of food left in the west. 'The lowest point of food supply started on 28 January,' Hirschfeld wrote in his memoirs. The bread ration, up till then 1000 grams a week, had to be reduced to 500 grams, and the official rations were no more than 460 calories a day, which fell to 350 in February.

The cities had gone deathly silent. 'Those who are hungry shout, but those who are starving keep still,' a newspaper reported on 30 January. 'The traffic has stopped, all enterprises are paralysed. Footsteps are smothered by the thick snow and this immense silence is penetrated by one single thought, that of the daily bread which is lacking. . . .'

Nothing was so important as food – with fuel on its heels. I remember getting up in the morning thinking of food; the whole day long we talked about food; and I went to bed hungry and dreaming about food. 'It is devastating to discover', the author Maurits Dekker remarked, 'that a human being, under certain circumstances, is so little different from an animal and in the end consists only of a stomach plus some instincts and tools.'

A Dutchman had to be very hungry before he asked a German for something to eat – but it happened. 'When the trucks full of foodstuffs arrived at the German garrison, people clustered around in the hope that they would spill something,' an Ams-terdammer reported. 'Now and then a German would give away half a loaf of bread or some biscuits, which led to desperate scuffles.' People fought over anything that was edible; a potato lying in the street was a treasure. The contents of an accidentally spilled bin for the central kitchen were scraped off the streets with spoons, and nobody bothered about hygiene.

Rotterdam, too, was overcome 'by a quiet oppressive apathy', a citizen wrote. 'The streets were empty, children stayed at home and only in some of the shops were people queuing for hours.'

Somebody else remembered in particular the faces of the people, 'sunken, grey and without life'. He went on: 'We have become paupers. We have no soap and our clothes are worn out. We all look dishevelled. Perhaps we believe that only others look so old and that we're not like them, decrepit little men with collars too wide and sloppy, shiny suits. . . . But one look in the mirror is sufficient. The poverty and anxiety of the last years are imprinted on our faces. . . . And we haven't laughed for ages.'

A sixty-five-year-old draughtsman in Rotterdam who went to see his doctor on 3 January noted with shaking hands: 'He could not give me anything. It was the common complaint and was caused by too little and fatless food.' A trip out to some farms had secured a few cabbages. 'I was blown over in the mud, but trudged home, stiff with hunger and cold.' Not far from home he had collapsed – 'Was only able to grab a lamp-post and two men carried me home'.

Douwenga, still at his evacuation address in Naarden, had also lost his zest for life. 'It has been snowing the whole day,' he recorded on 20 January. 'There was hardly any daylight and dark clouds were hanging over the snow-covered meadows. We stayed inside. Why should we tire ourselves? The rations were small again.' He looked now and then at the clock, but it was too early to go to bed and, while his wife was reading a story to the boys in the hope that they would not feel their hunger so much, his mind wandered: 'What are we eating tomorrow? There are still a few potatoes and a piece of sugarbeet.' But it was not nearly enough, and ten days later one of his boys fainted from hunger. 'If I look in the mirror I'm shocked by that thin hollow-eyed image and I do not dare to look at my wife. She's changed so much.'

'They were terrible: the trio of hunger, cold and darkness,' a young engineer in The Hague wrote, shivering in his hiding-place, 'and the worst is that they intensify each other.'

The sugarbeet that Douwenga mentioned was by now a normal part of our daily menu. Hirschfeld and Louwes were forced as early as November to supplement the rations with sugarbeets, but on 15 January it was for the first time officially announced that the beet was to be part of our future diet, and that every Dutchman would receive three kilograms of them instead of potatoes.

In every household the scrubbing, cutting and cooking of the filthy sugarbeets began. It was hard work and it was impossible to get one's hands clean for days afterwards. Dutch food experts had experimented with different methods of preparation, and published a series of booklets with recipes. The principle was very simple: wash the beet, slice it and then peel it. Cut the slices even finer with a cucumber-slicer and cook them for hours. Take the slices out of the juice, which thickened into a treacle, and mash them to pulp. The treacle could be improved by adding apple-juice or vinegar, while the pulp could be made into pancakes or a sort of porridge. 'Until I saw the first load of those monsters lying on the kitchen floor, I never knew that this wood in the shape of a turnip could be eaten,' Maurits Dekker wrote. But after all the work he had his reward. The pulp, 'together with a little onion and a gravy-cube, was a delicious meal'. Others left the pulp to ferment behind the stove for a few days and it then tasted almost like sauerkraut, while someone in The Hague wrote how she mixed it with some finely chopped onions, a touch of oil, some curry spices and sambal – 'it was just like nasi-goreng', a popular Indonesian dish. But few learned to love the beet, and I always found the pulp revoltingly mushy and sweet but, having no choice, ate my mother's pancakes or porridge almost daily, retching in spite of my hunger.

Another 'delicacy' the Dutch devoured was tulip bulbs. At the beginning of the war doctors had pronounced the bulbs fit for human consumption, but withdrew this in 1942. In the winter of 1944–5 they were rediscovered, and the Office for Food Supply again published some booklets to tell the Dutch how to handle the bulbs. 'They contain a lot of starch,' they told us, 'and when cooked their consistency will be slightly mealy.' It was impossible to say how many bulbs were needed for the recipes that followed, but we were advised to peel them, cut them in half and remove the bitter little yellow core. Almost everybody tried it out and nobody liked them, but the Dutch saying, 'Hunger sweetens even raw beans', was now more true than ever, and Dr Mees discovered that the bulbs were 'not too bad' when boiled like potatoes. They had cost him 8.75 guilders for five kilograms. Rather better was the tulip soup the authorities had devised. 'Take one litre of water, 1 onion, 4–6 tulip bulbs, some seasoning and salt [40 guilders à kilogram on the black market], one teaspoon of oil and some curry-substitute. Cut up the onion and brown together with the oil and the curry. Add water and seasoning and bring to the boil, while grating the cleaned bulbs into the boiling liquid. Add salt to taste.' It had virtually no nutritional value, but it filled the stomach. One had to be careful not to eat too many tulip bulbs as they could cause indigestion, but nevertheless the price rose to a staggering 60 guilders for one kilogram.

We were warned against other bulbs by the experts as they could be poisonous, and spinach seed, very popular for a while, was just as dangerous. The information service of the Office for Food Supply announced that it could cause constipation so bad that some people needed surgery. Dahlia tubers were also tried, but they never became as 'popular' as the tulip bulbs, of which that winter 140 million were consumed. One tulip grower later told an English journalist that he alone had sold 2500 tons of bulbs – 'crocuses for coffee, daffodils and hyacinths for fodder, and tulips for the humans'.

During the Hunger Winter, with humans reduced to eating tulip bulbs, house pets had a dangerous life. It was difficult to feed an animal – 57 per cent of animal lovers nevertheless succeeded – and dogs and cats were widely hunted. A straying dog ran a great risk of ending up on someone's table, and cats were sold as 'roof-rabbits'. A housewife in The Hague mentioned in her war diary how she received a piece of meat in exchange for a sack of coal. 'Later, I discovered it had been the hindquarter of a dog. It was delicious', but she was happy not to have known at the time. In Wassenaar, near The Hague, the police caught two women who were luring dogs into the house. 'The police investigation disclosed that their husbands slaughtered the dogs and sold the meat for 80 guilders a kilogram,' a newspaper reported on 12 March. 'Both men have been arrested.'

On 4 February I celebrated my eleventh birthday. In Yalta, Roosevelt, Churchill and Stalin began the conference that was to decide the future of the world after the war, Berlin had its heaviest bombardment ever, the Russians were only sixty-five kilometres from the German capital and the Americans captured Manila. All this affected my life not at all that day. I had to deal with a world that revolved around the next meal, the problem of how to keep the 'miracle-stove' burning, where to find grass for our rabbits, how long it would take to grind the last bit of rye in the long-suffering coffee-mill, how to keep my feet dry and warm in my clog-shoes. I can't remember what my presents were but I'll never forget my birthday treat – as many rye-pancakes as I liked. The result was disastrous. Not only was my stomach no longer used to the quantity I dispatched, but the rye had not risen properly and in the middle of the night I woke up in excruciating pain, fearing that my stomach was going to explode. My father had to massage me for hours before the pain subsided.

There was no school for us. Initially schools had operated on a half-day basis as most of the buildings were confiscated, and we had to share with others, but the bitter cold soon forced them to close down completely. My days were spent in cutting and sawing wood and, for the great part, in queuing for whatever the ration-cards promised us, mostly for bread. It was agony to stand in the cold for hours, taking turns with my brother, at the Reef bakery – a name I'll always remember as it was painted on the windows I had to watch for hours – and smell the fresh bread, even if I knew that the result was a very greyish, rather moist loaf. Walking home with the bread under my arm, I could never resist picking at the crust and scratching some crumbs off it as invisibly as possible and hoping that nobody at home would find out.

Even if there had been school, hunger and lack of clothing would have stopped many children going. One schoolteacher later found a stack of letters from October 1944 written by the parents of her pupils – 'Miss, Alie is unable to come as there is no tram and she has no shoes,' one of them read. Another told that a boy had gone out with his mother at four o'clock in the morning to get some potatoes. 'We came back at half-past eight and had been walking all the time. He had to go to bed.' A third one: 'Miss, Johan broke one clog. Our neighbours gave him another. He has now two left clogs but at least he can go to school.' And that was before the worst part of the winter began.

According to a yearly medical examination, children between the ages of ten and fourteen suffered most during that winter. The average schoolboy of fourteen, so stated the report, whose weight in 1940 was generally around 41 kilograms, weighed 37 kilograms in the spring of 1945. He was also two centimetres shorter than a boy of the same age in 1940. Girls suffered even more; they were 7 kilograms lighter and 6 centimetres shorter than those of 1940.

151

For mothers it was a desperate sight, and it often drove women to irresponsible and emotional actions, like the demonstration in Haarlem in March, when several hundred women stormed the Town Hall. They had heard that a ship full of potatoes had arrived in the small port, and the NSB mayor, S. L. A. Plekker, besieged in his office by the raging crowd, had to release them in spite of the fact that they were meant for the Wehrmacht. Other demonstrations were held in Amsterdam, where women forced Mayor Voûte to taste the food of the central kitchens, after which it improved suddenly.

The writer Bert Voeten saw one of these hunger marches on 28 February. 'About eighty women walked from the Waterlooplein to the Town Hall,' he recorded. 'They shouted only: "We are hungry, we want food for our children, hunger, hunger." It was not shocking, not dramatic. It was without fierceness, without that bitchy sharpness women can have. It was just the saddest, most hopeless and shabbiest group of people I've ever seen.'

In various other places a committee of housewives began to control the central kitchens after the food got worse, and in Purmerend a delegation of women penetrated the office of the Ortskommandant, the local military commander, with the result that every citizen received ten kilograms extra potatoes and a load of peat.

Women were not only the toughest and strongest, they were in fact the ones who fought hardest for survival; life revolved around them and they had by far the most difficult task. With so many men deported, in hiding or on hunger trips, the burdens of daily life came down completely on their shoulders.

Queen Wilhelmina, in a speech on 28 November, recognised this by saying: 'And I don't want to finish without thanking all those housewives, who lack absolutely everything to keep their households going. My thoughts are constantly with them. . . .'

A housewife's day was filled with constant anxiety, as many husbands realised. 'In the morning, while still in bed, she starts to puzzle what to eat,' one of them wrote. 'She has to queue at the greengrocer and the baker, where very often nothing is available, is forever busy with her ration-coupons, has to cook on one stove in the living-room.' Another added: 'No pen can describe the troubles women have. Even the most uncaring husband, who in the past never uttered a word of praise because everything was just as he thought it ought to be, had learned another view of his wife's task. That at least is some profit from the war.'

A great problem for the Dutch housewife, proverbially so clean, was the total lack of any cleaning material. Soap was missed most, and the substitute absolutely inadequate. It looked like clay, did not smell or foam and, finally, did not clean. Research done in 1944 revealed that, apart from soap, the items most in demand were chamois leather and beeswax, followed by haberdashery, brooms, brushes, sponges and needles. Clothing took second place, with the exception of shoes, underwear and stockings. Garments were patched and darned over and over again, and if one outgrew a sweater the wool would be pulled out, steamed to straighten out the kinks and made into mittens and stockings.

The clicking of knitting-needles in the long, dark evenings was to me a very familiar sound. Everywhere in Holland those evenings had suddenly taken on a different character. It was impossible to go out because of the curfew, and people did not entertain each other because there was nothing to offer. So the family circle became again the hub of society. Sitting around the little stove we played word games, told stories or sang. If the moon was full, the curtains were opened wide, but if there was no moon a little candle or an oil-lamp was the only source of light. We were lucky enough to have the battery from my father's car, which was hidden in a farmer's shed, and were sometimes able to read or write by the miniature lightbulb it fed. Some people had a windmill on their roofs to generate electricity and others used a bicycle on a stand.

Outside, in the streets, it was pitch-dark and very silent. Only with a special pass was one allowed to go out, and the rare footfalls were those of police patrols or German soldiers. An anxious silence would fall while they passed. Each house was in fact a prison, but, as someone wrote, 'a very special one, where those who are locked up create a warmth, which gives the courage to go on'.

Everybody went early to bed. It was warm there, and while you were sleeping you forgot the hunger, though very often I would lie awake in the middle of the night, listening to the screeching sounds of Hitler's V-weapons or the reassuring, heavy humming of the Allied bombers on their way to Germany. The strong beams of searchlights would suddenly light up my bedroom, and sometimes an anti-aircraft gun would make a desperate effort to stop the stream, but its rattle soon stopped and I knew that the German gunman had realised how hopeless it was.

On 1 March the Dutch food authorities, with the permission of the Germans, closed the Ijssel to hunger-trippers. During the month of February their number had still increased and they were endangering the last stocks in the north-east now that, after the thaw which began on 31 January, transport by water from the north-east to the west had started again. The announcement of the closure created a small panic in our household. My parents had decided to send my elder brother Wim to Friesland, north of the Ijssel, to our grandparents, to alleviate the food problems at home and also to give him the opportunity to build up his strength as he, then fourteen, was growing too fast for his rations. Preparations were hurriedly made and on 28 February Wim left on a long and lonely journey of 180 kilometres on a dilapidated bicycle, reaching his destination, Oudega, two days later. He had been lucky; the German commander at Kampen, where Wim had to cross the Ijssel, had given him permission to go on.

Other travellers were less fortunate. Restrictions on the hunger-trippers had been increased and led to many desperate scenes. For someone who had travelled for days, sometimes bartering his last possessions, a confiscation was a tragedy. Some resorted to ruses, and one famous story is that of a man who had got hold of a large piece of meat. Knowing very well that he would never get it past the nearby control post, he took a large box, put a dog in it and cycled up to the post. When the German ordered him to open it the man warned him: 'I've got a dog in it and he will escape.' But the soldier insisted and what was predicted happened: the dog ran away. Muttering something about nosy Germans, the man followed the dog back, put the meat in the box and half an hour later again rode past the German, who now waved him sombrely on.

The hunger trips, more extensive than ever in spite of the controls, became more difficult, too, because of the attitude of the farmers. Many of them had heard that their foodstuffs ended up on the black market in the cities and, even if this was only partly true, many innocent Dutchmen became the victims of the myth. The black market was as old as the war, and gave to those who had the money, bartering goods like gold and silver, and the contacts the opportunity even in the Hunger Winter of living a life of luxury. Prices were horrendous, considering that the average income of a Dutchman was not more than 2000 guilders a year – and much less during the winter of 1944–5 as economic life had come to a standstill. For a hectolitre of wheat one paid 4000 guilders in February, twice as much as in November 1944. A hectolitre of potatoes was 450 guilders, a kilogram of meat 100 guilders and the same price bought a kilogram of sugar or cheese. Multiply these figures by fifteen and one can compare them with present-day prices.

The Central Office for Statistics later calculated that in the Hunger Winter the price of bread on the black market was 210 times as much as the official price. Potatoes were 70 times more expensive, fat 100 and wheat 230 times.

The black-marketeers – often called the BBC, 'Black Business Company' – had their beats and one of the most famous was the Jordaan, the popular district in Amsterdam. 'The streets there are crowded,' the student Jan Peters wrote to his father in Amersfoort concentration-camp. 'Everybody shuffles slowly past the men and women with their boxes, and big business is done in the cafés. Absolutely everything is for sale and the police don't even bother.'

If the black market was one ugly aspect of war-time circumstances, the growing violence was another. It was mainly induced by starvation, but was very often organised by gangs whose loot ended up on the black market. 'Thefts, assaults and plundering are the order of the day,' a food inspector in Amsterdam reported. 'The transport of foodstuffs is seriously hindered and, though they try to protect the transports as well as possible, they cannot prevent thieves disappearing with the goods.'

'They had one special tactic,' a Dutchman wrote. 'The gang used to put some children near a corner and when the baker's cart appeared the children would begin to annoy the baker, pulling at his cart or jumping on his back. While the baker defended himself, the gang would jump into the chaos and open the cart with a crowbar. They would then disappear with the bread within a second.'

Many Dutch people worried over the question of how their children would come out of this war. With the fathers away and the mothers busy, many were left to their own devices, hungry and unkempt. 'Demoralisation increases by the day,' read an official report. 'The difference between mine and thine has disappeared . . . small or even big thefts are the order of the day. Schoolchildren are often sent into the streets with orders to steal.'

A report to the Allies dated 16 February put it somewhat more solemnly. 'As long as hunger and cold rule, those who are in need will follow the law of life, i.e. the urge to stay alive and try to defeat every obstacle in the way.' The conclusion was unavoidable. 'This has to be done by means which are in conflict with normal standards of morality.'

For those at 'the other side' it was an incomprehensible and frightening picture, but they could judge the seriousness of the situation by the rise of the death rate in Amsterdam alone. 'Whereas about 107 people died in the first week of September 1944, this number had increased to as many as 517 in the first week of February 1945,' a report disclosed on 27 February.

The medical profession was no longer able to cope. Drugs were not available, nor bandages or other material. Some hospitals had their own generators, but fuel soon ran out and there was no gas for the laboratories. Surgeons had to work in unheated operating-theatres and suffered as much as anybody else from hunger. The ration for a doctor in one hospital in Rotterdam for a day in February was one slice of bread and a cup of substitute tea for breakfast, two potatoes and some vegetables for lunch, and for supper a cup of broth and two slices of bread. My mother, who fell seriously ill in March and was taken to hospital on a stretcher pulled by two cyclists, remembered mainly the daily portion of beetroot that was supposed to help her recover.

Most cases the doctors had to deal with were of hunger oedema, of which the first occurrences were reported in February. Hardly anybody had not suffered from the effects of lack of food – pain in the limbs and an increasing apathy – but real oedema had up till then not been recorded. It spread rapidly and soon it was no longer unusual to see the victims with their swollen faces and legs, shuffling along the streets. Dr Herweijer, a physician in The Hague, guessed that 65 per cent of his patients were oedema cases, while in Rotterdam a total of 14,000 people suffered from it.

Other common diseases were those of the skin, caused by the lack of soap, hot water and, of course, vitamins. Every little scratch I had would fester, and boils were common. Scabies was also on the increase and one hospital in Utrecht registered 10,994 cases at the beginning of 1945 – against 100 in 1940. More serious were the epidemics of diphtheria (1.25 cases per 10,000 people in 1937, against 66 in 1944) and of typhoid (2 per 100,000 in 1938, against 225 in 1944). The hunger was further responsible for the fact that women often stopped menstruating and a great number of men became temporarily impotent.

That so many old people died is not surprising. The situation in homes for the aged was heartbreaking: there were no lifts, telephones or laundries working, and in one of them the staff demolished rooms and the attic in order to have at least some wood for a fire. In one home in Amsterdam they lost 315 of the inmates in the first six months of 1945, twice as many as the year before, and in another 60 corpses were waiting for burial at a time.

This was one of the cases that convinced Mayor Voûte of Amsterdam that funerals should become a municipal concern. The death rate had risen so fast that private undertakers, lacking men, transport and coffins, could not handle it any more. On 13 January, Voûte called the city surveyor, V. Feltkamp, to his office and asked him to take on the unsavoury task of finding the dead and burying them. He explained the difficulties: there was no wood for the coffins, there was hardly any transport, the horses who pulled the hearses had either been confiscated or were so weak that they would only trot very slowly, and finally there were too many people dying. It amounted in the first half of 1945 to 2.6 per cent of the Dutch, that is, one out of every 38 inhabitants of the Netherlands, but in Amsterdam it came to 3.5 per cent, in The Hague 3.6 per cent and in Rotterdam almost 3.7 per cent. In Hilversum 1371 people died in that period, against 511 in the same period in 1944.

Feltkamp's first question was, how many people was he supposed to deal with? The guess was between 1000 and 2000 unburied corpses. An empty church, the seventeenth-century Zuiderkerk, was given to him for use as a morgue. 'When I arrived the first day there were already 113 bodies,' Feltkamp remembered. 'I will never forget the sight, and the smell was terrible.' He at once installed some sort of air-conditioning, the rattling sound of which soon led to rumours that they were using a rattle in the church to keep the rats out. Next, he organised the church in such a way that the dead had a bit of privacy, by dividing it into cubicles with cardboard partitions. In an aisle he made a mortuary chapel, and in another room he placed an enormous urn of disinfectant. 'We were lucky that it was such a cold winter,' he said later. 'It was agony for my staff, but it prevented the bodies from decomposing too quickly, which could have led to epidemics.'

It was not easy for Feltkamp's team to find the bodies. Sometimes neighbours reported a smell, at other times the family came to them in despair. But not always. 'I remember a case of a dead husband who lay for five weeks in the room where the family slept, because they wanted to keep his ration-cards,' Feltkamp wrote in a later report. In some cases people who penetrated a seemingly empty house to look for wood would find a dead person.

The seventy oak coffins Feltkamp had to begin with were soon used up, and he had cardboard coffins made with a loose bottom so that they could be used again. But even supplies of these soon ran out and most bodies had to be buried in a sheet or, if the family couldn't spare one, in a large paper bag. In the four months of its existence, Feltkamp's municipal office dealt with 2800 funerals – not including those handled by private undertakers.

The Hague and Rotterdam managed without official interference, but the undertakers had great problems. A visitor to a cemetery in Rotterdam looked in horror at the rows of corpses. 'The shrunken bodies were lying next to each other. No flesh on thighs or calves. Most had bent arms and legs, the hands clenched as if the poor devil was still asking for food.' The attendant told him that many just died in a doorway or shelter. But often they were found on a bench, or thrown in a canal.

Amongst the anonymous dead were often Jews, who had died in their hiding-places, and had to be disposed of without anybody noticing. But sometimes they were the victims of a German bullet, like the pretty girl Feltkamp recalled who was carried in, shot dead as she had tried to steal some coal.

Some victims of German terror Feltkamp never saw: the hostages who were killed in reprisals. 'The Huns themselves took care of them.'

CHAPTER FIFTEEN

Trouble in London

IN THE middle of all their tribulations the Dutch in Occupied Holland listened incredulously to Radio Oranje when it announced that the Gerbrandy Cabinet had fallen on 25 January. To us it seemed incomprehensible that, while the country was suffering under hunger and terror, political problems could destroy the unity of the Government-in-Exile, our moral and practical supporters. For the NSB weekly, *Volk en Vaderland*, it was a unique opportunity to launch an attack on those people who, after almost 'five years of working against their common enemy, Germany', were basically still so divided, and mistrusted each other so greatly, that they were unable to agree about the future of the Liberated Netherlands. There was a certain truth in this biting remark, but the crisis was much more complicated and the cause much deeper.

Throughout the war there had been conflicts and problems in the Government, a group of men who had come together in London more or less by accident and who had often felt obliged to sacrifice their own principles and opinions for the sake of unity. But the first cracks began to appear in November 1944, after the visit that Prime Minister Gerbrandy paid on 18 October to Bedell Smith at Versailles. One of the subjects of conversation was the return of the Dutch Government to the liberated part of the Netherlands. 'We did not make a formal request,' Gerbrandy wrote later, 'as that would have been incompatible with the position of the Government.' Bedell Smith had been worried about Montgomery's reaction, but – always willing to oblige his Dutch friends – had nevertheless asked the Field-Marshal. Shortly afterwards the message arrived that an advance party of Ministers were welcome. Before any Minister could leave, however, objections were raised from a completely unexpected quarter. The

Militair Gezag, Netherlands Military Authority (MG), created by the same Ministers whose return it now resisted, told them from its temporary base in Brussels to stay in London. A confrontation was inevitable.

The MG had been formed in 1943, when the Allies asked the Dutch Government to set up a body that could provide a link between the Allied Command and the Dutch authorities. In May 1944 a Civil Affairs Agreement had been concluded that gave SHAEF full military authority in the Liberated Netherlands, while the Dutch Government preserved its sovereignty through the MG. A young colonel, H. J. Kruls, was appointed organiser of the operation.

Only after the Allies arrived in the Netherlands in September was he made a major-general, and on 1 October he left with his staff for Brussels, from where he 'ruled' the liberated Dutch provinces.

The creation of the MG had never been very popular with the Ministers in London, especially when they discovered that, as Queen Wilhelmina put it, 'it meant the curtailment of their own powers'. And in the south Kruls' régime was soon resented. His staff, mainly civil servants or important entrepreneurs who had hastily been turned into officers, developed the sense of 'the exquisite and surprising force of military rank and power', and often felt that they could give London a lesson in governing. They soon found themselves completely alienated from the Dutch people and the Ministers, who abhorred the fact that 'Liberated Holland was ruled by people who had the impression that the Dutch needed a strong military hand'.

The relationship between the MG and the Resistance in the south, now known as the Forces of the Interior, the BS, was perhaps the most difficult. The latter refused to act as errand-boys for men who had spent the war safely in London, and the former considered the one-time Underground as a bunch of scruffy partisans. Most of the conflicts arose over the purge of Nazis and their collaborators, and the MG felt that the BS was hindering it in maintaining law and order, one of its main tasks.

Another task was to prepare for the return of the Government but, when it came to the point, the MG's reaction was totally unexpected. On 12 November, Kruls wrote a letter to London which struck the Ministers like a thunderbolt. There was abso-

Children and old people suffered most. They could not manage a hunger
trip to exchange goods for a few potatoes, some eggs or wheat, and very
often they had to survive on the meagre rations served out by the central
kitchens. No wonder that some scrambled for the leftovers.

The owner of a car was lucky—even if there were no petrol he could always literally return to horse-power.

If transport was difficult to find for the living, it was almost impossible to find for the dead. This undertaker, looking like death himself, makes do with a three-wheeler.

The undercarriage of a pram was not ideal and, indeed, hardly built to stand up to long hunger trips, but for these women there was no alternative.

Without trains, cars or buses, every possible means of transporting food or firewood was exploited

The sight of nuns pushing a pram full of goods no longer caused a surprise.

Not only food was scarce; fuel for cooking or heating was as hard to come by:

A few branches were a gift from the gods and were dragged home only too willingly; and empty houses were robbed of the last little sliver of wood, many of them collapsing in ruins.

To those desperate for a little warmth, nothing was sacred: even the wooden blocks between the tramlines on this bridge in Amsterdam vanished into thin air.

Right While wood was so precious, Dutch housewives struggled with their 'miracle stoves,—economical but highly unreliable.

Two slices of bread, two potatoes and half a sugarbeet: a day's ration for one person in April 1945, a few weeks before the Liberation.

When the Germans at last capitulated. Allied rescue missions often found the most appalling situations, especially in families where the father had been deported or was hiding from the Nazis.

Water, the eternal enemy and friend of the Dutch, made the ordeal even worse for many of them:

Dykes were blown up by the Germans, as in the Wieringermeerpolder, in the hope of halting Allied landings and resulted in a fleeing population that left its empty houses behind. Only the statue of the 'Sower', symbol of the newly reclaimed polder, remained, staring gloomily over the waters.

In Walcheren and elsewhere the Allies also bombed the dykes, to force the Germans to flee. The result was the same, with thousands of Dutch people made homeless.

For five years Queen Wilhemina had been the symbol of hope and inspiration to the Dutch. When, in March 1945, she returned for a visit, albeit a short one, everybody knew that the end of the horror was near. Freedom was in sight.

It came on 5 May 1945. After five years of oppression and destruction, the Germans capitulated and the time for celebration had come. The Hunger Winter was over.

lutely no reason for the Ministers to come back yet, he stated boldly. 'The MG now has the whole business reasonably under control', and the interference of Ministers would create chaos. He warned the Cabinet that it was unpopular in the country, and that he feared most that their return would lead to the resurrection of pre-war political life, where 'prospective parliamentarians and job-hunters will jostle each other', hindering the work of the MG.

It was too much for the Ministers, and they urged Gerbrandy to recall Kruls to London. He obeyed, but only to give him a reprimand. A chance to establish a healthy relationship between the MG and London had escaped him, and the rot had set in.

The pedantic and stubborn Kruls was not in the least impressed by the Prime Minister's warning, but he was polite enough to be there when on Saturday, 25 November, at 4.30 p.m. Professor Gerbrandy stepped on to Dutch soil for the first time in four and a half years. Accompanied by four Ministers, he had crossed the North Sea in a Dakota, escorted by Spitfires, to land at Gilze-Rijen, near Breda. He had some difficulty in hiding his emotions, but recovered quickly and told waiting journalists that he had come for a reconnaissance of sorts. 'We want to observe the situation in the three provinces, take certain measures and give support to the military authorities.'

The 'quartermasters', as they were called, settled down in the Bosch en Ven Hotel at Oisterwijk, twenty kilometres from Den Bosch, and a busy time began. 'The Dutch Ministers travel through Free Netherlands,' the war correspondent A. C. van Beers reported. Life was certainly not luxurious for them, the journalist assured his readers. 'They have their meetings by candlelight and wear their overcoats because of the cold.'

Gerbrandy in particular had a hectic programme. He visited the ruins of Flushing, the Princess Irene Brigade near Goes, heavily damaged Flemish Zeeland, and travelled through Brabant and inspected the Shocktroopers in Limburg. He was deeply concerned about the devastation, he reported to Queen Wilhelmina. 'In Flemish Zeeland most places flattened; Walcheren flooded; and in Flushing only 3000 of the 24,000 inhabitants have stayed behind; in Den Bosch 800 and in Nijmegen 4000 houses completely destroyed; the population of the Betewe evacuated and the land flooded.'

He also worried about the condition of the population, he told the Queen. 'From the outside the situation in Liberated Holland is quiet. The population in general bear their material hardships in an exemplary and resigned manner. There is law and order.' But beneath the surface he was aware of potential danger, caused by difficult living conditions, communist activity, the arrogant actions of some members of the BS and 'the considerable mental instability of our people after all that has happened'.

Those 'actions' of the Forces of the Interior even forced him to organise a special meeting on 30 November. Prince Bernhard, who had been invited, was ill and sent his Chief of Staff, Colonel K. Doorman. In round terms the Ministers told him that they were upset by the fact that the Forces contained so few real Resistance fighters, and so many opportunists, who excelled in unjustified arrests. They very often acted, they told him, 'as if the country was theirs'. People had complained that they were liberated from the German dictatorship only to fall under that of the BS; and the fact that they had received the nicknames of 'Orange thieves' and 'the Prince's Nazi police' could seriously damage the position of the royal family.

Doorman tried to soothe the Ministers, pointing out that recruiting had been stopped since 11 October, and that Prince Bernhard had announced on 7 November that new BS units could only be formed with his personal approval. The Ministers were not completely satisfied and demanded an immediate end to the arrests and the removal of unwanted elements.

Prince Bernhard thought the question important enough to get up from his sickbed, and to meet Gerbrandy two days after his return to London on Friday, 8 December. The Prime Minister had by this time backed down slightly and denied being critical of the role of the BS. He only wished to prevent further irregularities, as he felt that the reputation of the Prince was at risk.

Another chance to re-establish his authority had been let slip by Gerbrandy and it was becoming increasingly obvious that he had lost control, and that the Dutch Government was drifting without a sense of direction. It was an embarrassing situation, especially as it did not go unnoticed in Allied circles, where it weakened the Dutch position. 'Holland today has two governments, existing side by side, working against each other,' was one American comment, and even that was too kind. The MG completely ignored those Ministers who had stayed behind in Holland, and when their colleague Dr Jan van den Tempel, the Minister for Social Affairs, paid them a visit in December he described the mood in Oisterwijk as 'very moderate' and he, too, soon had the impression 'that the government had no grip at all on events in Liberated territory'.

For all that, Kruls could not resist complaining about their presence in reports he sent to Gerbrandy. It hindered him in the speedy taking of decisions, he complained, and 'the population receives an impression of uncertainty and indecisiveness'.

Gerbrandy made one more feeble effort to control his MG chief: on 19 January he wrote to Kruls instructing him to follow the Government's directives unconditionally. Then he left it at that.

'A study of the relations between the Confidential Council, the Military Authority and the London Government would give a picture of chaos and reciprocal ignorance of each other's activities,' a Dutch politician wrote later. It was all too true. Quite apart from its failure to deal firmly with the MG in Liberated Dutch territory, the Government had hardly any dealings with its representatives in Occupied Holland, the Confidential Councillors. Telegram after telegram proved that contacts between The Hague and London were very unsatisfactory and sometimes nonexistent. 'We often discovered that what we reported to London and got through was not always passed on to the proper authority,' Councillor Willem Drees wrote later.

In consequence, the Council hardly knew what was being decided in London about the future, and in January they sent a delegate, J. J. van der Gaag, to England to find out what the plans were. Only then did he discover that the Government had decided to install a military authority for the whole of the Netherlands after Liberation, and that on the face of it all the preparations the Councillors in Holland had made were useless. A disappointed Van der Gaag cabled on 27 January to The Hague: 'Found little confidence in Confidential Councillors, whose task is considered vague and unimportant.' These were tough words for the men in Holland who had worked so hard, and were, as Drees remembered, 'running for our sakes at night like hunted birds from one place to the other in the hope of not being arrested by the Germans'. London clearly had the impression that, when Liberation came, the Councillors would simply read a proclamation, wave the flag from the balcony of every Town Hall and, one of them bitterly joked, 'everybody will live happily ever after'.

Another Dutch institution, the National Support Fund, the NSF, had the same problems with London, but for different reasons. The NSF was the paymaster of the Resistance and, with the usual Dutch caution in money matters, the Ministers expected miracles on the cheap.

The NSF had its origin in a fund for the families of Dutch sailors who were working for the Allies. In 1941 its work called for no more than 12,000 guilders a month, but when the Resistance increased, together with the number of 'divers', the sums rose to millions. Hiding Jews for the duration of the war alone cost 4.5 million guilders, and the Resistance itself cost Holland six million.

The most expensive period started with the railway strike. The railway managers expected at first to be able to pay their employees themselves, but when the strike lasted much longer than was hoped for they reluctantly knocked on the NSF door and borrowed a total of 34.4 million guilders.

Even if London were prepared to give a guarantee, the problem remained of how to raise the actual cash. One Resistance group thought of solving it by the most spectacular bank robbery ever, tipped off by, of all people, a former President of the Netherlands State Bank, Mr L. J. A. Trip. He heard that Seyss-Inquart had sent an enormous amount of money to Almelo and warned Derk Smoes, the commander of a group of 'Fist-fighters' in that town. On 15 November 1944, Smoes, with ten men, raided the bank and disappeared with the money – 46 million guilders. The Germans were furious and offered a million-guilder reward.

A few weeks later Smoes was arrested by chance, and after heavy pressure and consultation with his men told the Gestapo where the money was, in the hope of saving the lives of himself and others. But, in spite of all the promises made to him, Smoes was shipped off to a concentration-camp, and the last his wife heard of him was a letter: 'You know, darling, that I joined the Resistance with conviction and never would have wished it differently, even now my life is in danger. . . . Be strong, and try to live happily.'

Safer and surer ways had to be found to get the cash and a former seaman, Walraven van Hall, thirty-eight years old, who had from the beginning headed the NSF, designed a perfect system with the enthusiastic help of some bankers. They knew that in the vaults of the State Bank was stored a large supply of Government promissory notes, safely under the eye of the NSB president, Rost van Tonningen. A forger was asked to make copies of these very elaborate documents and, with the help of the Head Cashier, Mr C. W. Ritter, they were substituted for the real ones. The NSF succeeded, through various channels, in cashing them, and collected the two million guilders it needed.

Walraven van Hall, one of the most respected leaders of the Resistance, never knew of their success. He was arrested on 27 January, at an Underground meeting which the Germans had been tipped off about. He had already been sentenced to death in absentia, and, on 2 February, two days after his thirty-ninth birthday, he was executed on the corner of a street in Haarlem – near the Spaarne, where he had sailed so often as a boy and which gave him the 'love for the sea', his brother wrote later.

The foundations were thus laid for an efficient financial operation, something that could never be said of the monetary help the Government gave the NSF. Many appeals had to be sent before the Ministers put their hands deep enough in their pockets. 'It took a lot of time to change their minds,' an NSF delegate once reported from London, but in the end he succeeded in convincing them that support of the Resistance and the victims of the Occupation was not a question of 25,000 or 50,000 guilders, but that they had to think in millions. The Cabinet gave the necessary guarantees.

The great difficulty for the Ministers and others in London was to imagine and to understand what it meant to live under German Occupation. The Socialist journalist G. J. van Heuven Goedhart, arriving in London in 1944 after a very hazardous journey through Belgium, France and Spain, noticed at once how different the atmosphere was. Another socialist, J. A. W. Burger, who had arrived in 1943, was struck by the same fact and was amazed to discover that the thinking of the Government-in-Exile was at least a year behind that of the Dutch in the Netherlands.

Encouraged by Queen Wilhelmina, Gerbrandy made at least some effort to bridge the gap, and took the two Englandvaarders into his Cabinet at once. It was a brief and shocking experience for them.

The initial single-mindedness after the disappearance of De Geer in 1940, and later under the newly appointed Gerbrandy, was a thing of the past. No longer united in Stratton House, but dispersed all over London, the Ministers were tired men, while the Queen's influence and stature had grown. The myth, created by many of the Englandvaarders, that the Dutch wished for total change had had its demoralising effect on the politicians, and they had to fight a constant battle against a tendency towards totalitarian attitudes in London. The enemies of the movement called it 'Orange Fascism', and spread rumours that its followers wanted to make the Queen an absolute monarch and Prince Bernhard a king.

Wilhelmina never encouraged this attitude, but she made no secret of the fact that she wished – after consultation with the Resistance – for a change in the Constitution. She once wrote: 'I am pro-Constitution, [but] no slave of the Constitution or any law, because experience has taught me that these are very often the enemy of a truly democratic life.' What exactly she wanted is not certain, but at times she hinted at a more important role for the monarch, who could, for instance, appoint Ministers and preside over certain Cabinet meetings.

At first Gerbrandy had not been averse to these ideas, but gradually he changed his mind, and to the fury of a large number of Englandvaarders the Ministers – 'those fossilised bureaucrats', as they called them – passed legislation in the autumn of 1944 which reinstated the old local and provincial institutions. One problem, however, remained – that of a future Parliament. Over the years long discussions had taken place about the shape it should have, but when Van Heuven and Burger joined the Cabinet the balance came down in favour of a normally elected Second Chamber, just as before the war. Van Heuven was convinced that it was wrong to involvé the Underground movement too much, as it would mean a breach with the past and, he warned, 'there has never been a good government which did not acknowledge the continuity of history'.

This did not endear him to Queen Wilhelmina, and her warm relationship with Burger also cooled rapidly. Waiting for the delegation from the Resistance which she had invited, she obstinately refused to sign the Royal Decree that would summon Parliament after the war. One Minister wrote: 'Crown and Government began to drift apart.'

The situation became even more precarious when some very respectable inhabitants of Eindhoven sent a letter in which they told Wilhelmina that the restoration of the pre-war political institutions was 'totally undesired'. They even rejected speedy elections 'as these would inevitably lead to the resurrection of the numerous political organisations of the past'. General Kruls had obviously made some converts in the Netherlands.

After all the discussions with the Englandvaarders, the letter had a familiar ring to the Queen, and for her it was at last the advice she longed for. At once she sent for one of the signatories, and in December Professor Dr J. E. de Quay arrived. As a young Catholic politician he had been one of the trio that in 1940 formed the Netherlands Union, the only non-Nazi movement the Germans ever allowed to exist – and that only for one year. He had been for a time in concentration-camps since then, and the Queen saw in him the ideal man to keep her informed about the possibility of immediately forming a new Cabinet with Ministers from the Liberated sector. De Quay hesitated and advised her to let a proper delegation come over. Seventeen people were chosen, amongst them one woman, and their arrival in February could not have been better timed: Gerbrandy had offered his resignation to the Queen.

The direct cause of the Government's collapse was completely irrelevant to all the problems it faced, but a significant indication of its lack of cohesion. A speech made by the Minister of the Interior, Mr Burger, on Radio Rising Netherlands on 14 January, had been the *coup de grâce*. In the speech he had mentioned the purge of Nazis in Holland, stating that it was less important to persecute those who had 'made errors' than those who had 'completely erred'. 'A nation does not consist of heroes alone,' he remarked, 'nor of diplomats, but of a majority of people with normal worries about their daily existence.'

It seemed a sensible speech, as Gerbrandy later admitted, but in the unforgiving mood then prevalent in London and to the people of the still suffering northern part of Holland it was inexcusable. On 24 January, Burger was dismissed, and without hesitation two of this three socialist colleagues in the Cabinet resigned in protest. The choice was now between a reconstruction of the existing Cabinet with some new Ministers, or a completely new Government.

It was probably Queen Wilhelmina who gave Gerbrandy the final push. With the seventeen from liberated Holland in town, she saw a chance to take at least some steps in the direction of her 'new society' and she readily accepted his resignation when he offered it her. 'In the course of January 1945 I received the Cabinet's resignation,' she wrote coolly in her memoirs. 'The crisis was not easy to resolve at that moment for several reasons, not the least of which was the lack of persons of ministerial stature abroad.'

It was not the whole truth. During a weekend of discussions at Stubbings the Queen tested the seventeen, and she discovered several whom she thought would make able Ministers. The problem was whom to make Prime Minister. She had thought of De Quay, but settled for her Minister of Foreign Affairs, Eelco van Kleffens. He, however, at once put an end to all speculation. When two of the seventeen came to consult him about a change of leadership, Van Kleffens listened patiently and then, as he wrote in his diary on 5 February, explained to them why 'it would be frivolous, reckless and unjustifiable to replace Gerbrandy'. His main argument was that Gerbrandy was highly respected by the Allies, and he later told the Queen the same thing.

She accepted his advice, in the knowledge that Gerbrandy had promised to resign at once when the war was over, to make room for someone who had lived through the Occupation. And on 8 February Radio Oranje told us that the Queen had asked Gerbrandy to form a new Cabinet with the emphasis on 'fresh' personalities from the southern provinces. Gerbrandy, well aware that he must drop some of his loyal colleagues, confessed that he found it a 'highly unpleasant task', but he accepted 'with a heavy heart'.

It took him fifteen days to create a new team, which indeed included some new faces from the south, and which was – the Government's declaration stated – formed with the 'intention of expressing the spiritual trends which exist in the Netherlands'.

168

Wilhelmina, who had not got exactly what she wanted, was nevertheless satisfied, and on 24 February she spoke to the Dutch over Radio Oranje, telling them: 'We as a nation would show bad faith towards the many who sacrificed themselves, undergoing tortures and suffering in silence . . . if we did not set to work, even now, to prepare the new era of our national existence.' She was convinced that, with 'the recently completed reconstruction of the Cabinet, this need was taken into account'.

Not everybody in London agreed with her. The new Cabinet contained no more socialists – the last one, Van Heuven Goedhart, was not asked to rejoin, only learning the fact from a journalist – and so was not in fact wholly representative of the Dutch nation. Dr Jan van den Tempel, deeply disappointed not to be given the chance to finish the task he had taken on in 1940, was dismayed. He knew all too well the problems Gerbrandy now faced – chief of which was the Military Authority with its dictatorial and anti-democratic tendencies. It had consolidated its power now, he wrote, adding: 'The hope for a political adventure lives on in certain circles.'

CHAPTER SIXTEEN

Help at Last

THE FOUR AND A HALF million Dutch in the northern Netherlands may have felt isolated during that winter of 1944–5, but Queen Wilhelmina and Gerbrandy took care that they were not forgotten. It was hard work and brought little reward. In spite of Gerbrandy's publicity campaign in November and his visit the same month to General Walter Bedell Smith, Eisenhower's Chief of Staff, nothing but reassuring promises and soothing noises had come from the Allies, and little help had been given.

In January the Dutch Government hoped for a time that something was going to be done at last. Gerbrandy was again invited to Versailles and this time was actually to meet Ike himself. The Cabinet composed a directive whose harsh tone betrayed their concern and impatience. 'It might be useful to make SHAEF feel . . . that the British and American public, who believe that at least the relations of their Governments with the Netherlands Government in London are excellent . . . would be extremely surprised if they knew what difficulties the Netherlands Government were experiencing in their very legitimate endeavours to organise relief for the Netherlands.' And that was not all, the angry Ministers went on. 'Public opinion in Occupied Holland will be deeply disillusioned if they find that all the fine talk over the radio, in the papers and pamphlets dropped over Holland, about the relief operations in preparation does not amount to a row of pins.'

All those past months it had seemed hopeless to the Dutch Government. Whatever they had suggested in order to help their people disappeared into a bureaucratic fog. In long statements to all sorts of authorities, proposals had been put forward to land supplies on the beaches of Holland, to send ships from Zeeland through the inland waterways, or even trucks through the front line, but no reaction had followed.

Even the plans for immediate relief after the Liberation were inadequate, and in a note of 24 November 1944 the Dutch warned the Allies in despair that 'on the basis of historical experience, especially of catastrophic floods in the Netherlands, the conditions we must be prepared to find may well be of such an extraordinary nature that only a flexible plan can meet the situation'. Hoping to find some understanding amongst the British, the Dutch Government added that they had in mind something like 'glorious improvisation, as for instance at Dunkirk'. Just how bad communications were was proved by the fact that a request to send some of the stockpiled food supplies to the Liberated area, made on 21 September, was only answered by the British Foreign Minister, Anthony Eden, on 24 November. He told the Dutch that he was in favour of the idea and had sent it on to SHAEF, where it was once again shelved.

Gerbrandy's concern was understandable when he wrote on 16 December to Eisenhower that 'if the now Occupied part of the Netherlands has to go through the same procedure as the Liberated part, we shall witness such a calamity as has not been seen in Europe for centuries, if at all'. The Prime Minister left little to the imagination in his vivid description of what the Allies would find – 'no stores of food, no livestock, all the bridges lying broken in the rivers, the countryside sown with mines, the big towns inaccessible, the power stations blown up, the ports demolished, all transport destroyed, the population exhausted, men of the Resistance armed and desperate, *agents provocateurs* left behind by the Germans'. It was therefore urgently necessary for him to come and see Eisenhower himself. 'The Netherlands Government cannot accept the liberation of corpses.'

'His letter is quite moving,' was Eisenhower's reaction and he sent it on to Bedell Smith, pencilling in the margin: 'I think we have to see him – but Lord knows what we can promise.' And he invited Gerbrandy to come in the beginning of the New Year. When the Dutch Prime Minister arrived on 5 January, Ike himself received him.

The little Dutchman did not mince his words and told Ike straight out that he had hesitated for eight weeks before making this approach, knowing on the one hand how busy the Supreme Commander was, and hoping on the other that a little time would bring a solution to the problems. But now the Dutch Government could wait no longer. 'It would be criminal negligence on their part to assume the role of interested but inactive onlooker while events with regard to the Occupied Netherlands are taking a course which . . . can only lead to a catastrophe.' Gerbrandy assured Ike that his letter of December in which he had warned of a 'calamity' was no 'morbid fancy'. It had stated the plain facts. 'It is a matter of life and death, of health or a lifelong disability for millions of Netherlanders.'

He was especially worried by the fact that whatever the Dutch proposed was 'smothered in routine and bureaucracy' by SHAEF and explained that the Nazis planned to leave the Dutch completely destitute when they pulled out and the Allies would be faced with 'the well-nigh insoluble problem of immediately organising relief'. A delay of two or three weeks would be fatal, and SHAEF must be ready to fulfil its promises in order to avoid unrest. In practical terms, Gerbrandy told Ike, this meant that every day 2000 tons of foodstuffs must be sent to Antwerp – scarcely 4 per cent of the daily tonnage needed for the Allied armies.

Gerbrandy's tough speaking had an immediate effect. A letter was sent out by SHAEF reminding 21st Army Group, which had been assigned to Dutch relief, of its duty and announcing that the War Office in London had agreed to the forming of a District Headquarters for Planning, with the Canadian Major-General A. Galloway as its commander. 'He is expected to arrive in Brussels . . . in the immediate future.'

Another initiative resulting from Gerbrandy's visit came to nothing. Eisenhower's Deputy Chief of Staff, Major-General Grasett, had been so moved by the Prime Minister's plea that he proposed to issue an ultimatum to the Wehrmacht Commander in Holland to do something about the situation. His colleague, Lieutenant-General Morgan, thinking about the constant Allied air-raids on trains and ships in Holland, thought it better to discourage him. 'If I may say so,' he wrote to Grasett, 'it appears to me a trifle illogical to be threatening the man with punishment if he doesn't feed the Dutch, while we are at the same time doing everything possible in the way of destruction of communications, etc. to make it impossible to do that very thing.'

Gerbrandy was not dissatisfied with the results of his visit.

Queen Wilhelmina wrote in a letter to Roosevelt ten days later that he had found in Eisenhower 'not only a sympathetic and understanding listener, but also a man who fully realises the great importance of working out plans for immediate relief' after the Liberation. She was convinced that from now on SHAEF would do 'everything humanly possible'.

Their optimism did not last very long. Gerbrandy discovered by chance in January that the stockpile of relief supplies, stored at Oss, had been reduced from the promised 30,000 tons to a mere 5000. Montgomery had used them for his troops and for the Belgians. And the new District Headquarters had been unable to start work as Major-General Galloway, its commander, had been transferred to another appointment. But, worst of all, SHAEF and the 21st Army Group were constantly squabbling about the question of who in fact was actually responsible for the relief operation.

Unaware that Eisenhower was expressing the same concern in a letter to Washington a day later, the Dutch Minister for Foreign Affairs, Eelco van Kleffens, tackled the problem vigorously when he met the British Ambassador to the Netherlands, Sir Neville Bland, at a luncheon party on 13 February. He told him of his anxieties about the inadequate preparations that had been made for Holland's liberation, and next day Sir Neville reported to the Foreign Office that Van Kleffens 'appeared to feel that there was a lack of appreciation of the gravity of the problems on the part of British Military Authorities'.

But relief after Liberation was now no longer in fact the main preoccupation of the Dutch Government. Everything suggested that the situation in Holland was so dramatic that immediate liberation was needed. And with this in mind Gerbrandy approached Churchill on 20 January, five days after the Queen's appeal to Roosevelt. Military action was needed.

Walking to the map in Churchill's room, Gerbrandy reminded the British Prime Minister of the original Allied plans to advance to the Ijsselmeer and so cut off the German troops. What was happening now, he remarked, was something completely different. The Allies pressed on to the Ruhr, leaving western Holland to one side. Churchill listened with sympathy but had only one reaction: 'I must leave this to the Generals.' He confessed that he was unable to influence them and that in any case the best help for

Holland was a quick end to the war as a whole. He was convinced that it would be a mistake to stage a diversion into Holland when the whole German defence might collapse if the Allied armies pushed forward to the heart of Germany.

Gerbrandy was not so quickly discouraged, and he asked Churchill if he once again could go to Eisenhower, not only as Dutch Prime Minister but also as a representative of the British Supreme Command. Churchill shook his head. He did not wish to put any pressure upon Eisenhower. And, bitterly disappointed, Gerbrandy departed. He cheered up slightly when Churchill's secretary, Desmond Morton, came to Gerbrandy's office in Arlington House the next day to tell him that the British Prime Minister certainly felt that something had to be done, and had no objections if Gerbrandy wanted to go to Paris to speak with Eisenhower. A sly suggestion from the Dutchman that he should take Morton with him was, however, refused by Churchill.

The formation of his new Cabinet delayed the Prime Minister's visit to SHAEF till 24 February, and he was on his own when at last he arrived at Versailles. Ike was absent, and Gerbrandy had to deal with Bedell Smith. 'I stated that we thought it necessary to ask for a special military operation aimed at the liberation of Holland,' Gerbrandy reported to Churchill. But Bedell Smith, as Churchill expected, told the Dutch leader that it was impossible. 'We have not got the necessary divisions and equipment at our disposal,' he admitted frankly. He revealed to the baffled Gerbrandy that the war, as it was then going, might last till the autumn and that Holland might be liberated in the second half of May. That would be too late, protested the crestfallen Dutchman. 'The future of our nation is in the balance.' But Smith was adamant and explained that it was not possible to win the war without the Russians, and that therefore it was necessary to advance to the heart of Germany. The liberation of Holland was a diversion the Allies could not afford.

Heartbroken, Gerbrandy flew back to London to report to his new Cabinet and to Churchill. His visit had, however, at least one result. Once again Bedell Smith promised to pressure the 21st Army Group about its relief plans, and this was actually done. When Gerbrandy wrote to the British Prime Minister on 7 March, General Galloway had returned to his post at the Relief Headquarters and was hard at work. But, so concluded the Dutchman's letter, 'I cannot conceal the fact that the trust of the Dutch Government has been shaken by the course events have taken. The fact that, in spite of promises given to us, there has been neglect on the part of the 21st Army Group and that an intervention by Gen. Bedell Smith has been necessary, is most disquieting. . . . I can not forbear from making this plain to you.'

While the Dutch and the Allies argued over relief plans, other countries had acted. Neutral Sweden and Switzerland, with the help of the International Red Cross, had sent help, but even that operation had taken months to organise.

The first steps had been rapid. The Swedes accepted the Dutch appeal for help on 2 October; the Queen, Gerbrandy and the Dutch Ambassador in London approached, respectively, Roosevelt, Bedell Smith and the Chiefs of Staff. Even Churchill, after some hesitations and impressed by Gerbrandy's pleas, gave permission on 16 October to open negotiations, and Ike followed suit on 29 October. It was now, however, the Germans who made problems. They refused to open the ports of Amsterdam or Rotterdam to the relief-ships, and only after a lengthy correspondence with Berlin agreed that the port of Delfzijl far up in the north could be used. From there Hirschfeld's Central Shipping Company was to handle transport to western Holland in barges.

On 14 November the deal seemed to be settled, when suddenly a new problem arose. The Germans insisted that the Dutch Red Cross should be responsible for distributing the food, and that was unacceptable to the Allies.

With the departure of Princess Juliana, the Dutch Red Cross had lost its President. The Germans used this opportunity to Nazify it, and appointed a member of the NSB as its new President. At the same time a representative of the German Red Cross, Dr F. Reuter, was put in charge of foreign relations. The Dutch Committee had accepted these appointments, but refused further co-operation when on 19 November, five days after the deal with the Swedes and Swiss was sealed, the Germans appointed the notorious Nazi, C. Piek, as new boss of the Red Cross. Piek had first become known as the fanatical leader of the Winterhulp (Winter Help Netherland Foundation), the Nazi monopoly in the field of charity. He had been rather too charitable to himself, was sacked and banished to the Baltic States to

175

explore the possibilities there for Dutch farmers. When, instead of farmers, the Russians arrived, Piek returned to Holland and, as there were not many reliable Nazis left after Mad Tuesday, the Germans gave him the Red Cross.

When on Monday, 20 November, Piek arrived in his office in The Hague, he found all his staff gone, together with the records and the contents of the storerooms. The Red Cross had gone underground, and Piek had to form a new organisation, charged by the Germans with the distribution of the Swedish and Swiss relief supplies. The Allies made it known that with Piek in charge there would be no relief and, while the ships loaded with the foodstuffs waited in the Baltic, the dispute raged on. But in the third week of January an arrangement was reached with the Germans, and on 28 January the first Swedish ships arrived in Delfzijl. The Allies had won, and Piek's men had to look on – they were not even allowed to board the ships.

The two most welcome ships the Dutch had seen in years were *Noreg* and *Dagmar Brat*, with a combined cargo of 3700 tons including 2256 tons of flour, 513 tons of margarine and 10 tons of codliver oil. They were less welcome to the Germans and, although their representative, Dr Reuter, had given every support to the operation, the Nazi authorities began to create trouble. They pointed out that the waterways were still frozen, that there was no fuel for the barges and even less for the bakers, and when it started to thaw on 31 January they made difficulties about opening the sluices, but the Swedish Consul-General in Amsterdam, Walter Ekman, overcame all these obstacles with immense patience and tact. On 15 February the first barges arrived in Amsterdam, each covered with an enormous Red Cross flag as a protection against air attack.

We had received the first news of the magnificent Swedish present on Tuesday, 13 February, when pamphlets and posters announced: 'BREAD, MARGARINE AND CEREALS FROM THE SWEDES' and then went on: '125 grams of margarine for everybody; 800 grams of bread for all persons over four; 250 grams of cereals for children under fourteen.' It was incredible, but soon enough we could see it with our own eyes.

While the bickering with the Germans went on, the Dutch food authorities had been improvising a complete organisation, and with amazing speed everybody went to work as soon as the barges arrived. Transport workers, dockers, bakers, administrators, printers, they all toiled day and night without pay – even the police who guarded the bakeries.

Hilversum, like every town in Holland, changed overnight. Swedish products in their original colourful wrappings appeared in the usually dismal-looking shop windows; the drab streets were livened up by Swedish flags; pictures and maps of Sweden appeared from nowhere; girls in Swedish costumes helped in the grocery stores; and for a whole week there was only one subject of conversation: Swedish bread and what one would do with it. 'It was like the week before St Nicholas,' someone remarked.

The Swedes had made it a condition that nobody would have to queue, and a perfect rota system was set up, but it was agony not to be among the first when distribution began on 27 February. Like everybody else, I watched with envy the people who rushed home with their real white bread and margarine. 'With joyous faces the people left the shops, and it was a wonderful sight to see mothers going home with their bags full of bread,' a food inspector in Amsterdam could report to The Hague, happy after all the misery of the last months. 'The margarine has also been well received and everybody praises the taste.'

There were people who just could not hold back and took a nibble in the street; others carried it home like treasure. 'Some ate the whole lot, in one or two days; others only took one careful slice every day,' the inspector's report went on. We were indeed excited as never before in those grim years, and I thought the bread tasted like the most delicious cake I'd ever eaten. Hardly anything found its way to the black market and, as one Dutchman wrote, everyone celebrated. 'Sweden's gift made that week a golden page in the dark book of war history,' someone else said. High-flown words perhaps, but that was just how it felt to us. Anything could happen now, the journalist Diemer in Rotterdam believed, 'because we know that the International Red Cross has stretched its helping hands out to the starving crowd'. It was a ray of hope, a sign that the end of all misery was within reach.

The publicity for Sweden and the pleasure of the Dutch people during those unforgettable days did not please the Nazis at all, as Count Hakon Mörner, the representative of the Swedish Red Cross, was one of the first to discover. He arrived in Delfzijl on 28 February with the second load of Swedish foodstuffs and medicine, on board *Hallaren*. The ship was immediately boarded by the Customs and port officials, accompanied by Dr Reuter and a grim-looking local head of the SD, a staunch German Nazi in spite of his French name, Bordeaux. There was no sign of Ekman or Hirschfeld, and the atmosphere, Mörner reported to Stockholm, was decidedly cool. Reuter was embarrassed and explained, as soon as he had the opportunity, that Seyss-Inquart, in town the day before, had been highly displeased at the boycott of the Nazified Dutch Red Cross when the first ships arrived. He was also furious with Ekman, who, according to him, had created too much good publicity for Sweden. He had therefore decided that Ekman was out and the Dutch Red Cross in.

A hurried meeting in the Delfzijl Town Hall followed, and Mörner made it clear that in that case *Hallaren* would return to Sweden, with the cargo. A telephone call to the State Commissioner from Dr Reuter was sufficient and the German doctor, visibly relieved, told the Swede that Seyss-Inquart had changed his mind.

In the next few days all Mörner's skill and diplomacy were needed to avoid fresh trouble while the cargo was unloaded, but he could not prevent a new German attack, this time from Otto Bene, the representative of the German Foreign Ministry in the Netherlands. On 9 March, Bene summoned Ekman to tell him that he could no longer tolerate 'this state within a state' and demanded the immediate liquidation of his relief organisation. The Swedish Consul-General exclaimed that the Dutch people were dying in the streets, but Bene ended the discussion brusquely with the threat to shoot the Dutch if they should ever dare to rebel.

Bene told Mörner the same, in more polite terms, in a letter on 10 March, and the Swedish Count saw only one solution: to go and see Bene himself. 'Only good can come of it,' was Reuter's hopeful comment, and five days later the two left for the German headquarters in Apeldoorn, preceded by a motorcycle patrol, intended to keep a lookout for attacking planes – a necessary precaution, as Mörner noticed. 'A number of burned-out cars along the roadside showed', he wrote to Stockholm, 'that these attacks have not been without effect.'

Bene received him courteously, explaining that he had nothing personal against Ekman, but that he only wanted to prevent the

Dutch Government in London getting involved in the Swedish relief programme; for the rest, it was a matter with which Seyss-Inquart was dealing. In Bene's well-armoured car, Mörner and Reuter were taken on to Spelderholt, the State Commissioner's residence near Apeldoorn, where Mörner was again very politely received. It was obvious that the two Nazis wanted to make a good impression on the Swede, who listened in some amazement to Seyss-Inquart's expressions of gratitude and satisfaction at the work that was being done.

When the conversation turned to Ekman, the State Commissioner repeated Bene's argument that the Dutch should not become involved, not only in London, but in Occupied Holland also, and they reached agreement when Mörner proposed setting up a Swedish Committee under the Consul-General to control distribution. After a delicious dinner where 'only questions of an entirely non-political nature' were discussed, Mörner returned to Delfzijl, highly satisfied. 'I consider that all questions concerning the relief work ... have for the time being been solved in a satisfactory manner,' he reported to Stockholm. Where Ekman was to find enough Swedes in Holland to help him was a mystery but, as the Germans never checked if the promise was kept, the operation went ahead as before.

While Mörner was with Seyss-Inquart, the unloading of *Hallaren* was completed, and after some delay the ship was able to leave Delfzijl on 23 March, just as *Dagmar Brat* and *Noreg* arrived on their second mission. Sailing from Delfzijl at the same time was another ship, the Portuguese *Henri Dunant*, which had docked on 8 March. Its arrival had been watched by Mörner's dinner guests in *Hallaren*, among whom was Dr W. Pfister, a representative of the International Red Cross, who had organised the Portuguese mission. The ship had in fact been chartered by the Swiss Government for aid to Holland and had made a difficult journey that had led to another confrontation between Germans and Allies about the relief.

Coming from Lisbon, but going via Sweden to pick up more food supplies, nobody could agree which route *Henri Dunant* should take. The Germans proposed the Kiel Canal, but the English had no desire for a truce in this strategically important target area. On 28 February *The Times* reported that the talks had reached a deadlock, but suddenly common sense returned and concern for the Dutch won. The Kiel Canal would not be attacked during the ship's passage – a decision that applied for every relief ship that followed.

And there were quite a few. The operation worked perfectly in the coming weeks, and both Swiss and Swedes reported a happy collaboration with 'mutual visits and invitations on board the ships'. Even the relationship with the German Dr Reuter remained relaxed, and that the Dutch were happy needs no emphasis. They honoured the donors by giving each week the name of either 'Swedish', 'Swiss' or 'International Red Cross' Week.

For Hirschfeld and Louwes, the Dutch food authorities, the relief meant working day and night, but they were grateful to do it 'even if it came rather late', the former grumbled, but he added at once: 'The Red Cross shipment will make it possible in the coming weeks for us to give 400 grams of bread extra.' This, together with the 800 grams of the official ration, was not much, but it was more than the Dutch had had in the severe winter months.

CHAPTER SEVENTEEN

Bullets and Bombs

SPRING 1945 arrived early in Holland. After the wettest autumn in eighty years, and one of the coldest winters for a long time, a very welcome sun appeared in the second week of March to stay with us for a few weeks. It was a tonic which the starving Dutch badly needed. Little had changed – thanks to the Red Cross aid we received now about 525 calories a day; sugarbeets were still an indispensable part of our menu, but the tulip bulbs – which had begun to sprout – were disappearing, and gas and electricity were nonexistent. But at least we no longer needed to heat the house and only lit the fire for cooking. The manhunts were not as frequent as before – there were few men left and those who had escaped detection were deeply entrenched in their hiding-places. But German terror had by now reached a peak in another field: the execution of hostages. 'You saw them lying everywhere in groups of twenty – and they left them there as a warning,' a Dutchman wrote in anguish.

In July 1944, Hitler had ordered that all trials of Resistance fighters in occupied countries should stop, as these turned them into heroes and martyrs. Instead they were to be summarily executed. To implement this new rule, his already notorious SD in Holland acquired a new boss, Dr Karl G. E. Schöngarth. This alcoholic, who had learned his trade in Occupied Poland, gave a large degree of independence to his local officers, and in some regions a reign of terror began.

Shots were heard the whole winter through and – as Hitler had ordered – they were fired in public. The victims were men who had been arrested and held in prison as so-called 'death candidates', until they were needed for reprisals after an attack on a German or an act of sabotage. Until September 1944 their execution had been in private, but now it was to be witnessed, and like Walraven van Hall they were shot on street corners or in the squares. In Rotterdam alone, more than 100 Dutchmen died this way, and in Amsterdam 200, while a dazed and horrified public, driven into the roped-off streets, was forced to watch.

The Dutch thought they had seen the terror at its worst, but one incident late on Tuesday, 6 March, led to a bloodbath without parallel. The cause was an attack on Hanns Albin Rauter, after Seyss-Inquart the most powerful official in the Netherlands, and through his constant flow of decrees and threats certainly the best known and most hated of the Nazis. Rauter – an Austrian like the State Commissioner – who on my eleventh birthday, 4 February, had celebrated his fiftieth, was a fanatical Nazi and a great disciplinarian. A dry, tough man, he lacked all charm and could be extremely rude. Seyss-Inquart called him 'a big child with the cruelty of a child', and without any qualms he had hundreds of Resistance fighters killed and thousands deported, which gave him the well-deserved reputation of being the 'evil genius' of the Nazis in Holland. Since Arnhem he had played a more important military role, too, and was made commander of a number of German and Dutch units defending a zone along the Rhine. But on the night of 6 and 7 March, between Apeldoorn and The Hague, his gruesome career came to an end.

The attack on his life was in fact an accident. The commander of a Resistance group in Apeldoorn had heard that evening of a German army transport of 3000 kilograms of pork, just what his men needed. Being short of transport, he first ordered the capture of a car, and at ten o'clock four men, one a German deserter called Sepp, dressed in SS uniforms, cycled to a spot near the Woeste Hoeve inn on the road from Apeldoorn to Arnhem. Stopped by a German sentry who asked them the password, Sepp bluffed his way out by shouting 'Frankenstein', and when the astonished German answered that his was different Sepp – in good SS manner – snarled: 'I have only to do with our own unit; yours doesn't interest me.' The perplexed soldier let them go.

Near the Woeste Hoeve they hid their bikes and waited. A few cars flashed by, but all of them were too small. At last, just after midnight, a heavier sound was heard and a large BMW was flagged down with lights. The driver was furious and, reaching for his gun, called: 'But, man, don't you know who we are?' They were his last words. After a total of 234 bullets had been fired, the four Germans in the car appeared to be dead and the four men cycled away, leaving the BMW and its bullet-riddled passengers behind. The 150 German soldiers lodged nearby heard the shots but didn't dare move, and it was only at three o'clock that a Red Cross car arrived and discovered that one of the four men was still alive: it was Rauter.

He was rushed to hospital in Apeldoorn and his adjutant, Wilhelm Heissing, was next day already able to report to Himmler that his life was saved, in spite of bullets in the lungs, his right shoulder, his left thigh, jaw and right hand. Himmler wired to Seyss-Inquart that he would be very grateful 'if you would do anything that can contribute to his recovery'. But the SS boss had done more. Although Rauter, on regaining consciousness, had begged with unusual generosity that there should be no reprisals, on 7 March Himmler ordered the execution of at least 500 people. Seyss-Inquart thought it excessive, but he could not prevent executions beginning all over Holland.

The most monstrous was near the Woeste Hoeve where on the morning of Thursday, 8 March, three coaches loaded with 117 death candidates from the prisons of Arnhem and Apeldoorn arrived at the place where Rauter had been hit. While the sun was rising over the heath, 150 'Greens' of the Order Police pushed and bellowed them into a long row. At the same time the Apeldoorn Resistance group, who had heard the news, were racing with all their arms to the spot, but by the time they arrived the 'Greens' were busily arranging the bodies for exhibition at the roadside.

Other executions took place in Amsterdam that day, where seventy men were shot, and in Ouderkerk, where the SD claimed fifty-three victims. But the mass murder did not stop there. While here and there in Holland little groups of five and ten men were being killed, twenty-six young men were executed on a rubbish dump on 12 March in the centre of Amsterdam.

It is difficult to calculate how great the number of the victims was. The German Headquarters simply stated that 'after a cowardly attack on the night of 6 and 7 March . . . some hundreds of terrorists and saboteurs have been executed'. The most cautious guess is a total of 250, but it almost certainly came to about 400. 'It was,' *The Times* in London said on 28 March, 'merely a new example of the unparalleled terror to which people in Occupied

Holland are now subjected.'

The Resistance leaders reacted at once. They asked the Government in London to protest vehemently, which it never did, and they ordered their men to become even more active and 'not to accept the brutal actions of the enemy passively'. The BS commander, Colonel Koot, warned the men, however, not to kill war criminals and German soldiers at random, as he did not want to give the Dutch the impression that the BS was just a gang of murderers. Many Dutch people agreed with him, like Dr Mees in Rotterdam, who wrote on 9 March in his diary: 'Rauter of course deserves the death penalty, but such a bandit has to be judged by a qualified judge. This way he gets off too lightly and he will be succeeded by someone who is worse.'

His prediction was right. Karl Schöngarth took over from the convalescent Rauter and went on a rampage. In Rotterdam particularly, his murder squads hardly ever stopped. 'This afternoon – it's now 13 March – I was standing here on the Hofplein, looking at the bodies of twenty men and boys, murdered this morning on the same spot,' a deeply moved Rotterdammer wrote. 'Somewhere else in town another twenty men were shot in public. . . . They were lying there as they had fallen, higgledy-piggledy, next to each other and half over each other, unbelievably still. Silent accusers. . . . One man had his lunch box under his arm and there was a boy of fifteen, picked up on his way to school. . . .' Many witnessed the same scene. 'Nobody talked, just hate and horror in their eyes.'

Three weeks later there were another twenty deaths in Rotterdam. 'They were taken from the police station and shot for something of which they were completely innocent. . . . You just look and feel punch-drunk, shattered, and you don't know what is stirring in your soul.'

The Dutch papers kept silent about these mass murders, but Seyss-Inquart had his comments. In his last speech ever for Radio Hilversum, on 10 March, while the Nazi revenge was raging, he talked about Germany, 'a developed country and the responsible representative of the European classical and humanist culture and mentality', a country that according to him would never resort to the methods of the 'Bolsheviks, who do not just murder and destroy individual opponents but entire groups'.

The State Commissioner not only had nerve, he was ill-informed as well. On 19 March, Hitler issued an edict ordering the destruction of everything in Occupied Europe that could be of use to the enemy. This included all electrical plants, water-works, gasworks, bridges and railways. Holland would certainly not be spared. Himmler, with his pathological hatred for the Dutch, would see to that. He had been involved in plans to destroy the administrative capital of the Netherlands, The Hague, with Germany's latest secret weapons, the V1 and V2, but the plans were cancelled. Ironically it was to be those same V-weapons which brought on The Hague its greatest disaster in that early spring of 1945. But for once the Germans had nothing to do with it – directly.

The V1 and its successor, the V2, were Hitler's last hope for victory. They were called with reason 'retaliatory' weapons, because both were lethal, and between them killed almost 9000 people in Britain and 3500 on the Continent. While the V1 was a flying bomb, the V2 was the first rocket to travel with a speed faster than sound, and after the Germans lost France both were launched from sites in Holland. About 4000 V1s left the launching-pads near Haarlem and Delft for Antwerp and the south of England, while about 1300 V2s were fired from bases near Wassenaar and The Hague. Many of them never reached their destinations and fell somewhere in Holland, killing many people. For instance, on New Year's Day a V2 missile crashed on Ockenburg near The Hague and killed thirty-eight people. We always listened tensely for the rumbling sound overhead to stop – which could mean disaster.

The first two V2s, fired from Wassenaar on 8 September 1944 at 1844 hours, fell five minutes later on Chiswick, in west London, killing three people, and in Epping Forest. The British Govern-ment pretended initially that the weapon did not exist, but when the Germans boasted over the radio on 8 November that the V2 was creating havoc in southern England the time had come to react. Three days later Churchill made a statement in the House of Commons, reassuring the harassed Londoners that 'the scale and effect of these weapons have not hitherto been significant'. A month later the British Air Ministry released the first official details of the fourteen-metre-long rocket, revealing that it had a range of 300 miles and travelled at a speed of 3000 miles, or 5800 kilometres, an hour.

All the reassuring noises could not prevent the V-weapons having their effect in London. The Radio Oranje broadcaster Henk van den Broek mentioned that in August 1944 – and that was before the V2 was launched – 14,000 houses in London had been destroyed, while 800,000 had been damaged. The V2s had less immediate effect on the capital itself. Only forty per cent of the rockets crashed in London, while the rest fell somewhere in the country. They nevertheless killed 2724 people, with the worst disaster in Deptford, where a V2 hit a department store and claimed 160 victims.

For those who lived near a rocket site in Holland the weapons were a frightening sight. One eyewitness wrote: 'Cycling to The Hague I watched the departure of a V2 from the sportsfield near Rijswijk. I heard an indescribable noise, shrieking and thundering, and saw a long torpedo-shaped monster with a long fiery tail appear.' The rocket took off rapidly and disappeared out of sight. 'With trembling knees, I climbed back on to my bike, under the impression that I'd seen the coming of hell.'

The Dutch Underground made all possible efforts to inform the British of the exact location of the sites, but it was hard to keep up with the Germans, who moved them around constantly. One thing was certain. The V2s, a spy informed London, were stored in a part of The Hague woods which had not been cut down for fuel. 'From there a narrow-gauge railway leads to the Queen's Palace' – the 'House in the Woods'. Some preliminary preparation was carried out in the stables, and the rockets were then transported by truck to the sites. It seemed straightforward enough, and in the second half of February the RAF started to bomb the launching-pads, but with remarkable inaccuracy. Hundreds of houses in The Hague were damaged, 'in some cases at a considerable distance from the target area', someone sighed. 'The situation in The Hague is getting impossible!'

Apart from hunger and cold, the inhabitants had to take shelter at least ten times a day from the RAF planes, but they understood it was for their own good. 'In spite of everything we have to go through, we cannot get angry with the English,' a schoolteacher whose house had been destroyed wrote in her diary.

On Saturday, 3 March, the usual fleet of RAF Mitchell bombers arrived over The Hague. The fifty-six planes seemed to be heading in the direction of The Hague woods, but suddenly dropped

186

their bombs over the Bezuidenhout, a residential district at least a mile from the target. Twice they returned, unloading their deadly cargo, and within a few minutes the whole neighbourhood was a sea of fire. 'The first refugees appeared in our street,' Raatgever, whose house had been spared, wrote. Some of them were only half dressed, 'with pale faces, bleeding . . . with trembling lips and staring eyes', and they described the horror: 'The Bezuidenhout is in ruins, whole streets are on fire.'

It was no exaggeration. Not only were 511 citizens killed and many more wounded, but also 3250 houses were destroyed. The fires raged till Monday night while the firemen from surrounding towns looked on helplessly, because of lack of petrol for their engines. More than 12,000 people became homeless and lost their possessions, like the BS commander, Henri Koot, whose invaluable stamp-collection and precious library were destroyed together with his house in the Adelheidstraat.

The bombardment led at once to wild rumours. Raatgever remembered how people were predicting an immediate invasion. 'The English have landed on our beaches,' they said, and Alkmaar has been taken. According to some, the bombing of the Bezuidenhout had been necessary to give cover to airborne troops, but the truth was much simpler and more painful. And it led to the most dramatic confrontation of the war between the Dutch Government-in-Exile and their British hosts.

The reaction of the Dutch in London to the news of The Hague's latest torment had been at first one of incredulity, and then of fury. Queen Wilhelmina, normally so composed, for once could not control herself. 'She was not only shocked,' her aide Gerard Rutten remembered. 'She personally gave the authorities responsible a piece of her mind over the telephone and even Churchill did not remain ignorant of her opinion.'

On 7 March the Dutch Ambassador, Michiels van Verduynen, sent a very sharp protest to the Foreign Office, stating that, although the Dutch Government realised that bombing always entailed risks to civilians, 'they are of the opinion that the specific attack against a target surrounded by densely populated districts was highly irresponsible'. The Ambassador demanded an instant enquiry and asked Anthony Eden to prevent a repetition.

The Queen's intervention with Churchill had an immediate effect. The Prime Minister wrote an unusually sharp letter to the

Chiefs of Staff, pointing out reproachfully that the Dutch complaint 'reflects upon the Air Ministry and the Royal Air Force in two ways'. In the first place, Churchill went on, it showed how feeble the RAF efforts have been to intervene against the rockets and, secondly, it had led 'to this slaughter of the Dutch'. He just did not understand how it could have happened, as the RAF had received sufficient information about the sites. 'Instead of attacking these points with precision, all that has been done is to scatter bombs around this unfortunate city without the slightest effect on the rocket sites, but much on innocent human lives and the sentiment of a friendly people.' He, too, demanded a thorough enquiry.

The first result was what Radio Oranje called a 'frank admission' that the bombing had been an accident. 'A more detailed enquiry is still going on,' it told us on 23 March, 'and measures will be taken against those who are responsible.' The British Government and the RAF expressed their deep regrets, which led to a bitter remark from Joseph Goebbels, who said that when the Germans bombed Rotterdam in 1940 the British had shouted 'Murder', using it then as an excuse to 'ruin the Reich', while when they bomb The Hague 'it is just a mistake'.

A few weeks later investigation revealed that the tragedy of The Hague had been the fault of the officer who briefed the aircrews. The Air Ministry explained to the Foreign Office that the officer concerned 'through most culpable negligence read the horizontal and vertical co-ordinates the wrong way round'. The Foreign Office, in its letter of apology to the Dutch Ambassador on 7 July, thought it more tactful – or less embarrassing – not to go into too much detail. It only mentioned that the cause of the 'unfortunate occurrence' had been an error on the part of the officer who supplied material for briefing the crews. It added: 'The officer concerned has since been convicted by court-martial and punished.'

CHAPTER EIGHTEEN

Holland SOS

GOD MADE the world, but the Dutch made their own country, it is sometimes said, and how true that is was shown in the Hunger Winter. 'Largely dependent on dykes and canals, Holland is a sort of man-made machine that must function as a unit or not at all,' the American civil affairs expert, Harry L. Coles, explained to Washington. The soil will produce little without fertiliser; the fertiliser cannot be brought in unless the water is at the right level in the canals; the water level cannot be controlled unless the locks and sluices are operating; these in turn are dependent on the mining and transport of coal, and on the production of electricity. In short: 'A large population depends on the operation of this intricate network of machinery.'

The shortage of coal and other fuel was indeed one of the basic problems in starving Holland. 'Today there is no bread at all, as the bakers have no flour and others no coal,' Dr Mees recorded on 7 March. And Dr Pfister of the International Red Cross reported around the same time to Geneva that upon the solution of the coal problem 'will depend the lives of 4.5 million people', explaining that there were practically no coal reserves left. The consequence was that the transportation of foodstuffs had become an almost insoluble problem; while the lack of electricity had paralysed agriculture. 'It is impossible', the Swiss wrote, 'to describe what radical and dire consequences the lack of coal is having for the Netherlands, and how incredibly primitive life has become.'

Pfister, who had the chance to look around during his relief negotiations, had a frightening story to tell. 'At the beginning of March Dutch estimates placed the proportion of flooded arable land at between twenty per cent and thirty per cent: the sewerage systems in the cities no longer work since the pumps cannot be used. In rainy weather the water level rises in the lavatories – and in the Netherlands the weather is often wet.' It was a serious threat to health. 'In the middle of February, about 10,000 people were in the most primitive emergency hospitals, suffering from famine oedema. At the same time many patients in the ordinary hospitals, comprising 19,000 beds, were suffering from symptoms of deficiency diseases.' And if nothing was done 'the three western provinces will no longer be able to exist'.

The Dutch food authorities had told him that 15 May was the date by which urgent action must be taken and that after that 'the greatest calamity ever to befall the Dutch people will become bitter and terrible reality'.

His Swedish colleague, Count Hakon Mörner, had only been able to see a little, but he had listened a lot when in Delfzijl in March, and he confirmed the Swiss report, warning the Swedish Red Cross that the food situation was expected to deteriorate rapidly after the middle of April, 'when it is calculated last year's crop of sugarbeets and vegetables will be exhausted'. It was therefore considered urgently necessary that after 15 May about 4000 tons of flour, 500 tons of margarine and 500 tons of barley a week should be brought in.

All these reports, shattering as they were, came from outsiders, but on 17 March a cry for help from inside Occupied Holland, and written in English, reached London. The writer began by warning that words had – through constant exaggeration – lost their meaning:

> The expression 'starved to death' has been used so often in a figurative sense that it is difficult to realise that people are dying in the streets from exhaustion and privation. I do not mean that these people are 'deadly' tired, but quite definitely that their corpses can be carried away. And when the question arises: 'But how can people stand it?', my answer is: 'Those people cannot stand it; they are really going completely to pieces' – Holland SOS.

He went on to give a few examples of hardship. A friend, a professor in Amsterdam, had not tasted a potato for three months and survived on pancakes made from sugarbeets. A doctor in The Hague had tried to join a sort of dining club, in order to eat his fill for once, but was put on a waiting-list. When, after two weeks, his turn came, the menu consisted of 'a tiny

190

pastry, a teacup full of watery soup, a toy piece of meat, four small unpeeled potatoes and a little pudding made of water, custard and glucose'. The price of the whole gastronomic treat was the equivalent of 30 American dollars.

The writer had himself survived the winter because his landlord once had a shop which sold fountain pens, of which he had kept thirty, bartering them now for food. The worst were the hunger trips, he wrote to the free world. 'An absolutely reliable informant told me how he had to break the news of a workman's death from starvation to his family. He found that the mother, too, was dying.' His story must have sounded unreal to outsiders, but they could at least understand one thing: the Dutch impatience to be liberated. 'Simply nobody believes that Liberation is technically impossible,' the Dutchman stated. 'They try to find an explanation and their only conclusion is that there is no strategical need to liberate them.' It gave the Dutch the feeling that they were being sacrificed. 'The Allies are admired,' he warned, 'but they are at the same time regarded as callous egotists', and as a very pro-British friend had said to him: 'To let an ancient and civilised people like ours die without lifting a finger – by God, how can they do it?'

The Allies had, however, made some plans to come to the aid of the Dutch. On Wednesday, 7 March – the day after the attack on Rauter – the Americans marched for the first time across the Rhine over the bridge at Remagen. Three days later the armies of Montgomery, at the north flank of the front, reached the river, too, ready for action in Germany – and, if possible, in the Netherlands.

Churchill was one of the first to hear the news. He had received Gerbrandy's appeal to save the Dutch – 'if it is not already too late' – on 8 March, sending it on to his Chiefs of Staff with the comment: 'This frightful letter from Dr Gerbrandy . . . requires your immediate attention.' He added the surprising advice that a plan at once be made 'to prevent the horrors of the Dutch', and at the same time to extirpate the V-weapon sites in Holland. 'I consider that if it were inevitable, which I doubt, a certain delay might be accepted in the main advance to Berlin,' he concluded.

Churchill was not acting completely on his own. He had just returned from a visit to the front, where he had had long conversations with Bedell Smith and Eisenhower, and they had given him reason to be somewhat more optimistic. He was in an ebullient mood that week, highly delighted by the fact that on Saturday, 3 March, he had been the first British statesman to set foot in Germany since Chamberlain's visit to Munich six and a half years earlier – and four years after Hitler had announced his own intention of coming to London.

The British Prime Minister and Mrs Churchill had arrived on 2 March and were rushed to the front. His journey was slowed down by the wildly cheering American soldiers, who lined the roads, shouting 'How are we doing?' and yelling promises to bring Hitler back alive. The *Daily Telegraph* reported that Churchill acknowledged them with his famous V-sign.

He visibly enjoyed the trip and was very amused to discover, not far from the famous West wall, a sign, 'This was the Siegfried Line', and a little farther on a clothes-line with the words 'This is the washing', a reminder of the popular war-time hit 'We're Going to Hang Out the Washing on the Siegfried Line'. His hosts had great difficulty in keeping him away from dangerous sectors, but nobody could stop him next day from firing an artillery piece, loaded with a shell on which he had chalked 'Hitler – personal', joking: 'I didn't aim the gun, so they cannot blame me if I missed him.'

The shell missed its target indeed, but Churchill's visit was hurtful enough for the Nazi leaders in Berlin. Joseph Goebbels wrote with venom in his diary: 'Churchill is at the moment with Montgomery. The old criminal doesn't want to miss the opportunity to be present at such an important event and to play first fiddle.' The Dutch reaction was different, and when Churchill, on his way back from the front to France, stopped in Den Bosch the citizens lined the streets in spite of bitter cold to welcome the most popular Englishman ever with delirious enthusiasm. One paper reported how an old lady, celebrating her twentieth wedding anniversary, gave him her bouquet. 'Churchill thanked her warmly and promised to give her regards to Her Majesty the Queen.'

In Reims, where SHAEF had now settled, long talks with Ike and Bedell Smith began, and it was there that Churchill heard for the first time that the Allies might have two divisions available to liberate the suffering Dutch 'after the crossing of the Rhine'. He was delighted but, although he mentioned it in his letter to his Chiefs of Staff, in the one he wrote to Gerbrandy on 14 March he was more careful. He talked only about 'the difficulties which have confronted the military authorities in the question of diverting the Armed forces of the Allies from the major operations against the German armies'. He was convinced, he told Gerbrandy, that the course they had been pursuing was the right one, for which the British had been willing to endure the 'constant winter bombardments by V-weapons, which operations in North-West Holland would have eliminated'.

That same afternoon Churchill made his first full statement about the situation in Holland to the House of Commons. He began, *The Times* reported, by expressing the deep concern and sympathy 'we all feel for the Dutch people in their present ordeal'. He had added that he was very much aware that such expressions were of little comfort 'unless followed by practical help', but he admitted that there was very little that could be done apart from sending relief, and preparing stocks 'which will be sent into Western Holland with all possible speed as soon as the Germans are driven out'. But there was one assurance he could give: all efforts would be made to support the Netherlands Government in their relief programme, which had – at last – been approved by SHAEF.

The Prime Minister perhaps felt obliged to give this assurance after the discoveries his deputy, the Labour leader Clement Attlee, had made in Zeeland. Attlee, who returned on 14 March, had told him that only a quarter of the food that was available had reached the Dutch in the Liberated area, and that something must be done, especially if a speedier Liberation was a possibility. He had long discussions with the Dutch authorities 'about the practical means of bringing assistance to the people in Occupied Holland as soon as it is possible', Churchill notified his Dutch colleague, adding: 'He is fully alive to the urgency of the problem and he has reported to the War Cabinet, who are no less determined that no effort shall be neglected which might help to alleviate the tragedy which threatens to overwhelm the Dutch people.'

Despite these pleas for help and expressions of sympathy, the Dutch Government in London once again had to wait for further action, which, as Churchill knew by now, was delayed again.

Eisenhower, who about this time wrote to a friend about 'moving into Holland before strictly military consideration might dictate such an operation', had not approved a plan that the Combined Chiefs of Staff had prepared, and even less its consequences. On 27 March he informed Washington that operations west of Utrecht 'would inevitably involve very heavy casualties among Dutch people through bombing and shelling . . . as well as from starvation and flooding'. The main difficulties were, Ike wrote, that most of the area was flooded and that the towns were prepared for all-out defence. The safest way therefore to liberate the Dutch 'may well be the rapid completion of our main operations', and he asked the Chiefs of Staff to tell this to the Netherlands Government, emphasising 'the great cost of Dutch lives and property that any other course would necessitate'.

'We here in Occupied Holland are still no-man's-land,' a desperate Diemer recorded in his diary in March. 'It saves us from the destruction of warfare – apart from the air-raids – but the suffering caused by the lack of food and fuel doesn't diminish.' And he wondered if Holland would remain the 'dead corner . . . until the end of the gigantic struggle'.

Only thirty kilometres south of the Dutch front line, in Tilburg, the town that had given the Princess Irene Brigade its fame, a group of Dutch people were meanwhile working very hard at the relief preparations Churchill had referred to in the House of Commons. Headed by Colonel M. M. van Hengel, in peacetime director of a large enterprise in nearby Oss, they were responsible for that area in the western Netherlands that was hardest hit, the provinces of Noord-Holland, Zuid-Holland and Utrecht, in official terms the B2 area.

It had taken a long time to get the operation off the ground. As early as October SHAEF had prepared in principle a relief plan, which divided the Netherlands into three areas, of which B2 with its 3.6 million inhabitants would be the problem child. As Gerbrandy had discovered, however, the stockpiles at Oss had diminished rapidly after the Liberation was delayed; the so-called Netherlands District Headquarters under Major-General Galloway had been slow to organise matters, and only after Washington had intervened and Churchill had received Gerbrandy's complaint of 7 March had things begun to move.

Gerbrandy had to use strong language before it ever got that far, stating that if more people died after Liberation because of lack of preparation it would 'not only be a shock to public opinion, but a scandal, the responsibility for which will be laid at the door not only of the Dutch Government, but also, I fear, of the British'.

Towards the end of March, the programme drawn up in Galloway's office was ready, the stocks were being built up again, and as soon as it was possible an enormous relief apparatus could be set in motion. According to the plan, supplies would be rushed in by road through Arnhem, by barge along inland waterways to Rotterdam, and by ship to Antwerp. In addition there would be supplies by air. The Allied armies had assumed responsibility for the transport of all the foodstuffs to the thirteen Civil Distribution Centres which would be installed in western Holland, and from there the Dutch Military Authority would take over.

The MG had already in 1944 appointed Van Hengel head of a semi-military body called the 'Directorate for Emergency Supplies B' and he had begun at once to recruit his staff, which at the first alert would travel north to help. 'It seemed so simple,' one district commissioner remembered. 'At the end of 1944 I received the message that my service might be required to help my compatriots, people who, as we knew too well, would have suffered terribly,' and after a talk with Van Hengel – 'he told me everything in sober words and in a tone that could not disguise his emotions' – he had joined. The housing was very simple, the Textile School in Tilburg, where with 'some pencils and paper and a few fanatic chaps' the schemes were developed. Growing bigger, the organisation moved to the Ave Maria convent where the plans were finalised on 10 March.

Immediately after Liberation 285 kitchen centres would be opened, which would provide food for 972 issue points. A further fifty-one specialised nutrition groups, each consisting of one doctor, six nurses and five welfare workers with an ambulance, were to move in to help the worst cases. A special mixture of predigested proteins was devised which could be administered orally or intravenously – a total of 70,000 doses – and special camps would be opened for those who returned from Germany, while forty groups were trained for general assistance.

Now the long wait for action began – and it was a frightening wait. 'I can only say that we all worried terribly, knowing that with

195

every day that passed our compatriots in the B2 area came closer to starvation,' one collaborator remembered. 'It was awful, the fear of coming too late.'

The fear was certainly not unjustified. *The Times* reported on 24 March: 'The number of deaths in Rotterdam . . . is now put at 40 a day. Most of the deaths occur among people below the age of 14 and over 40.' And a report from the IKB, the Churches' relief operation, on the first half-year of 1945 was further proof.

The IKB had been able to do a great deal since it was formed in December. Helped by the farmers in Friesland and Groningen, the organisation had succeeded in transporting at least four tons of food from north to west to help the special cases, those whose weight was twenty per cent below normal. They needed a doctor's certificate, but the applicants were so many that the examination had to be double-checked, and soon the weight-loss qualification was increased to forty per cent below normal. Of people over sixteen years, only 'those who are directly at risk to life through undernourishment' could be helped.

In spite of these limitations the IKB, which in January in The Hague alone fed daily 5703 children and 200 adults, was helping 28,313 children and 11,750 adults in The Hague area by March. More than 500 cases registered each day, and in April the number of daily rations had increased to 60,000. For NSB leader Anton Mussert, alone in Almelo, the impact the IKB made was a reason to make a last effort to recover a little of his influence. He wrote to Seyss-Inquart on 9 February to propose the appointment of NSB officials to assist the IKB organisers with the work. He argued that this was necessary, because 'otherwise only churchgoers and democrats will gain and the NSB will be the loser'. He demanded at the same time that one-tenth of the IKB goods should be given to the 'comrades'. Seyss-Inquart rejected Mussert's idea without an explanation.

His refusal was certainly not inspired by love for the IKB, as was shown by the efforts the Germans made to hinder the special transports, even those of 50,000 children who were evacuated from the west to the north. But the Churches simply went ahead and made it clear to Seyss-Inquart that any direct interference by either Dutch or German Nazis would lead to an open conflict with them. And to this united front the Germans gave in: it saved the lives of at least half a million people.

CHAPTER NINETEEN

Back for Ten Days

'I HAVE been doing everything I could on the food situation,' President Roosevelt wrote to Queen Wilhelmina on 21 March 1945. 'We are, all of us, laying aside large supplies of foodstuffs to use when the British and American troops occupy more of the large cities.' The American President really had a soft spot for the Dutch. 'I have written to General Eisenhower to do his best to save food in Germany and keep it for use in Amsterdam, etc. You can be very certain that I shall not forget the country of my origin.'

Princess Juliana had spent a weekend in the White House, and discussed a possible date of a return to Holland. 'I told her to tell you to be sure not to go back too early. It must be an absolutely safe date.' The ailing President had read in the papers that the Queen, whom he admired enormously, had already made a flying visit to the Liberated provinces of her country, and he wrote in melancholy vein: 'I wish I could have been with you to even that small area.'

Queen Wilhelmina had no longer been able to suppress her homesickness, and had spent ten days in the southern provinces. The territory had not yet been transferred to the Dutch authorities, which led to the bizarre twist that the Queen had to ask SHAEF for permission to visit her own country. 'Strange situation, to be on Dutch soil without ruling,' she herself remarked. She had no desire to risk a refusal, and put careful feelers out first. The reaction from the Supreme Command and the Dutch military authorities was not very favourable. Fighting was still going on, V-weapons were frequently fired from Holland to England and Belgium, and the chance of meeting German saboteurs or SS deserters could not be ruled out. But Wilhelmina knew what she wanted, and felt that, if King George VI and Churchill could visit her country, she certainly had a right. She

197

put pressure on, and SHAEF relented.

The whole expedition was treated as 'top secret', and only a few were to know where and when she was going. She was to travel in a military column under the command of a British or American officer, and would have a bodyguard of Dutch soldiers. Two Dutch adjutants were added, but no lady-in-waiting, so the Queen had to do her own packing and unpacking every night. A couple of journalists and radio reporters were allowed to come, but they had to promise not to write or talk about the trip before the Queen was back in England.

On Monday, 12 March, Queen Wilhelmina left England in a military Dakota, escorted by twelve Spitfires. In the plane with her were Baron Baud, Juliana's private secretary, Gerard Rutten, the Englandvaarder who had become a sort of press spokesman for the royal family, and her lady-in-waiting, Mrs Verbrugge, who would stay behind in Breda. The journey was, Wilhelmina noted, quite different from any of her previous tours. There was no luxury at all 'and the luggage was extremely restricted'.

The Queen had decided to accept an invitation from Queen Elizabeth, the widow of King Albert of the Belgians, to stay with her in Brussels on her way to the Netherlands. 'This had the advantage that I would arrive at an airport not far from our frontier'. And late that afternoon travellers at Brussels airport watched surprised while Allied soldiers surrounded one of the runways. A huge limousine appeared, and at half-past four they saw a Dakota landing, from which a small and plump old lady, dressed in a brown suit decorated with an enormous marguerite, descended. Queen Wilhelmina was back on the Continent.

She was greeted by Prince Bernhard, some officials and the Belgian Prince Regent, Prince Charles, who whisked her away to the Palace at Laeken. It was not a happy visit. The Germans had taken King Leopold and his family as prisoners to an unknown destination, and everybody was very concerned. The atmosphere in the colossal palace was gloomy, and the Queen found the meeting with Queen Elizabeth and her son – 'usually so gay and active' – this time very sad.

In the early morning of Tuesday, 13 March, a long military column took shape on one of the Brussels boulevards not far from the Palace. First some jeeps, which were to 'sweep' the road with the help of black-and-white chequered flags and sirens, then some with American military police and one with an anti-aircraft gun, followed by jeeps with Dutch soldiers, and at last the Queen's car. Eisenhower had sent his own limousine, an enormous monster of three tons, with bullet-proof windows and tyres. On the roof and the doors was the American emblem, the circled star, but for this occasion it carried also the Dutch flag – Wilhelmina had refused to travel with the usual royal standard.

While the column was formed outside, her two companions, Baron Baud and Gerard Rutten, waiting for the Queen, looked around them in amazement at Laeken Palace. Time seemed to have stood still, Rutten thought. There was still a very strict protocol, and he compared his court dress, a British battledress, with that of the Belgian footmen, 'still dressed in beautiful old-fashioned uniforms with short blue silk knee-breeches and white stockings'.

As soon as the Queen appeared with Elizabeth and Charles the party left, waved goodbye by their Belgian hosts from the terrace, and went to the column, ready for departure. 'I saw in one glance that the Queen was not in the least pleased with the armoured limousine waiting for her,' Rutten recorded, and she was even less pleased when the procession drove away and the sirens began to scream. The royal car stopped at once, and Wilhelmina asked her aide to stop the noise. 'I'm not a fire-engine.'

The journey to the Belgian border was made in silence and at great speed, through a deserted Antwerp – destroyed by the flying bombs which for once stayed away – to the border town of Eede-Aardenburg in Flemish Zeeland. The sky was grey, but when the Queen stopped near the frontier the traditional 'Orange sun' appeared.

An hour before her arrival the town crier, Toon van den Broeck, had alerted the inhabitants of Aardenburg with his gong – 'The Queen is on her way'. Within minutes all the houses and ruins were covered with flags, the children were lined along the street, and a few minutes before the Queen was to cross the border the Commissioner of the Queen in Zeeland, J. W. Quarles van Ufford, together with the MG boss, General Kruls, took up their positions. A long stick with a Dutch flag was planted on the borderline which, for lack of paint, had been indicated with a line of white flour.

'I crossed it on foot,' the Queen stated simply in her memoirs,

199

but those who were present never forgot that moment. It was exactly 12.29 p.m. when Queen Wilhelmina set foot on Dutch soil for the first time in almost five years. 'She was pale, but very composed,' Rutten remembered. 'It was still, so still that one could hear the flapping of the flag.' Nobody cheered, and the greeting by the officials was quickly over. It led to a little scuffle among the dignitaries, who all wanted to be the first to welcome the Queen, but Commissioner Quarles won, to the irritation of General Kruls. Professor L. J. M. Beel, recently appointed Minister of the Interior, also made sure he was noticed as he felt it his constitutional duty that the monarch should return accompanied by a representative of her Government.

The few hundred people who had rushed to the border were not aware of these bureaucratic manoeuvres; they simply stared at this small aged lady in her brown suit, brown lace-up shoes and the white marguerite, for whose return they had longed so much during those terrible years. Suddenly one hoarse voice began to sing the Wilhelmus, the Dutch national anthem, and others followed, tears running down their faces.

The tension was gone, and a sudden outburst of joy followed. It was a reaction the Queen would meet during her whole trip – 'the same emotion and enthusiasm', she wrote. At least one of the members of her entourage felt as if a mother had returned to her children.

From the border they went on to Aardenburg itself and from there to Sluis. Walking through the streets of this small town, the Queen could see for the first time the damage the terrible eighty-five days of battle for the Scheldt had done. Hardly any house was not seriously damaged. And it was the same in every town or hamlet she drove through that first day. Whenever she could, she would stop to chat to the people, listening to their stories of terror, death and destruction.

Her first meal in the Netherlands was in Oostburg, where the carillon of the Town Hall chimed the Wilhelmus over the ruined market-place. An invitation to join the local notary and his wife for lunch was refused by the Queen. Conscious of the food shortage in Holland, she had brought her own provisions, a basket full of sandwiches, and had it fetched from her car. 'The reader will easily understand the great joy it gave us to share them with our host and hostess,' the Queen wrote later, but that basket was in fact the cause of many disappointments. Wherever the Queen travelled, the population had – with joy and love – scraped a meal together, but in the first days the Queen consistently refused to accept it. She insisted on eating her own sandwiches, which she shared with her staff who, noticing the disappointment of the people, began to hate the basket.

One of the last towns she visited that day was Breskens, the most badly damaged of all, where one-tenth of the population had been killed during the fighting in October. Wilhelmina talked to a few orphans, dressed in track-suits made from army blankets; and a young Jewish girl who had survived in a hiding-place nearby offered her some flowers.

The night was spent in Sluiskil in a simple house, where, as Rutten noticed, the lights in her room stayed on till late – the Queen wanted to be well prepared for the next day – and where Ike's enormous limousine looked out of place. Prince Bernhard had given orders to keep the car always within reach in case of a bombardment or any other danger, and that order had to be obeyed, even if it meant that Eisenhower's personal driver had to spend many nights sleeping in the car.

Next day the eastern half of Flemish Zeeland received the Queen. The first stop was at Terneuzen, where in September 1944 the Germans had shot five men who had tried to remove the explosives from the sluices. 'I took the marguerite I had pinned on my coat and laid it at the spot where these heroes had fallen,' the Queen recorded. A sixth man, who had been present but who had escaped, was introduced to her, and after a short prayer she went on, asking that a monument should be erected on the spot. In Hulst again a meeting with Resistance men and again a refusal to lunch. But at least she accepted an apple from the mayor's garden.

Thursday, 15 March, was possibly the most heart-rending day of the whole visit. The Queen crossed to Walcheren, the island once called the Garden of Zeeland, now still completely flooded. One of her former Ministers, Van der Tempel, had already visited the island in December, like Gerbrandy, and wrote: 'Here really reigns the terror of war, complete and raw. The lustre of Middelburg was knocked down or has floated away. Dirty, sad and wet, and irreparably damaged – the glory of Zeeland.' Now the Queen could see it for herself and she was shattered. 'It was a cold unforgettable journey,' she recalled later. 'How tragic was the aspect offered by the Island of Walcheren, once so picturesque: a sheet of water as far as the eye could reach, with church spires and roofs rising out of it, and trees that would never put forth leaves again.'

Crossing the island in an amphibious vehicle, she visited the big hole in the dyke at Westkapelle, made by hundreds of English bombs, and was told the story of the forty-four people who on 3 October had taken cover in a mill, and she remembered later how that drama had affected her. 'Without any hope of assistance those inside it had watched the water mount higher and higher until in the end it carried them all away.' While the stench of drowned horses and cows was penetrating, she quietly talked with people who had lost everything and lived miserably in the former German bunkers, and only when she left did an old woman in Zeeland costume begin to sing the Wilhelmus, hesitantly joined by others.

From Westkapelle the party continued to Domburg and Oostkapelle, past the deserted and half-drowned farmhouses, in which furniture could be seen floating. Windows and doors moved with the waves, but even here the red, white and blue flags fluttered. Some inhabitants had returned by boat especially to hoist them. The Queen was visibly moved and stammered once: 'I had never thought it was that bad.'

Lunch in Oostkapelle was at the house of the village doctor, as it was the only undamaged one. Someone had assembled a delicious but very sober buffet, but the Queen instead took a piece of bread out of the famous basket. It was by now so hard that she was unable to cut it properly and started hacking away. Her aides decided there and then that the basket must disappear, as the performance was becoming pathetic. When the Queen asked for a sandwich next day, one of them told her that the store was finished. She looked surprised and puzzled, but there was nothing she could do and from then on the Queen could enjoy Dutch hospitality, to the joy of her hosts – and her staff.

The night was spent in Middelburg, where on Friday she made her first official speech. 'After almost five years' expectation we hold out hands to each other again, we look each other in the face, deeply moved by all that has passed through your lives. It is difficult to imagine the emotions that have overwhelmed me now

I am being reunited with you. My trip through Walcheren and Flemish Zeeland will always be one of the greatest events in my life. . . .'

The visit to Zeeland was over and it was now Brabant's turn. Breda was the first city, and the difference was at once obvious. The province had suffered much less, and the improvisation of the visit to Zeeland gave way to much greater formality. Meetings in town halls, discussions with churchmen, conferences with officials and industrialists, and, after one night in a mansion near Eindhoven, even a Guard of Honour from the Coldstream Guards. Wilhelmina was not pleased at all and she told Rutten to take care that the people she wanted to meet, the Resistance fighters and their families, were not kept away by the authorities. He passed the message on to all the mayors of the places she visited, and it worked.

The Queen was very much aware that her visit had a special significance. Since the Liberation the southern provinces had lived under the autocratic Military Authority, which had not been able to improve the situation as quickly as the Dutch had hoped. They felt disillusioned and dissatisfied, and the arrival of the Queen gave them the feeling that the Liberation was now real and that a better future was at hand.

This was very evident in Eindhoven, where thousands and thousands lined the streets, and where the Queen was mobbed when the police could no longer hold back the hysterically enthusiastic crowd. She staggered, but was saved by her soldiers, who lifted her and almost carried her to the waiting car. A few people were hurt.

The visit took place on Monday, 19 March, exactly half a year after the town was liberated by American airborne troops, the 'Screaming Eagles', and it almost became the last stop of the tour. In spite of the press embargo on the Queen's trip, a local daily paper published a large article about her reception in Eindhoven. The whole edition was suppressed before the paper had reached the street, but there could have been a leak. That same evening, the French Radio, followed by the BBC, gave the news of the royal visit to Brabant. An emergency meeting was organised, but Wilhelmina wouldn't hear of cancelling the rest of the journey, and the next day she travelled on unperturbed to Den Bosch.

There again they had blundered, this time by hoisting the

national flag on the spire of St Jan's Cathedral, telling nearby German artillery that something important was happening in the town. The flag was hastily pulled down, and the Germans only began to shoot after the Queen had left, but it convinced her that she would be unwise to insist any longer on a visit to Nijmegen, which was directly on the front line.

Limburg was the last of the three provinces that welcomed Queen Wilhelmina. Passing through Belgian territory, the whole cavalcade drove to Maastricht where the Americans, as the liberators of that part of her kingdom, took over her protection from the British and Canadians. The atmosphere changed instantly. Enormous black drivers in trucks decorated with Orange ribbons, cameras, multi-starred generals noisily trying to catch a glimpse of 'Queenie' – it was a complete circus. Wilhelmina kept her dignity, but watched amazed and amused while travelling from Maastricht to Heerlen, where she met a large group of mineworkers from the mine named after her.

The men had just come from the night shift and were still as black as the coal they dug, and there were threats of a strike as a protest against the small rations, but the Queen ignored both and, shaking their dirty hands, thanked them for helping so much with the reconstruction of the country. One thirty-six-year-old miner, Peter Toussaint, suddenly stepped forward and declared solemnly: 'Majesty, we have been loyal to you during the war; we will be loyal to you now.' The Queen bowed her head and grasped his big black hand again, while his colleagues cheered.

The last day of the tour, Thursday, 22 March, also gave the Queen a last chance to see the horrors of the war: she visited Venlo and Roermond, liberated exactly three weeks earlier after a fierce battle of which the scars were very visible. Most inhabitants had been evacuated – in Roermond only 6000 of the 20,000 had stayed behind – the streets were filled with rubble, and there were still mines and booby-traps.

The stop at Roermond was short, but in Venlo the Queen stayed longer. In the market square, surrounded by ruins, a few thousand people were gathered, many of them on stretchers. But the sun was shining and the atmosphere was excited. The Queen talked with many of the wounded, and with people who had lived for weeks in their cellars while shells were flying over their heads. And when she left the town she told the mayor with unusual emotion: 'My heart will always be in Venlo.'

By the time Radio Oranje told us in Occupied Holland about the visit on Friday, 23 March, the Queen was already safely back in England. She had been driven from Venlo to a nearby airport, where Prince Bernhard waited. It was noticeable that she was tired, but she made no secret of the fact that she would have loved to stay. It was impossible, and after a short conference with Bernhard – pacing up and down along the runway – she thanked all her guards and drivers, before stepping into the Dakota that would fly her back to exile. Three cheers from the bystanders, followed by the Wilhelmus, and the engines began to roar. Escorted again by twelve Spitfires, the Queen left at 2.20 p.m. 'Those unforgettable days belonged to the past,' she sighed.

The secrecy surrounding her trip had been so tight – in spite of the two leaks – that, on her arrival at an airfield not far from Laneswood, nobody was waiting. Not even her car had been sent, and Wilhelmina drove home in a jeep lent to her by the base commander.

'All those busy, happy days had demanded more of me than a human being can give, spiritually and physically,' she admitted in her memoirs. 'I returned to Mortimer radiant and grateful, but exhausted.' She had been bothered by sciatica, 'in consequence of all the excitements of my return, which I could not work off by giving rein to my feelings like my compatriots'. The years of royal training took their toll. 'I had to be ready all the time and show my sympathy to all. And this is possible only when one has one's emotions under complete control.'

Before the Queen began a short period of rest and recovery at Laneswood, she sent through Radios Oranje and Rising Netherlands on Saturday, 24 March, a message to Liberated Holland, expressing her thanks for the welcome. 'Words are not enough to tell you my impressions and what it all did to me,' she told the Dutch people, and she was immensely encouraged by the enthusiasm with which they were tackling reconstruction. Finally, she was very happy to notice 'the unity and co-operation, which had grown in our nation these last years . . . '.

CHAPTER TWENTY

Race through the East

THE QUEEN's broadcast on Saturday night, 24 March, was followed by the long-awaited news that the great Rhine Offensive between the Dutch border and the Ruhr had started. American, Canadian and British armies had crossed the river in four places. On the eve of the attack Field-Marshal Montgomery had sent a personal message to his soldiers: '21st Army Group will now cross the Rhine – having crossed the river we crack about the plains of Northern Germany, chasing the enemy from pillar to post.'

The signal for the offensive was given on 23 March, at 2.30 p.m., ten minutes after Queen Wilhelmina had left Venlo airport, and after a barrage of heavy artillery fire the first troops crossed six hours later. 'The final phase of the war in Europe had begun,' Bedell Smith, Eisenhower's Chief of Staff, commented.

To have the war so near and still so far made the Dutch restless, and in Resistance circles the possibility of a rising was being discussed. The German troops in Holland were not of the best quality, often refugees from battles in the east and as often without proper equipment or arms. The staff of the local German commanders had to hand over their weapons to the troops so that at least the appearance of an army ready for battle was kept. Ammunition was also scarce. But there was another, more important, reason for intervention.

Seyss-Inquart had always made it clear to Hirschfeld that Holland would be inundated if it were necessary for the German defence and, although 230,000 hectares of agricultural land in the west were already under water, the Germans were working hard at the mining of other dykes. 'We feared that the enemy would not stop at well-laid preparations but that, insensitive to the fate of the Dutch, they would go on to desperate destruction,' Major-General J. Kok, the leader of a Resistance group specialising in anti-inundation operations, wrote later. He explained that the Germans had placed explosives in the dykes that separated the low-lying polders from the canals which encircled them, as in the Haarlemmermeer-polder, the largest inland polder, the Ijsselmeerdyke near Amsterdam and the dyke of the Noordoostpolder, Holland's latest piece of reclaimed land. Should the explosions ever take place, then not only would the polders be flooded, but the man-made canals would also be emptied at the same time, their banks and beds would dry and crack, and Holland's whole system of inland waterways would be totally useless for years.

The consequences would be disastrous. The roads were almost impassable because of barricades and blown-up bridges, the railways were virtually non-existent as most of the equipment, rails included, had been carried off to Germany, and the waterways were the only hope of obtaining quick relief after Liberation, not to speak of the whole reconstruction of a country where 4.5 million people had to live.

Together with the German weakness, this threat – and the famine – almost begged for a concerted rebellion against the Germans. Prince Bernhard – and Ike – were not unaware of these feelings, but knew that a rising now would lead to a massacre, while the Allies would have to look on helplessly. It was therefore not surprising that, on the same night as the announcement of the Rhine Offensive, both men issued a warning to the Dutch Resistance. Ike repeated his orders of 14 September to obey their Commander, the Prince. He added three more points – no overt action in support of the Offensive; remain at your posts; and finally: 'when action is required of you to assist the Allied armies in driving the enemy from your homeland you will receive precise instructions'. The Prince underlined this message with the warning that 'under no circumstances should anybody take the initiative independently. The most strict discipline is required. . . . Beware of provocation.'

For the moment the Dutch had to remain passive, but hope grew that the Allied troops would soon march into our part of the world. Radio Oranje had good news every day. 'Five Allied armies are now driving in a united front along the beautiful motorways which Hitler built for his own armies, sometimes four lanes wide,' the radio teased the Nazis. 'The Third Reich is collapsing fast.'

207

Even the weather was promising. Days of uninterrupted sunshine and a gentle wind gave the spring an extra glow. The meadows around Hilversum, where not flooded, were lusciously green and the cattle could leave the stables much earlier than usual. The first fruit trees were beginning to blossom. And on 28 March Monty at last ordered the commander of the Canadian First Army, General Henry D. G. Crerar, 'to open up the supply route to the north through Arnhem and then operate to clear north-east Holland'. On 30 March the first Canadians marched over the German–Dutch border into Dinxperloo not far from Doetinchem. That same day the Germans dismantled their last V-sites near The Hague. It was Good Friday, and for the Dutch a very good Friday.

Easter Day 1945, on 1 April, was suddenly cold and windy, with some rain at times. It should perhaps have been seen as a warning to those who were becoming too optimistic and saw Liberation around the corner. But for the moment the news remained good, and with much lighter hearts we celebrated Easter with our half-loaf, some margarine and extra cereals received from the Red Cross. For my little sister, still under four, there was even an egg, but for the rest of the family an egg would have cost four guilders on the black market. The central kitchens had done their best, too. 'There was a thick but undefinable soup with vegetables and potatoes,' a housewife in Rotterdam recorded but, in spite of all the help from outside, sugarbeet was still our staple diet.

On that same day the first big town in the eastern Netherlands, Enschede, was liberated. 'No citizen was killed,' Radio Oranje reported. Not during the battle, at least; but on the eve of the Liberation the Gestapo had executed ten men, and, one hour before the Allied troops marched in, another two.

For us, with our unreliable newspapers and radio, it was difficult to find out exactly what was happening, and Radio Oranje had the same trouble. 'There is great secrecy about the movements of Montgomery's armies,' it said. But one thing was sure, a Rotterdammer wrote that Easter Day: 'Destiny is hanging dangerously and inevitably over the enemy. The Occupying Forces are nervous and defend themselves desperately.'

But the Dutch were getting nervous, too. Liberation had to come soon if the country were not to be completely flooded, food to become even scarcer and the country as a whole to disintegrate. Some, who had been in hiding for months, and dared to come out now the Germans were paying more attention to their own defence and less to them, could not believe their eyes. 'In streets half ripped up, people kneel down to look for coal, the parks are completely uprooted, many houses have broken windows,' a Rotterdammer reported. 'Here and there is a doorway, a half-dazed and emaciated old man or woman is sitting with closed eyes . . . children are digging in a rubbish heap for something edible.' Maurits Dekker, strolling through Amsterdam for the first time in four years, couldn't grasp it all at once. 'Was this decaying and neglected city, damaged by greedy looters, manhandled by indifferent barbarians and battered by desperadoes, my old, beautiful and noble Amsterdam?' Everything seemed to say 'Memento Mori'. 'Wherever I look these words were visible. They were floating in the gutter with the faeces that bubble from the wells now the sewerage is not working, they were lying in the muddy gullies alongside the tram-rails which before were filled with wooden blocks, which had now disappeared into stoves, they were hanging in the heavy yawning emptiness of the houses which were demolished from roof to cellar, as if eaten by termites . . . they stood over the door of the old church where they collect the corpses for which there are no coffins and no transport to the cemeteries.' It was a city in a death-struggle.

And so was the whole of western Holland but, although the front in the west was rapidly knocked to pieces, Berlin had no intention of giving up its last foothold there. In March, Noord-Holland, Zuid-Holland and Utrecht were declared 'Festung Holland' – Fortress Holland. Ike learned of this in advance and warned the American Mission in Moscow on 29 March that the enemy was going to hold on 'to the last isolated areas', expecially to coastal fortress-areas like Holland.

General F. Christiansen, who had left Hilversum in November for Delfzijl, handed over command of the German 25th Army on 7 April to General Johannes Blaskowitz, who that same night crossed the Noord-Holland to set up his headquarters again in Hilversum. Blaskowitz, certainly no admirer of the Nazi régime, was in disfavour with Hitler after he had protested against SS cruelty in Poland, but he was a capable officer of the old school and incapable of disloyalty to his country. At once he started to

209

make preparations for the last stand. The famous Grebbe Line was flooded; explosive charges were placed in dykes all over the west; sluices were closed so that the water in the Ijsselmeer rose to an alarming level; the guns in the bunkers along the coast were turned round, pointing inland; and, finally, plans were drawn up for a withdrawal – if the Grebbe Line should fall – to behind the Holland waterline, west of Utrecht. The Germans were ready to obey Berlin and 'fight to the last man and the last bullet'.

Three days after Blaskowitz's return to Hilversum, the town suffered its worst air-raid of the war. Up till then we had seldom been bombed – only about seven times – and although Radio Oranje boasted on 26 November 1944 that four squadrons of the RAF had destroyed the German headquarters in Hilversum with 348 rockets the building showed hardly any damage.

The attack on Wednesday, 11 April, had nothing to do with the fact that Blaskowitz had established himself in Hilversum. Its targets were some munition-ships in the little inland port, about a kilometre from our house. It was midday when the raid started, and I was alone at home with my two-year-old sister and my five-year-old brother. My mother was still in hospital and my father had gone out to the farms to try to get some food. Suddenly, out of the blue sky, a couple of Spitfires dived over our roof in the direction of the port. Guns rattled, while a few bombers dropped their load. I was watching the spectacle with fascination from the first-floor window when I remembered that my brother was playing somewhere in the streets. I ran downstairs into the lane, almost hysterical with worry. People shouted at me to go inside but, unaware of the planes and the bullets, I just ran, searching in panic until a neighbour pulled me into his house, where I found my brother as well.

I remember very little of the rest of the incident but, according to official sources, two people were killed and seven wounded. The planes had for once hit the ammunition-ships well and truly, and two of them sank, together with a few barges and a sailing yacht. More than 170 houses were damaged.

The attack on Hilversum was only a pinprick. The war was raging now in the whole of eastern Holland. Almelo was liberated on 5 April, and one day later Canadian troops started to attack the old fortress of Zutphen. The German troops, 1500 paratroopers between the ages of fifteen and twenty, fought fanatically in spite of the fact that their equipment was totally inadequate. 'All the soldiers move around on bikes, even children's bikes,' one inhabitant reported, 'and the best means of transport is a horse and cart.' The Canadians had to burn the boys out one by one with their flame-throwers, an officer later revealed, before they surrendered.

Entering the city, the Allied soldiers were confronted by a ghastly sight: the bodies of ten Dutchmen who had been murdered at the last minute. They herded some German prisoners-of-war to the spot, compelling them to bury the mutilated bodies. CBC correspondent Matthew Halton reported: 'As the frightened paratroopers looked on, Sergeant-Major Austin, cold with hate, bent over the dead men and showed me things too horrible to describe. Some of these men had been tortured and then shot. Their hands were still tied behind them, but some of them hadn't even been shot. They had been tortured to death in an unspeakable way. The worst things you've ever read about in any account of Nazi atrocity were there. I saw and was sick.' He looked at the German prisoners and asked one of them what he thought about it. The young, unshaven, red-eyed paratrooper rose to his feet and stood, shaking, at attention. 'Das ist ein Schweinerei,' he said in a trembling voice. 'That's a swinish thing. The Gestapo did it.' Halton looked at him and asked: 'Do you understand why the world hates your country?' And for the first time he heard a German say: 'Yes, I understand.'

The next town to be liberated was Deventer and on Saturday, 14 April, the capital of Overijssel, Zwolle. A BBC correspondent, Robert Dunnett, was present and reported how the Dutch were busy putting the collaborators into the school 'that they had all known for four years as the Gestapo prison'. They told him that there were 300 known collaborators in town and with typical thoroughness they were out to get them all. 'Many were young girls who had been too kind to the occupying forces.' The Zwolleners surrounded Dunnett and had hundreds of questions. 'A young man wanted to know if potatoes, bread and beans were rationed in England, another if London had been badly damaged by bombs, and one girl chipped in to ask: "Is Deanna Durbin still alive, and Shirley Temple?" '

Meanwhile, other Canadian troops had tackled the province of Drenthe, and on 12 April, with the help of French airborne

211

troops they reached Westerbork camp, where the 850 Jews still remaining were liberated amid scenes of enormous enthusiasm. That same day Eisenhower visited a concentration-camp in Germany, Ohrdurf near Gotha, for the first time, writing later: 'I have never been able to describe my reaction, when I first came face to face with the indisputable evidence of Nazi brutality and ruthless disregard of every shred of decency.'

The liberation of the north-east was taking on the speed of an avalanche. Faster and faster the Canadian troops, with the support of the French and the Poles, moved from town to town. Assen was freed on 12 April, the capital of Friesland, Leeuwarden, was reached on 15 April, and Groningen captured after a bitter fight on 16 April.

For many people in the north their liberation came almost unnoticed. My elder brother Wim, who had since the beginning of April been staying with my grandparents in the small and isolated village of Oudega, happened to hear it from his grandmother, who had visited friends in a neighbouring village. It was 17 April, and later that afternoon he saw a couple of men with Orange armbands cycling past. It was the Friesian Underground, who had played a very important role in liberating their own province.

A Jewish 'diver', who had been hiding in a village near Heerenveen, remembered another picture of Friesland. He was liberated on 14 April, and that afternoon the village looked 'like a Sabbath afternoon in the good old days'. He counted about sixty Jews, who had survived in the small place without knowing about each other. Next day, he went to Heerenveen to see the entry of the Canadians, and he watched with amazement the Frieslanders, usually so phlegmatic, but now mad with excitement. 'I had never thought that they could cheer that loud,' was his comment.

That same day Polish troops reached the Dollart, an estuary in the north of Groningen, completely cutting off the Germans in Fortress Holland from their homeland, the Reich.

CHAPTER TWENTY-ONE

A Russian Drama

ONE SMALL corner, up in the far north of Holland, remained occupied while the northern provinces were liberated, and it became the stage of an unusual and very murderous battle. It was Texel, a windy weather-beaten island consisting of Ice Age dunes and polders, which had been reclaimed in the Middle Ages, its meadows the grazing-grounds of Texel's famous sheep and the breeding territory of rare birds. The island was thinly populated, with here and there a thatched farmhouse, surrounded by some windswept trees, the little towns and villages sheltering behind the dunes or the bold dykes that protect it against the seas.

Part of the island's occupation troops were formed by Georgians from the southern Soviet Union, most of them staunch Communists, who had been forced like so many citizens of the Soviet Union to join the German Army, or had volunteered in the hope of obtaining independence for their different republics after a German victory. Now that the end of the war was approaching, whole battalions of Russians had mutinied and, to be on the safe side, the Germans took their arms away. The 882nd Georgian Battalion – 800 Georgians and 400 Germans – based since 6 February on Texel had, however, been allowed to keep theirs, and when on Wednesday, 4 April, the commander of the island, Major Breitner, gave orders to 300 Russians to prepare to leave their leaders thought it time for action.

That afternoon a strange meeting took place in the dense fir forests in the west of the island. Six Georgian officers in their German uniforms gathered to plot the arrangements for a rising. First to speak was Eugene Artemidze, a former schoolteacher who acted as a sort of political leader for the Communists in the battalion. He stated that a mutiny had become inevitable now that the Germans were going to send only 300 of them away. He feared, rightly, that if those 300, as they planned, went over to the Allies the Germans would vent their rage on the Georgians who had stayed behind.

The military commander, Sjalwa Loladze, a former Russian Air Force pilot who had joined the Wehrmacht to escape the horrors of a German concentration-camp, agreed with him. 'It is very fortunate that the Germans have allowed us to keep our weapons and have even given us extra ammunition for the journey,' he remarked. 'It will be their own downfall.'

It was decided to form six groups, each of a hundred men, who would attack strategic points on the island, such as the northern and southern batteries, the little airfield, the headquarters of the local commander and the different barracks.

On the night of 5–6 April, at one o'clock, Loladze gave the signal for the operation, christened Day of Birth, by ordering the Georgians to murder their 400 German colleagues. Dr Veening, the local doctor in Texel's little capital, Den Burg, heard the shots and grenade explosions as he returned from visiting a patient at one o'clock. Major Breitner, who was spending the night with his mistress in the town, heard the same sounds and ran to the nearby little port of Hoorn to cross from there by the ferryboat, *Voorwaarts* ('Advance'), to Den Helder on the mainland.

After the bloodbath in the barracks it was the turn of the German headquarters to be invaded by the Georgians. The local commander and three of his clerks were shot on the spot, but one German escaped and ran barefoot and half-dressed to the German fortress at Oude Schildt and, while this was being prepared for defence, the escaper went on to Den Helder to summon help.

Everywhere on the island fighting had by now broken out and, three hours after he had gone to bed, Dr Veening was woken up by two Georgians who came to ask for help for their wounded men. He followed them, but did not get far. A German patrol stopped their car, and the doctor and the two men narrowly escaped by disappearing into some gardens.

The plan for the attack had been very simple – on paper at least. But the Georgians were guilty of one fatal oversight. Although they had occupied the post office and destroyed the telephones, they did not know that the German headquarters had its own signals system. A soldier who had remained undetected was able to alert the northern and southern batteries, which, surrounded by barbed wire and a minefield, could easily be defended against any attack. Just as fatal for the Georgians was the fact that only a few days earlier the battery guns had been modified to swivel round completely so that the whole of the island was within reach of their fire.

When, early in the morning of 6 April, the local Resistance leader, Mr W. H. Kelder, was woken up and taken to Loladze, the rising still looked like a success. The stocky and resolute Georgian asked for 200 Dutchmen to join their struggle as a show of loyalty, and two large English flags. These would be spread out somewhere on the island to show the British where they could drop their paratroops. Four hours later 200 men had reported to Kelder, and Loladze addressed them in front of his headquarters in the Texla bunker. His speech was made in his own language, but a German-speaking Georgian translated it. 'The rebellion against the hated oppressor has started in the whole of Holland,' Loladze announced. 'I appreciate it very much that you've come to fight with us as comrades. We have reached the point of no return. Long live Holland. Long live the Soviet Union.'

Fifty of the Dutchmen received arms, but before they could go into action the Germans, who had discovered that Texla was the heart of the rebellion, began to fire on the bunker complex, killing the first Texeler. At the same time German soldiers arrested fourteen inhabitants of Den Burg, shot ten of them and threw their bodies into the sea in reprisal for the sympathy that the Dutch had shown to the Georgian cause. For the Texelers, too, the war had started.

Voorwaarts and another ferryboat meanwhile returned with reinforcements for the Germans, and Breitner, who came back at the same time, sent two envoys to Loladze at midday with the demand that the Georgians surrender by three o'clock or they would be fired on. Breitner's ultimatum was ostentatiously torn up by Loladze, and at three, as promised, the bombardment started. There was only one solution: to abandon the Texla bunkers and retire to the woods. The Georgians disappeared, leaving five seriously wounded men behind with a Dutch nurse, who a few hours later had to watch helplessly as a German officer shot the men in cold blood in their beds.

The shelling lasted the whole day, and the little emergency hospital in a former youth hostel near Den Burg was over-

215

flowing. Dr Veening, recovered from his early-morning adventure, could hardly cope but got assistance from the German military doctor, Piechler. Some Georgians who were brought in were also tended, but efforts to hide them failed and next day a screaming SS officer kicked them out of their beds to be executed outside.

It was that day that the inhabitants of Den Burg could see how much damage the shooting had done to their town. At least fifty houses were destroyed and ninety heavily damaged, and it was only the beginning. Later that day, the batteries began their bombardment again, and in the coming days at least 1800 shells hit the place. Meanwhile the Georgians had made at least one important conquest: the lighthouse and the bunkers around it at the northernmost tip of Texel. All their attacks on the batteries and the airfield, however, had been beaten off and the leaders decided to switch to guerilla tactics in the large Eierland polder while waiting for help.

On Friday, 6 April, plans had already been made for asking for support from the Allies. The Resistance leader W. H. Kelder, who by now had sent his men home, had been in touch with the only man on the island who knew how to handle signalling apparatus, K. van der Kooi. Checking the set at Texla, they discovered that it was no longer working and that the only way to get in touch with England was to send the lifeboat *Joan Hodshon*. It was Sunday night before the boat could be launched, painted white, covered with a Red Cross flag and with a crew of ten Dutchmen on board. Only three Georgians were intended to join the delegation, but when they were at sea Van der Kooi discovered a fourth as stowaway who told him that he had had enough of the battle.

It was too dangerous to go back. The moon was full and it was pure chance that the motor of the lifeboat had not been heard by the Germans, so the man was allowed to stay. It took *Joan Hodshon* twenty-four hours to cross the distance of 240 kilometres, arriving near Cromer. Van der Kooi swam ashore to tell the coastguard what was happening on Texel. London was contacted at once and a bombardment of the batteries requested, but the only reaction was a cool order for Van der Kooi and his men to be sent to the capital. He arrived there next day and, instead of immediate action, six days of exhausting interrogation followed before the English handed the men over to Dutch intelligence.

Peter Tazelaar, the leader of the Friesland Resistance, also reached London to look for support for the Georgians. He had gone to Reims to see Prince Bernhard, who was there with Gerbrandy for talks with Eisenhower, and on his arrival the Dutch Prime Minister at once gave him a lift in his own plane to London. Tazelaar got in touch with the War Ministry, but met the same noncommittal reception as Van der Kooi. Not until around 20 April was Monty informed about the rising by M16, with the message that 'even now the Allies could occupy the island very easily', but nothing was done.

On the day the lifeboat left Texel, the Germans ordered all the inhabitants of the island to report at once the presence of any Georgians hiding in or near their houses. To prove that they meant business, they dragged Melle Zegel and his wife out of their house after they found a Georgian there. The couple were shot, and the Georgian hung from a signpost, until a Dutchman cut him down later that day. 'Texel is under a reign of terror,' a Texeler wrote. 'The awful, dirty Huns shrink from nothing.'

Monday began quietly – the diarist noted that he had been sowing – but in the afternoon the shelling started all over again. 'And there are fires all over the place,' he recorded. 'Farms, sheds, barns, they're all in flames. I saw a smoke column in at least seven places and the whole polder is burning.' Around four o'clock the entire island was covered by a pall of black smoke which hid the sun. At night, especially, the spectacle was fantastic and frightening: the dark polder was dotted with forty burning farmhouses, whose flames leaped high in the air.

For the Germans it was the only way to drive the Georgians out. 'They don't dare to enter a suspect house, because they're too frightened,' a farmer noticed, and they were afraid with reason. Some Dutchmen who were forced by the Germans to help clear the corpses discovered that almost all the Nazi soldiers had been killed by a single bullet through their heads. 'Terrific sharpshooters, those Georgians,' at least one Texeler wrote with satisfaction.

On Tuesday, 10 April, the first thirty local victims of the small war were buried, while the German batteries were silent for once, and the German commander came to pay his respects. But once the funeral was over the shooting started again, and for the coming week Texel was a hell of fire, smoke and noise.

Ten days later it was obvious that the Georgians had lost the battle completely. The longest they held out was in the Eierland polder, where no German soldier at first dared to set foot. But in the end the 400 Georgians there were no match for the 3600 Germans, mainly SS, shipped over on 8 April, who were constantly attacking and shelling them, and they withdrew to the lighthouse and the bunkers up in the northernmost tip of the island.

This complex, like the batteries protected by barbed wire and mines, had been in their possession for two weeks since the first attack by the Germans had been beaten off. On Friday, 20 April, the Germans made another effort. They surrounded the tower with fifteen guns and started to shell it mercilessly, supported by the nearby northern battery. Some of the Georgians escaped, but on Saturday afternoon the others were forced to surrender under the constant battering. The lighthouse was a ruin and its light smashed to pieces.

There was no mercy for the fifty-seven Georgians who gave themselves up. A Texeler who drove by later in the day saw the wounded lying along the road, guarded by Germans, who afterwards executed them. A farmer who witnessed the massacre later said: 'I watched from the roof of my kitchen and saw the completely naked Georgians digging an enormous hole.' When it was finished the prisoners were put in front of it in rows of ten and executed at close range. 'It took the whole afternoon before the last men were slaughtered. The last four had to fill in the grave first before they were shot', and were buried by the Germans themselves.

It was the end of the battle for the Georgians. 'They are beaten and scattered,' a Texeler wrote on Monday, 23 April. 'They're roaming around and are hunted down by the Germans.' The day before, the Nazis had started combing the island with a line of men walking ten metres apart searching the fields and the houses. 'But they're still afraid. We had to open all the cupboards and doors ourselves, and had to walk in front of them.'

That night the Georgian commander Loladze fell. He had been hiding with nine of his men in a house which the Germans encircled and set on fire. Eight Georgians were killed, but

Loladze, and one other man who had survived the fire, made an attempt to run when dusk fell. The Germans, who had been waiting patiently, shot him in the back and forced the owner of the villa to bury the body.

For a long time the Germans didn't realise they had killed the leader of the rebellion, and two days later they published an appeal to the Dutch to look out for this dangerous man, recognisable by his high forehead covered with warts. At the same time they published an announcement that no more executions would take place if the rest of the Georgians surrendered. A Russian doctor and two soldiers were the first to discover that it was a trap. After receiving their arms, the Germans at once forced them to undress and, in front of a terrified Dutch family, all three were killed. Returning next day, a Dutchman discovered that the bodies had been mutilated, the eyes gouged out and the skulls shattered.

Another Texeler saw ten Georgians, standing naked in front of the grave they had dug for themselves, suddenly run for it, scattering in all directions. Eight of them were shot, but two escaped.

The last remaining Georgians – many hidden by the Texelers in spite of all the Nazis' threats – were determined to kill as many Germans as possible. A farmer saw two of them, hiding in a bush, shoot twenty-eight Wehrmacht soldiers out of a search-party of thirty. And one Georgian soldier hit three men in one burst before he himself was killed. On 26 April the Germans, however, could announce that 'the total destruction' of the Russians was almost completed and, although an erratic guerilla struggle went on for weeks, the island was once more completely in German hands.

The little war had claimed a lot of victims. No less than 117 Texelers lost their lives, either in the bombardments or by execution; around 800 Germans were killed, while of the 800 Georgians only 235 survived. The material damage was at least ten million guilders.*

The Dutch and Georgian delegations in England received the news of the German victory with great dismay. Their trip had

* The survivors of the rising left Texel, only liberated on 20 May, for Den Helder on 18 June. From there they were taken to Wilhelmshaven in Germany and handed over to the Russians, who were reported to have rehabilitated them.

been in vain, and the British had never had any intention of helping the island. One of the Georgians, who after their arrival in *Joan Hodshon* had at once been interned without any explanation, wrote later bitterly: 'We had risen against the Hitler tyranny, we had made great sacrifices, but instead of receiving help we were betrayed and abandoned.' Operation Day of Birth had ended in a struggle to the death for most of his comrades.

CHAPTER TWENTY-TWO

Stop at the Line

A NAME which had made history seven months earlier came back into the news on Friday, 13 April. Arnhem was attacked by British troops. The advance on the town began when the troops made a surprise crossing of the Ijssel near Westervoort in 'Buffaloes', and after hard fighting established a bridgehead on the west bank. An enormous pontoon bridge assembled at Nijmegen had been pushed along various waterways to the point of attack and was at once swung into position, and at two o'clock on 12 April the first tanks rolled across it, moving first north and then swinging round to assault Arnhem from the east. The struggle lasted a whole day, but on 14 April the capital of Gelderland was in British hands.

The town was ghostlike. CBC correspondent Matthew Halton, driving in from the south, looked in wonder at the powerful German forts and redoubts which now encircled the town and had been shelled to pieces by the Allied rockets. 'The town itself was a deserted, burning shell. . . . The whole thing was a dreary, disheartening sight – another of the destroyed towns of a beautiful continent.'

But Arnhem was not only a burning shell, it was also a completely empty shell. Directly after the evacuation of its 100,000 inhabitants in September 1944, German soldiers had at first simply stolen whatever they fancied, but on 1 December an organised marauding expedition started. Seyss-Inquart received orders from Hitler that household linen, and other goods as well, should be taken out of Arnhem and sent to Germany for those families who had suffered bomb damage. 'I gave my permission and listed the town for indemnification,' the State Commissioner said later at his trial. It was meant as a punishment for those citizens of Arnhem who had helped the Allies during the battle in September.

Everybody was ordered out of the town, except a small fire brigade under the command of Willem Onck. They had to watch helplessly while special 'clearance commandos' swooped over the city like locusts. In their brown uniforms with the swastika on their sleeves the Nazis broke open doors and windows and took away everything of any use. It was done with German thoroughness. There were teams specialising in textiles, others in china, there were squads on the look-out for sewing machines and others for vacuum-cleaners. Specially trained women, led by a woman with the inappropriately sweet name of Frau Gazille ('Gazelle'), were experts in the detection of hiding-places. Floors were ripped apart, wallpaper torn away and gardens dug up in the hope of discovering the treasures the evacuated Arnhemmers had left behind. Finally, the goods were stowed in trucks and driven to the different regions of Germany that had received Arnhem as a 'gift' from the Führer.

What they could not take away was smashed to pieces or just left to rot in rain and snow. Boys from the Hitler Youth followed the official looters and kept Willem Onck and his men constantly busy by setting houses on fire. Many Dutchmen, labouring on the German defences around Arnhem, joined the Nazis and took away what was left. 'There was a group of men from Bussum who left the town with cars full of stolen goods every night,' a journalist, Henri Knap from Arnhem, recalled. 'They took it to 't Gooi and sold it with ease. We once found a note on which an order was written for a Persian carpet and a dinner-service – as if the place was a department store.'

Most of it ended up in Germany, however, and the Red Cross official Dr van der Does discovered after Liberation that 98 per cent of all the houses had been robbed of their household linen. To restore even a semblance of normality the town needed – to begin with – 60,000 chairs, 20,000 single beds, 10,000 double beds, 82,000 blankets and 20,000 stoves.

When Halton drove around the town the citizens had not yet returned and he was surprised to meet among the heavy military traffic one man in civilian clothes. They shook hands. 'You've come back,' the man said quietly to Halton. That was all.

After the liberation of Arnhem it was the turn of Apeldoorn, near where Queen Wilhelmina's favourite palace, Het Loo, lay hidden in the dense Veluwe forests, and where Seyss-Inquart had made his headquarters at Spelderholt. The first attack by the Canadians on the night of 13–14 April was beaten off, and the Allies, supposing the town to be heavily defended, prepared a more thorough assault for Tuesday, 17 April. The Germans – fanatical SS units – suddenly moved out, however, on the eve of the attack, and the Underground was just in time to warn the Canadians before they began bombarding the town.

The last phase of Montgomery's plan was reached. The troops now had to break through the Veluwe to the Ijsselmeer in order to complete the isolation of the Germans in Fortress Holland, not a very difficult undertaking as the Germans began to flee en masse to the west. Some went by boat over the Ijsselmeer, others by road. One enormous column of Germans marched straight into a Canadian armoured division near Otterloo, and a bizarre battle began between tanks on one side and German clerks, cooks, drivers and suchlike on the other side, until another Canadian force put an end to it with flame-throwers.

Putten was reached on 18 April. In the little town, which had had no news of its 589 deported men since the drama in October, women and children hid in the cellars of their burned-out houses, while shells howled overhead and the German soldiers fled. At nine o'clock that evening, the first Canadians were welcomed. A day later Harderwijk and Kampen were taken, and on 22 April the Allied troops stood at the Grebbe Line, where five years earlier the antiquated Dutch army had faced the mighty German forces.

On that day, Monty issued his last order of the campaign in Holland, ordering the Canadians to stay put and 'not for the present operate further westwards than the general line now held east of Amersfoort'. Further instructions would be issued if it should become necessary later on to attack the Germans in western Holland and to liberate that area. Radio Oranje commented: 'After a miserable long wait the east and the north of our country are liberated . . . but the three hunger provinces in the west are still occupied . . . the Dutch nation has begun to go under because of starvation.'

Radio Oranje had not exaggerated. Two days after the Canadians had reached the Grebbe Line on 24 April, the central kitchens in Amsterdam closed their doors – there was no fuel left. 'Only those who have a right to additional food, and children, will be supplied,' the announcement read. The 400,000 people who had survived the winter, partly thanks to the kitchens, had to look after themselves with nothing to look for. And, in despair and disbelief, they learned of the halt to Allied progress.

No one in Occupied Holland knew that Eisenhower had decided not to attack the Germans in Fortress Holland because he feared the total destruction of the area, as he had already explained to Washington in March. In his book *Crusade in Europe* he justified his decision. 'Montgomery believed, and I agreed, that an immediate campaign into Holland would result in great additional suffering for that unhappy country, whose people were already suffering from lack of food.' The Allied Commander had, however, decided to do whatever he could to alleviate the situation. And it was none too soon.

The winter months had been bad for the Dutch, but the month of April was far worse. The Allied advance in the north and east had cut off all food supplies, and stocks in the hunger provinces were down to nil. Hirschfeld wrote in his diary on 7 April: 'With our hunger-rations we will be able to get through to the beginning of May.' But these rations were not even adequate for survival as the 525 calories a day supplied in March were again reduced to 400. 'It is too crazy to be true, but it has happened. Next week the bread ration will be reduced again, and even with retrospective effect. That's just half a loaf a week, a slice a day.' It was the tram conductor in Rotterdam who wrote this. After his escape from the raids in November and the halting of the trams, he had joined the central kitchen teams, but it had not improved his food situation very much and he was now near starvation. He had asked for ration supplements, but there were so many 'special cases' that he had heard nothing about it. 'If help does not come soon, I fear the worst,' he wrote on 7 April. 'The only thing I can do is stay in bed. Today I got up at ten and was back in bed at seven . . . to allay the hunger. I just eat sugarbeet cakes. Supper consisted of seven of those. We bought one kilogram of rotting carrots for 2.50 guilders and are eating stew tomorrow. . . . I'm starving.'

Crime increased by the day. 'In our neighbourhood we have a lot of burglaries,' Diemer recorded on 11 April. 'And this morning I saw large gangs of men and women looting. They concentrated on bakers' carts and on potato transports. The police are invisible and the Germans don't pay attention any more. We are a nation without authority. Hunger is everywhere and shady elements are trading stolen goods for abnormally high prices – a loaf for 60 guilders.'

'Today there would have been frozen cherries, but the Wehrmacht had confiscated them,' a housewife in The Hague complained. 'The same with the frozen pork, which now turns bad. The Wehrmacht is baking bread with the flour that was meant for the civilians.' Her doctor had told her that the death rate among children was rising rapidly. 'This winter many children died of the cold, now they die of hunger. Recently they brought a boy of eight into hospital, who weighed 12 kilograms. The child was still walking and amazingly cheerful.'

In spite of their preoccupation with food, the news that President Roosevelt had died on 12 April hit the Dutch very hard. Close friends, like Churchill, had realised for some time that the President's health was failing, but his sudden death came as a shock to the whole world. On his desk he had a piece of paper saying '75 miles from Berlin', and Churchill wrote later: 'It may be said that Roosevelt died at the very climax of the war.'

Every Dutchman felt it as a personal loss. 'Roosevelt was so proud of his Dutch descent,' Diemer wrote. 'In 1937 he took the oath as President of the United States with his hand on the Dutch States Bible, an heirloom. And how proud we were when in 1943 our Queen became the first woman allowed to address Congress, and aroused such enthusiasm.' He was convinced that history would pay its due to this President – 'the enemy of all dictators'.

Another diarist recorded the same feelings. 'Yesterday Roosevelt died ... what terrible news, everybody says. "As if someone in your own family has died" – and that's how it feels. A disaster.' The big question for the Dutch was who was his successor? Would he be strong enough to carry on the war and to help in the post-war problems? We did not even know the name of the Vice-President and neither did the Underground press, who had to take it from the radio and consequently spelled Harry S. Truman's name variously as Crewman, Thewman, Threman, Froomen, Frulmer, Struwman and Croomen.

Radio Oranje asked the Dutch to keep one minute's silence on Sunday, 15 April, to commemorate the President, 'one of Holland's best friends', and Queen Wilhelmina and Prime Minister Gerbrandy were present at the memorial service in St Paul's

Cathedral in London on 17 April.

The Dutch, however, were stunned by a disaster of another kind on that day. Unexpectedly, the Germans blew up the pride of Holland's dykes, those guarding the Wieringermeerpolder, and flooded twenty thousand hectares of fertile agricultural land. 'With two huge holes, each with a width of twenty metres, the Germans inundated the polder . . . so that farms and roads are completely destroyed,' Dr Mees in Rotterdam wrote. 'This flooding has no strategic value at all, but it makes our food position still more difficult. Those vandals try to destroy as much as possible.' It was just twelve years since the Wieringermeerpolder had been created as the first polder to be reclaimed from the sea, and not, like all the others in the Netherlands, by draining lakes. Its huge, modern farms were an example of efficiency, and a great draw for hunger-trippers from Amsterdam. The Resistance had often used it as a dropping-zone and had received there, amongst other things, seven thousand weapons, ten tons of explosives and transmitters – a total of forty landings.

To blow up the enormous dykes which protected it from the sea had needed thorough preparations by the Germans. Shortage of explosives had made it necessary to construct special concrete mineholes, which were charged with unexploded Allied shells of 200 to 500 kilograms. The mineholes were connected to a master clock set in the dyke, which would detonate the explosive automatically.

The 7000 inhabitants had been warned to evacuate their homes on 16 April, but many of them hung on, in the hope that the Germans would change their minds. Dutch representatives sent to negotiate with the German commander on the morning of the seventeenth found him not unco-operative but, while the talks were still going on, a heavy explosion rocked the office. One of the German officers present turned round, exclaiming: 'Now the Wieringermeer is gone . . . we didn't give the order . . . how is that possible?'

It was 12.15 p.m. and the polder, 3.40 metres below sea level, would be flooded within forty-eight hours. There was not a minute to lose, and orders for evacuation were hurriedly circulated through the polder. 'Chickens were pushed into a crate, pigs into a sack,' one farmer recorded, 'the horse in front of the loaded cart, and another cart with chairs and a pram on top behind it . . .

then the cow tied to it.' Although the water had already risen ten centimetres, he went into the house for the last time. '[I] walked through the sheds and storerooms, took the grandfather clock, and put it on top of the cart. . . . We had to leave – until when? More than seven happy years were cruelly ended. We were driven away by Nazi terror and NSB treason. . . . A beautiful fertile enterprise (to be personal), where the seeds had been sown, was destroyed in one single day.' In the yard the plum trees were blossoming – 'for the last time', he wrote sadly. 'The garden, laid out by ourselves, was so radiant, twenty-four fruit trees seven years old, just beginning to mature, cranberries and gooseberries nursed up from cuttings, the raspberries we planted recently, and beds of strawberries, vegetables, lettuce and all sorts of cabbages. Today it saw the lovely sun for the last time, caressing with her warmth this mad, mad world.' The ditches around the farms were now brim-full. 'I took my bike and cycled away from the yard behind the cars. . . .'

The flooding of the polder meant that at one stroke the Germans had destroyed the granary of western Holland with its 512 farms. But even that was not enough. The fleeing inhabitants were checked at the polder exits by the Landwacht, who were looking for 'divers', discovered quite a few and shot twenty-nine of them in transit to Hoorn. Amongst the victims of the Landwachters was the deputy leader of the Resistance movement in the polder, A. C. de Graaf, who – as Raatgever bitterly recorded – 'came out of his hiding-place to save his wife and children, fell into their hands and was murdered . . .'.

The Dutch followed the Allied advance with increasing apprehension. Would they arrive in time, before the Germans had destroyed what was left of their provinces? 'We in the west talk mostly about food,' Diemer recorded, 'but we also wonder how heavy a defence the Germans are going to put up. We don't know how many Germans there are, but they have got reinforcements and there are a lot of those young fanatic guys, around twenty years old, but also tired old men, the opposite of the Herrenvolk who marched into our country in May 1940.'

At least the weather was good, and vegetables were freely available now the distribution system had collapsed and export was impossible – even to Germany. But prices were horrendous – a cauliflower for 7 guilders, rhubarb for 3.50 guilders a kilogram

– and only a few people could afford them. 'The walking corpses on the roads increase in number and the bedridden, too . . . you see many tragic cases in town,' Diemer's diary mentioned on 18 April. 'Often you can find someone lying down exhausted in the sun if he's lucky, and it strikes me how little attention is paid to this. In ordinary times everybody would have crowded round these people. Is it indifference? After a while the poor man struggles to his feet and staggers on.'

The tram conductor in Rotterdam described how it felt to be like that. 'I went to the barber this morning, but I didn't feel very safe in the streets. It is as if I am doing a cake-walk, foot after foot, like a drunken sot.'

His wife made a desperate effort to get him into one of the special oedema clinics and, waiting for the final approval, she began to get everything ready for his admission. It was not an easy task. 'I have hardly any underwear, and what I have is so filthy and faded that I cannot let anyone see it . . . ,' he wrote on 20 April. On that day, with Russian troops encircling Berlin, Hitler celebrated his fifty-sixth birthday. His projected Thousand-Year Reich was fast collapsing, and everybody agreed that this would be his last birthday in power. 'There are not even flags,' Dr Mees noticed. 'Last year they still had some. Nothing in the papers about Hitler, either.' The same day, Leipzig fell, the battle in the Ruhr was over, the Allies took 316,000 prisoners, and the Americans and Russians were only a hundred kilometres apart. In the Netherlands, Radio Oranje told us, Kampen had been taken, but the Canadian patrols east of Amersfoort had met strong German concentrations at the Grebbe Line. 'It's going well, except for us,' Dr Mees said. 'It's taking too long for us. Death, particularly from oedema, is increasing alarmingly even in better-off circles, chiefly because of lack of protein.' And the Rotterdam tram conductor, who was still waiting for admission to hospital, wrote on 22 April simply: 'Hunger, hunger. . . . It's getting worse. We don't even get our one slice a day. We don't know where to turn. We just stare at each other with hollow eyes.' Diemer had witnessed another assault by starving people on food transports. This time it was on a cart full of buckets of soup for the central kitchen. 'The driver laid his whip on his horse, and his companion gave the attackers a warm welcome by offering them the hot soup in a less than charming manner, in their faces. The gang reeled back. . . .'

By now hunger had even destroyed any interest in the war. 'Even if the Canadians were in Gouda, the people would think of nothing else but food,' wrote the tram conductor on 23 April, but for him the worst was over. He was at last admitted to the emergency hospital in Kralingen near Rotterdam. He was elated – 'I have a nice bed next to the window. That will be marvellous tomorrow when the sun shines' – and he recorded every meal. At ten o'clock his first glass of milk, at midday a stew of potatoes, cabbage, meat and gravy, at two o'clock a cup of tea – real tea – with sugar. It was incredible to him, but certainly came not a minute too soon. He had lost a lot of weight, but not as much as his neighbour in the ward, who weighed only fifty-two kilograms.

It was the last week of April and not only had the central kitchens in Amsterdam closed down, but even the extra help the Churches had been able to give through the IKB was in danger. 'We've reached the point that the last reserves of potatoes and grain have gone, so that 4.5 million Dutchmen will have to live on vegetables, meat and milk,' the IKB announced on 26 April. But most Dutch people wondered where to find the meat and the milk.

Shops were closing and trade was everywhere coming to a complete standstill when suddenly the streets of the big cities in western Holland began to show an unexpected sight: pushcarts full of flowers. 'The town is like a garden,' Bert Voeten in Amsterdam wrote. 'Everybody walks around with tulips, daffodils. One has nothing to eat, misery has hit rock-bottom and one approaches the stage of indifference. We buy flowers and we put them in our rooms, on the window-sill. We salute the new life that grows festively among the swollen bodies of the oedema victims, among the emaciated children and the garbage heaps in the parks. It is spring in Amsterdam and the water is rising.' In The Hague the chestnut trees in front of the royal palace were blossoming, a housewife reported, wondering if it was a good omen.

Many were too weak to appreciate the flowers and the spring, and every day that Liberation was delayed seemed like a year. 'Nothing is important any more,' Voeten recorded. 'This morning I received three kilos of potatoes from a charity. Some children were playing in the streets and a girl came up to me to ask for a potato. I gave her one and of course they all followed. I distributed the lot.' In another street yet another demolished house had collapsed. 'Three boys were lying under the rubble.'

The outside world seemed far away to the isolated and tortured Dutch, who could no longer imagine what normal life was like, and shrugged their shoulders at such news as that of the first United Nations Conference in San Francisco on 25 April. It was totally unimportant. The only thing that mattered was food, food and food again.

'Today I saw two children dying in the street,' Bert Voeten wrote on 29 April. 'They looked like small dead birds in winter, so sad and helpless. . . .'

CHAPTER TWENTY-THREE

The Side-Track

WHILE THE Allied armies stormed through the east and north of the Netherlands that month of April – watched impatiently by the Dutch in Occupied western Holland – startling and almost incredible developments were taking place behind the scenes, unknown to the starving population. These had begun with a visit paid by State Commissioner Arthur Seyss-Inquart to Reichsminister Albert Speer in Oldenburg on Easter Day, 1 April. Seyss-Inquart went to see Speer after receiving 'scorched earth' orders from Berlin.

'Without any military necessity for it, all technical installations were to be blown up,' he recounted later at his trial. 'That meant in effect the destruction of Holland, that is, the western Netherlands.' He explained to Speer that, if explosions were carried out in fourteen to sixteen different strategic places in Holland, the country would be completely inundated in three or four weeks.

Speer, who had been charged by Hitler with implementing his policy of destruction, was pleasantly surprised when Seyss-Inquart admitted openly that he 'did not want to inflict any more damage on Holland', and replied that he himself was ignoring the same orders in the Reich. He went farther. 'Speer told me at that time that the war, for Germany, would end in a relatively short period,' Seyss-Inquart told the Nuremberg tribunal, 'because armament production simply could not be kept up. He said two to three months.'

It had been a hard blow for the State Commissioner, who told the tribunal that up till that time he did not want to believe it. But Speer's eye-opener made him decide to end the defensive occupation of Holland, 'without violating my duties to the Reich and to the Führer'.

Before the State Commissioner hurried back to Holland, he

first telephoned Dr Ernst A. Schwebel, his delegate for the province of Zuid-Holland, in The Hague, and told the startled German official that he planned to disobey Hitler's instructions and let the Allies help the starving Dutch, on condition that they held their advance at the Grebbe Line. Schwebel, despite his very unattractive appearance – he was huge, flabby and had an amazing red nose – was one of the few decent Nazis in The Hague and agreed with his boss who, he later testified, was acting from humanitarian motives.

Early next morning Schwebel got in touch with the Dutch food official, Dr Hirschfeld, to inform him that Seyss-Inquart was on his way back and wished to meet him that evening. At eight o'clock the Dutchman came to Schwebel's house in The Hague, where three-quarters of an hour later a very composed State Commissioner arrived. Seyss-Inquart told Hirschfeld that he had just returned from a thousand-kilometre trip to Germany to discuss with Speer the orders to devastate Holland, and had that day agreed to ignore them. He had also talked to Blaskowitz, who as a military man felt that he must obey the Führer's orders and defend the Dutch coast to the bitter end, but was also ready to avoid unnecessary destruction if a way out could be found.

Hirschfeld answered coolly that that was all well and good, but, he added, 'there must be an end to the war. We are starving to death.' Seyss-Inquart at once made it clear that he could not consider capitulation. He reminded the Dutchman of the fate of a German general whose initiative in agreeing terms for surrender had ended in his execution – and Seyss-Inquart's own wife Gertrud in Salzburg was an easy victim for a possible revenge. He would of course reconsider this point of view, as soon as the German troops in Fortress Holland were cut off from the Reich. 'Then we will be our own king.'

Hirschfeld was less inclined than Schwebel to believe in Seyss-Inquart's 'love of mankind'. He was convinced that his gesture was more an effort to save his own skin when the war was over, and perhaps become the man who saved Germany by opening the road to negotiations with the Allies. His motives, however, were not in the least important; it was action that was now required.

Seyss-Inquart revealed to the astonished Hirschfeld that he knew about the existence of the Confidential Councillors, the agents of the Dutch Government in The Hague. He had even read their Liberation Manifesto, which had been confiscated, and found it 'very dignified' – promising with a smile to give it back one day. He now suggested that Hirschfeld should get in touch with them, and repeat to them what he had said, without mentioning his name.

Next day, 3 April, Hirschfeld met four reliable Dutchmen, amongst whom was A. M. Snouck Hurgronje, the temporarily retired Secretary-General of the Dutch Foreign Office. 'We all agreed that we had to act rapidly,' Hirschfeld wrote in his memoirs, and together with Snouck he composed a telegram which the latter handed over to the Confidential Councillors with the request to pass it on to London. In the message the Dutch Government was warned that 'according to reliable information from highest German authorities' orders had been given to defend the coast when the Allies moved west of the Ijssel, and to destroy and flood the country. 'Those who have orders to carry out this destruction and inundation can only disobey these orders, and are willing to do this, when Dutch territory is militarily isolated from Germany.'

It was hoped that the Government in London would read between the lines and understand that the Germans were willing to disobey Berlin as long as the Allies did not attack them in Fortress Holland, but concentrated on simply cutting them off. Hirschfeld's role in the operation had ended there. The Confidential Councillors themselves took over, represented by M. A. Th. L. van der Vlugt, who was not only the Consul-General of Finland in The Hague, but also one of the leaders of the IKB, the Churches' relief organisation.

On 7 April he approached Schwebel to discuss food problems. He had heard from a reliable source that, since his return from Speer, Seyss-Inquart had considered giving up Holland to join the war at home but, having rejected this, had unexpectedly changed his mind about capitulation. Van der Vlugt decided to bring up the subject, and to his surprise Schwebel reacted positively and even mentioned the one condition for possible capitulation: a 'correct' treatment of civil and military German authorities.

It was a sensational proposition, and Van der Vlugt passed it on at once to the Confidential Councillors, who met two days later on Monday, 9 April, and agreed that talks with the Germans should start as soon as possible, in view of the present emergency. They first wanted, however, to be sure that the German military authorities also agreed with the proposal, and that the negotiations would take place on the basis of Unconditional Surrender as the Allies had always demanded. Van der Vlugt was asked to get in touch with Schwebel again and discover the views of the German Army, while the Councillors would inform the Government in London, Prince Bernhard and the BS Commander, Colonel Koot.

Schwebel was a very busy man next day. At nine o'clock in the morning he received a visit from Van der Vlugt, who now discovered that the Germans were considerably more cautious than they had been three days earlier. Asking the Dutchman to consider the conversation of 7 April as a 'private occasion', he told him that Seyss-Inquart had confirmed the day before that Blaskowitz agreed in principle about stopping the organised destruction, but was sticking to his orders to defend Holland. It was thus impossible to talk about an official capitulation, only about some sort of neutralisation of a specified territory. The conditions were that the Allies would not attack, and that the Dutch would not provoke the Germans. For their part the Nazis would then be willing to stop the destruction, the executions of political prisoners and the raids, while the setting up of a relief headquarters by the Red Cross would be encouraged.

Van der Vlugt left to report to the Councillors, and Schwebel telephoned Seyss-Inquart in Apeldoorn. The State Commissioner agreed completely with his delegate's proposal to go on with the talks, but told him that in no way could phrases like 'peace' or 'neutralisation' be used. If necessary, he would handle the negotiations himself.

At four o'clock Van der Vlugt was back in Schwebel's office to hear Seyss-Inquart's reaction 'with satisfaction', Schwebel noticed. He proposed that Van der Vlugt should be accompanied by one of the Councillors, and assured him that, although the talks would at first take place without the presence of an army representative, they had the blessing of the German High Command. Van der Vlugt asked him to open negotiations as soon as possible because of the length of time that would be necessary to obtain approval from London. After Van der Vlugt had gone, Schwebel once again called Seyss-Inquart, and the two men agreed that the talks should begin the next day.

When Van der Vlugt got back to his office he found a message: 'Hurry. Schwebel asks you to come at 6.30 to his office, or at 7.30 to his house.' Van der Vlugt was only twelve minutes late that evening at the Sophialaan, where he heard that Seyss-Inquart wanted to meet him next day, and that he had no objections if the Dutch Government and the Allied authorities were informed about the coming talks.

On Wednesday, 11 April, the Confidential Councillors met again at ten o'clock to decide how they would tackle the talks with Seyss-Inquart. After all those years of oppression and terror it was almost repellent to them to sit at the same table with him, but the terrible plight of the Dutch made it necessary – they thought – to keep up at least the appearance of chilly politeness. Van der Vlugt revealed to them that Seyss-Inquart still believed that Hitler planned to let the Allies advance to a certain point and then employ a new secret weapon. The Nazi official knew very well that it would not help Germany to win the war, but it would certainly delay an Allied victory. In that case, the Dutchmen realised, there was no use in talking to the State Commissioner as the conqueror to the conquered – the Germans with their false hopes would never accept that – and all aid to the Dutch would be in danger.

The Councillors agreed, but asked Van der Vlugt to make it clear to Seyss-Inquart that they had no competence to make any settlement and were only able to accept a German declaration. This would have to be taken to the liberated sector of the Netherlands and discussed with the Dutch Government and Prince Bernhard as Commander of the Dutch Army, who could then get in touch with SHAEF. As Van der Vlugt's companion at the negotiations the Councillors appointed P. J. Six, the leader of the Order Service and the son of a famous professor who, as Schwebel ascertained, was highly respected and of 'unblemished character'.

The only problem was where the two Dutchmen would meet the German. According to the Dutch, they told the State Commissioner – who had asked them to come to Apeldoorn – that if he wanted to speak to them he had better come to them. Seyss-Inquart, on second thoughts, agreed with that. Up till now his talks with the Dutch had been kept secret from his underlings, and the arrival of two Dutchmen in Apeldoorn might arouse the suspicions of the other German officials who lived in the same street – with dangerous consequences.

Everything was settled, and only London had to be informed. That evening Prime Minister Gerbrandy received a telegram, promising a very important announcement in the near future which made it necessary that he should come as soon as possible to the Continent.

As seven o'clock on Thursday, 12 April, a meeting took place which only two weeks earlier would have been thought impossible: two Resistance leaders, Van der Vlugt and Six, sat drinking tea with Seyss-Inquart in Schwebel's cosy Dutch living-room in the Sophialaan. It was not exactly a pleasant or relaxed meeting. Van der Vlugt in particular took an immediate and strong dislike to the State Commissioner, whom he met for the first time and whom he thought 'utterly slippery and vain'. But matters were too important to be influenced by personal feelings and the talks came at once to the point. 'The State Commissioner drew their attention to the exceedingly difficult situation with regard to the supply of foodstuffs to western Holland,' a later report to the Dutch Foreign Office began, and declared himself ready to give his full support to any relief work – 'the military situation permitting'.

At least five thousand tons of food were needed weekly, which could be shipped to Rotterdam. The thousand tons of coal required for the same period could be brought from the Ruhr, where enormous stocks were kept. Politely, he listened to the two Dutchmen, who explained to him that questions like those of the inundations and the executions must be settled, too. They made no secret of their conviction that the war was lost by Germany, and referred to Hitler's remark in his book, *Mein Kampf*, that disobedience was allowable in order to save a nation from perishing. Further destruction, they pointed out, could never serve German war interests.

Seyss-Inquart did not react to the quotation from Hitler, but he confirmed that all orders for destruction had been withdrawn and that only the Dutch coastal region would be defended. He now promised officially that if the Allied troops stopped their advance at the Grebbe Line, 'and commit no further acts of war', the German military command in Holland would be prepared not to inundate more land or destroy further capital goods. He personally would see to it that all political prisoners were transferred from prisons to a decent camp, that no further executions took place, and that the raids stopped. If German personnel were attacked, the culprits would be brought before a proper court.

It looked as if the Dutch had a formal commitment at last, even though Seyss-Inquart made it a condition that an eventual truce would be carried out 'as inconspicuously as possible', and even after the State Commissioner replaced the phrase 'on behalf of the German Commander' in the Dutch report of the talks with the expression 'with the knowledge of . . .'. The meeting was concluded with the surprising promise by Seyss-Inquart to give a safe conduct to every Dutchman taking the proposals to 'the other side'.

The Confidential Councillors decided that same evening that Dr L. Neher would go as their spokesman, and that J. van der Gaag was to accompany him, as he had had experience in secretly crossing the German lines in January.

It was the latter who arrived first at the office of Seyss-Inquart in The Hague on Friday, 13 April, where he was received by the State Commissioner himself. 'You have immunity for everything you have done in the past,' Seyss-Inquart told him, 'but not for what you may still do against us.' Then, changing his tone, the German asked him to do his utmost to save the poor Dutch from starvation. To Van der Gaag's question about how he was to reach the Liberated southern provinces, Seyss-Inquart answered unexpectedly, 'You go exactly the same way you did in January', but he in his turn was slightly taken aback when Van der Gaag, leader of one of the largest Resistance groups, told him that he wanted to take his Allied uniform and pistol with him.

It was an unreal situation, which became even more so when Neher arrived with Schwebel and the latter personally picked up Van der Gaag's little suitcase, in which his uniform and pistol were packed, to carry it out to his car. Triumph changed rapidly into embarrassment, however, when the two Dutchmen arrived in Gorinchem with Schwebel in the large Nazi car and noticed the disgusted looks of the citizens there. The NSB mayor welcomed them with open arms, telling them in detail about the Resistance movement in his region and its hiding-places, while Schwebel made the preparations for a ceasefire along the River Merwede, which the two Dutchmen would have to cross.

Neher had decided that it would be better if they went separately – one never knew with the Germans – and Van der Gaag was
to go first. He asked for two German officers and a car, and at one
o'clock that night left with them. They drove for a while, and
when Van der Gaag asked them to stop and wait for him they did
so obediently, while the Dutchman went to see a guide and tried
to convince the man to come with him. Van der Gaag and the
guide had never met before, but the latter, who at first suspected
he was dealing with an *agent provocateur*, was in the end persuaded, and went back with Van der Gaag to the German car,
which drove them to an army headquarters nearby.

Nothing was impossible any more, it seemed, and Van der Gaag
was not even astonished when the thirteen German officers there
offered him a drink and insisted on being present when he put on
his Allied uniform, believing that he was a spy. The Dutchman
did not disillusion them and left at three o'clock for his boat,
waved out by the noisy Germans, who obeyed without any hesitation the orders not to shoot while he was rowed across.

On his arrival at the other side he was taken to Prince Bernhard
in Breda to arrange Neher's crossing. The Germans had agreed
to a rather complicated method to safeguard his journey. At
eleven o'clock on Saturday morning they would wave a white flag
at a spot three hundred metres east of the shattered bridge near
Huisden, and the Allies were to answer with a white flag from the
other side. An hour later the operation would be repeated in
order to confirm that a truce of forty-five minutes was about
to start. Neher would then cross in a rubber dinghy, rowed by
two German soldiers and accompanied by an officer. And so it
happened. At quarter-past twelve Neher was welcomed by a
Canadian officer on the southern bank of the Merwede, and
after a stiff salute the Germans rowed back.

When Neher arrived in Breda on Saturday afternoon he found
Van der Gaag already in conference with Gerbrandy. The night
before the Dutch Prime Minister, who had flown from London
after the warning of 11 April, had received another message
which, as he remembered, 'suggested the fantastic possibility of a
German capitulation'. He left next morning, nevertheless, for a
visit to Nijmegen, but had hardly arrived when he was telephoned
by Prince Bernhard, who told him that representatives of the
Confidential Councillors urgently wished to see him. While he

raced back, Van der Gaag was telling his story to the Prince and the newly appointed Dutch Minister of War, Professor J. A. de Quay. They reacted cautiously to the German proposals, but without waiting for Gerbrandy the Prince decided to fly to Reims to try to see Eisenhower. Neher would wait for Bernhard's return and Ike's comment, while Van der Gaag would fly with Gerbrandy to London at once to inform the Queen and Government.

Bernhard returned the same evening from Ike, who had stated that it was not up to him to decide. 'It is a question for the Governments,' he believed, adding, however, that he thought it a good proposal. With this message Neher flew on Sunday to London, where Gerbrandy asked for a meeting with Churchill, who, although ill in bed, asked his Dutch colleague to come to Chequers, his official country home.

Only five days earlier Churchill had intervened on behalf of the Dutch. On 10 April, two days before Roosevelt's death, he had written to his American friend to remind him of the plight of the Dutch. 'I fear', he said, 'we may be soon in the presence of a tragedy', and he suggested asking the Germans, through the Swiss, to allow additional supplies from Sweden. He even thought that the Germans might be willing to accept further supplies 'by sea or direct from areas under military control of the Allies', adding: 'we must avert this [Dutch] tragedy if we can. But, if we cannot, we must at least make it clear to the world on whose shoulders the responsibility lies.'

Roosevelt, in what was to be one of his last letters to Churchill, had agreed with the British Prime Minister and proposed to 'give notice to the German Government that it is responsible for the sustenance of the civil population in those parts of Holland that remain in German Occupation'.

The proposals of Seyss-Inquart went, however, considerably farther than Churchill had foreseen, and his reaction was 'initially reserved, if not adverse'. 'We have them in our grasp,' was his point of view. The Prime Minister of South Africa, Jan Smuts, present at the conversation, was more positive and managed, together with Gerbrandy, to talk Churchill into taking a second look at the Germans' offer. When the Dutch Prime Minister left, the British leader promised to get in touch with the Americans and, shaking his hand warmly, grumbled: 'Please don't believe that I'm rejecting it completely.'

Strangely enough, Gerbrandy met the same reserved reaction that evening when he reported on his visit to Churchill to the Council of Dutch Ministers. Van der Gaag and Neher were invited to join, but their reception was very cold. None of the Ministers knew who they were and one of them wondered aloud if the two men were not infected by the Nazis. Gerbrandy, however, came to their assistance and convinced his team that they were dealing with honest men who had come on an important mission.

Queen Wilhelmina, like her Prime Minister, had no doubts, either. She travelled at once to London where she and Princess Juliana, just back from Canada, installed themselves in Chester Square, 'so as to be available at any moment of the day or night, and to lose no time when important decisions had to be taken'. Next Monday she received Dr Neher and invited him and Van der Gaag to come and stay with her.

The final decision now rested with the Allies. 'They took a long time,' the Queen wrote in her memoirs, but one personal telephone call to Churchill was sufficient to have Gerbrandy called to No. 10 Downing Street on Wednesday, 18 April. What Churchill wished was a 'statement' from the Dutch Government, in which it would declare its own frank opinion on the question. Gerbrandy hurried back to consult the Queen and his Cabinet, and a lengthy discussion followed.

News had come in from Holland that the Germans had flooded the Wieringermeerpolder on 17 April. It was the second time since the beginning of the talks with Seyss-Inquart that the Germans had gone back on their promises. On 15 April they had executed thirty-four men in Amsterdam, and now they had breached the dykes of Holland's newest polder. Schwebel had at once asked Van der Vlugt to come and see him, and had explained apologetically that the inundation was a military necessity – the Germans knew that the polder had been chosen as a landing-ground for British paratroops. Van de Vlugt immediately sent a telegram to London repeating Schwebel's statement and it lay before the Ministers in London that evening of 18 April, together with a request from the Commander of the Forces of the Interior in western Holland, Colonel Koot, asking them for immediate action to prevent further flooding. The choice, according to Koot, was between an airborne landing or acceptance of the German proposals. He warned finally that 'with progressive conquest, foot by foot, nothing but water would be left'.

It was now up to Van der Gaag and Neher to plead for Seyss-Inquart's proposal as – so they explained – an Allied surprise attack made with the only three divisions available was doomed to failure. The Cabinet decided to put it to the Allies: either attack immediately with sufficient troops to ensure quick success, or consider Seyss-Inquart's proposals.

Churchill answered Gerbrandy next afternoon personally. 'My dear Prime Minister,' the handwritten letter began, 'I should not think there was any chance of clearance of Western Holland being accomplished in any relation to the date you mentioned, namely 30 April. In any case it would be marked by fighting and inundations and the destruction of the life of Western Holland.' He was sending Gerbrandy's demand on to Eisenhower, who 'I understand is not unfavourable to the course you originally proposed'. To keep Seyss-Inquart in check meanwhile, he thought it might be a good idea to make him aware that his hundred thousand officers and men, including himself, 'unless he flies like a coward, are in our grip and can certainly be placed high on the list of identified war criminals'. The letter ended 'with deepest sympathy for you and your much honoured country. Believe me – W.S.C.'

Churchill, once he had resolved to act, did so decisively. He gave his Foreign Secretary, Anthony Eden, then in Washington orders to take up the matter, sent a telegram to President Truman to warn him that a civilisation with a tradition much older than the United States was in danger, and forwarded the proposals to General George Marshall, the United States Army Chief of Staff.

Marshall himself had written on 18 April to Ike about possible aid for Holland, and when he received Churchill's message about the German proposals, with the Prime Minister's own ideas on neutralising Holland for two to three months, he passed the letter on to Eisenhower at once, asking for his views. Two days later Ike wrote back that he was only too ready to do something for the suffering Dutch 'even though it may be at some expense of our own operations against the enemy'.

The proposals made by Seyss-Inquart were in fact, he told Marshall, of military advantage to the Allies, 'as it would allow them to hold the Grebbe Line with minimum forces'. He hoped only that the Russians – the matter was being discussed with them in San Francisco at the United Nations Conference – would concur. If they did not, then he believed it would be necessary to press operations in the north-western area, 'because of the advanced state of starvation of the population in the larger cities'.

The delicate relations of the Allies with Stalin made matters no easier, while the death of President Roosevelt, the great friend of Holland, slowed things down even more, and Van der Gaag and Neher, both very much aware of the sufferings in Holland, began to get restless. On 19 April they sent a telegram to the Confidential Councillors assuring them that things were moving. 'Have full support from our authorities,' they cabled, 'but decision elsewhere.' And while Van der Vlugt went at once to Schwebel to report this, receiving the good news that the port of Rotterdam would be partially cleared for relief ships – 'a proof of the good faith of the Germans', he told London – Neher and Van der Gaag could not stand it any longer and on 21 April complained bitterly to Gerbrandy about the slowness with which the matter was being handled.

The Dutch Prime Minister, however, was helpless – he also had to wait until the Allies, heavily preoccupied with their first United Nations talks in San Francisco, had time to deal with the Dutch affair.

In the meantime a new complication arose in a completely unexpected quarter. While the question of relief was discussed in London, Washington and San Francisco, Seyss-Inquart's proposals led to a bitter conflict in Holland between the Confidential Councillors and the Resistance movement. Although the latter was often mentioned in the telegrams to London, their leaders were never officially notified of the German proposals. A raid on the house of Willem Drees, one of the Councillors and also Chairman of the Contact Committee (the Council of Resistance), had confirmed the rumours that were circulating in the Underground. The SD had found all the documents concerning the German initiative and Drees, who escaped, was confronted at the next meeting with an infuriated Contact Committee. The nineteen Underground groups, united in the Committee, rejected rigorously any kind of negotiation for a truce with the Germans, as it was, according to them, cowardly and in conflict with the formula of Unconditional Surrender.

The Resistance fighters also feared that it would halt the Allied advance and were actually convinced that the Allies had already walked straight into the trap Seyss-Inquart had set for them. Not knowing that the standstill at the Grebbe Line had been agreed in March at SHAEF, they pointed out to Drees that the Nazi governor had taken his main initiative only after the offensive west of the Ijssel had started and that he had succeeded in halting the Allied progress east of Amersfoort. On 21 April they composed a telegram to be sent to the Queen, Prince Bernhard, the Dutch Government and Eisenhower, urgently requesting the liberation of western Holland on the basis of Unconditional Surrender. 'Every kind of negotiation which does not lead to immediate capitulation is declined . . . *signed*: The Joint Resistance Movement.'

The telegraphist who had to send the telegram to London felt it his duty to inform the Confidential Councillors, who at once called the Resistance leaders for a meeting. On 22 April one of them appeared to talk first with the Chairman of the Councillors and later with Drees, but the two were not able to persuade him to withdraw the telegram. They therefore thought it wise to wire London that the Underground message was not only 'ill-informed', but certainly did not have the support of the whole movement.

It was all very confusing for the Government in London, especially when a day later another telegram from the Resistance arrived, reiterating its protests against the talks with the Germans. It was obvious to the Government that a bitter conflict was being fought out over the heads of the starving Dutch, and Gerbrandy decided to go ahead and ignore the pleas of the Underground. He knew all too well that the Allies wanted to avoid an attack on Fortress Holland at all costs. They had consistently told him that Holland was not only a side-track off 'the shortest road to Berlin', but that the flat country, intersected every hundred yards by dykes and canals, and now partially flooded, was also almost impossible to invade with the heavy armour and mechanical equipment of the Allied armies. Apart from this, Gerbrandy realised by now the extent of the damage a war in this densely populated area would cause.

Eisenhower restated this on 23 April in a letter to the British Chiefs of Staff: 'Due to present deployment of our troops we cannot possibly mount and carry out decisive operations in Holland for some weeks. When this does become possible, determined resistance by the Germans would inevitably result in even more widespread destruction.' He had, however, heard in the meantime from the Dutch Government that the supplies of food in Occupied Holland would be used up by 28 April and again urged that relief should start at once. Like everyone else involved, he was beginning to lose patience with the political bickerings with the Russians. 'I am aware that the Seyss-Inquart proposals are being discussed on a Governmental level in San Francisco,' he snorted, 'but it may take some time to arrive at a three-way agreement.' In the meantime he would like to have a free hand and send at least some help.

That same day he wrote to Marshall that the 'Holland Affair' bothered him deeply. He was not so much in favour of neutralising Holland, as the Germans might ask for more concessions, and he had a better idea. 'My personal solution would be the simple one of laying down orders to the German commander which he would be compelled to obey under the penalty of having himself and his entire command classed as violators of the laws of war or as war criminals.'

At last on Tuesday, 24 April, the Combined Chiefs of Staff by-passed San Francisco and cabled to Ike that they had 'decided to leave the matter in your hands with the proviso that you will not depart from the Unconditional Surrender policy'. The Soviet military authorities could 'if they so desire' have military representatives present at any discussion with the Germans. Ike acted at once and instructed the American Military Mission in Moscow to contact the Soviet General Staff and ask them to choose a representative without delay. The Russian Army, suddenly and very obligingly, reacted fast and appointed Major-General Ivan Susloparov, the Chief of the Soviet Military Mission in France, to represent them.

Ike still had one doubt. He had heard about the flooding of the Wieringermeer and asked BS Commander Koot in Occupied Holland what he thought of it. 'Understand flooding has taken place contrary to proposed agreement,' he wrote. 'Suggest therefore you point out that Allied forces have not advanced over Grebbe Line and therefore flooding unjustified in view of negotiations.'

Koot immediately sent Van der Vlugt to Schwebel, who contacted the German Army Command. The answer came that same afternoon and was still as arrogant as ever. The flooding had been in connection with the Allied advance, the Germans explained. The statement by the Allies that they had taken no action at the Grebbe Line was rejected – 'strong pressure and air-raids for several days' – but the State Commissioner had now nevertheless given the order to stop the inundations and only to make fresh preparations in case of enemy attack.

It was sufficient guarantee for Ike to agree formally to the negotiations, and late that afternoon a delighted Gerbrandy received the message that Eisenhower now had full powers to negotiate and to 'undertake operations to provide relief for the Dutch'. An eventual truce 'should ensure to the maximum possible degree that all German forces concerned cease all active operations, including naval and air activities, conducted from the area in question; and that the Germans freely admit and facilitate distribution of all forms of relief supplied to the Dutch population'. Inundations, executions, raids, etc., were to be stopped, and political prisoners were to be transferred to accommodation conforming to the standards of the Geneva Convention.

Gerbrandy dashed off a letter to Churchill to thank him warmly: 'Whatever the final result will be, I shall never forget your prompt action, through which I am confirmed in my conviction that you are the elected instrument to make the United Nations win the war.' He sent at the same time a telegram to the Confidential Councillors and the BS Command to inform them of the good news. It was confirmed to the Dutch on 26 April when, early in the morning, Colonel Koot received a cable from Eisenhower asking him to come with a German officer to the Allied lines near Amersfoort to start the secret negotiations.

At a quarter to eleven that same morning the message was in the hands of Seyss-Inquart, who left in a hurry for Hilversum to meet General Blaskowitz, and ten hours later Van der Vlugt was told that the State Commissioner had chosen Schwebel to represent him for the first talks, to be held on Saturday, 28 April.

Early in the morning of that Saturday – it was only seven o'clock – Van der Vlugt once again went to see Schwebel, now with the message that the Allies had ordered a ceasefire in the Amersfoort area between 0800 on 28 April and 0800 on 29 April 1945 in order to safeguard the delegates. They asked the Germans to take similar action. The Germans obliged, and one hour later an almost uneasy silence fell over the Veluwe. The active hostilities on the Dutch front had come to an end.

CHAPTER TWENTY-FOUR

Manna from the Skies

FOUR WEEKS had passed since Seyss-Inquart made his startling proposals and only now, on 28 April, were the direct talks between Germans and Allies able to start. For the Dutch in Occupied Holland they had been the longest four weeks since the beginning of the war. The official ration had shrunk to almost nothing – from 400 to 230 calories a day – and on Tuesday, 24 April, the Confidential Councillors wired to the Government in London that 'within ten days there will be no more food in western Holland'. From 27 April the bread ration was 200 grams a week, from 4 May practically nothing at all. 'It is already famine,' the telegram spelled out. 'In ten days it will be death.'

The same evening we heard on Radio Oranje that at least something was being done for us. Next morning the news was confirmed as dozens of hastily printed posters appeared on trees and fences. It was for us the most marvellous news in months: the Allies were sending food from the sky.

In an official statement from the Supreme Command it was said that, now the enemy was no longer able to prevent starvation, Eisenhower had decided to drop food supplies over the Occupied territories. 'We warned the enemy that this will happen and that he is not to hinder us in our efforts to help you.' The food parcels would be dropped by low-flying bombers. 'If you hear the planes coming, take cover,' the announcement warned – the parcels being heavy enough to kill people – and the message ended with the words: 'Don't forget it – we are your friends and we will do everything possible to help you.'

In the autumn of 1944, after the battle of Arnhem, the possibility of food drops had already, in fact, been discussed by the Allies, but it was then considered technically impossible. At the beginning of April the chances seemed better after the urgent appeals from the Queen, Gerbrandy and Prince Bernhard, and increased publicity about the situation in the three provinces. 'The Plight of Holland' had by this time reached the letter page of *The Times*, where Sir Frederick Godber, Chairman of the Help Holland Council (founded two months earlier), told readers that the daily ration of the Dutch was by now 'one plateful of thin soup with two slices of bread and a ration of twelve potatoes per week'.

The Allied reaction to the proposed food drops was at first cautious – they had plenty of other things to worry them – and Prince Bernhard, who had always supported the idea, became desperate. 'Do I have to knock on the Good Lord's door?' he exclaimed once. And perhaps the Good Lord had heard it – Ike gave the go-ahead.

On 8 April the Prince's staff and the officers of the Netherlands District Headquarters, charged by SHAEF with organising relief for the Dutch, met to discuss the possibility of the food drops, the organisation of the operation, the drop-zones and distribution in the western provinces. A telegram was sent to Colonel Koot in Amsterdam to ask him to take the necessary steps, and on 12 April the British Foreign Secretary, Anthony Eden, wrote to the Dutch Ambassador in London, Michiels van Verduynen, that 'in addition to the plans which have been in hand for some weeks for relief . . . via Sweden, we have now been actively examining the possibility of sending relief supplies direct . . .'.

A Dutch journalist, H. George Franks, head of the Dutch press agency in the free world, ANEP, began to travel around the RAF bases, telling the RAF crews about conditions in Holland so they would know why they were being sent, and on British airfields the RAF began to experiment. It was important to find out not only how to pack the food, so that the parcels would not be smashed to pieces, but also how to drop these parcels from a low altitude on to the field indicated. After a few weeks of training, a demonstration was organised for some of the officials of the British Air Ministry. Some of the Dutch Ministers were also invited, and Franks remembered later how one of them, very sceptical about the whole operation, changed his mind when a sack of flour landed at his feet. 'Unfortunately it exploded, and he looked like a Friesian cow.'

All these careful preparations slowed the operation down, but on 15 April the British Air Ministry decided that it could definitely go ahead. It had already calculated that the Allied strategic bomber forces could deliver 2200 tons daily without difficulty, and huge stores of eight million rations were built up at British airfields.

All that was needed now was a signal from Amsterdam, where at the BS headquarters they were working in secret on the organisation of the reception and the distribution with the official food authorities in Holland. On 23 April the plans were ready to be sent to London. According to them, dropping-zones a thousand metres long and four hundred metres wide would be laid out near the cities, so that transport could easily be organised. The BS were to guard the zones, which would be marked by three columns of smoke in the centre and by a large white T of twenty by twelve metres, whose top pointed in the direction of the wind.

Communications from Occupied Holland, however, had taken too long and the pressure exerted by Churchill and Gerbrandy on Eisenhower to do something for the Dutch – apart from the negotiations with Seyss-Inquart – had forced the General to break the news sooner than expected, on 24 April. It brought joy to the ordinary Dutchman, but panic in higher circles.

More than thirty-five of the forty places chosen by the Allies were unsuitable, and the fact that nobody in Occupied territory was completely ready would create chaos. Louwes, one of the Dutch food officials, heard Ike's offer on his radio. 'This plan would, I feared, given the circumstances in Holland, lead to murder and manslaughter,' he wrote, 'but, at the time I heard it, nothing could be done.'

The Germans thought differently about that. The same night at one o'clock Schwebel came to wake Van der Vlugt to ask him to intervene and stop the drops. The Dutchman agreed. The plan was too foolish, especially since the Germans intended to fire on the planes. He promised to send a telegram to London, if only the Germans would stop their radio snooping for illegal transmitters.

The two men hurried through the blacked-out The Hague, where Seyss-Inquart, after he had had to leave Apeldoorn to the Allies, was once again living at Clingendael, now more a fortress than a lovely country house. They woke up the State Commissioner, and in the presence of the Dutch mediator Seyss-Inquart

phoned the German detection station to order them to stop their
activities. 'It was a strange thing,' Van der Vlugt remembered
later. 'A delegate of the State Commissioner comes to ask if he
can, please, use our illegal transmitters to contact London.'

The Germans made it clear that they had to veto the drops for
defence reasons. It was also pointed out that no organisation for
distribution was available, so that the foodstuffs would end up on
the black market. Van der Vlugt added in the message that he,
too, was against the drops until he had had further talks with the
food authorities in Holland. He reminded London of the Nazi
decree which threatened every Dutchman with death if he picked
up something which came from an Allied plane.

Prince Bernhard, equally surprised by Ike's sudden announcement, was worried, too. Plans to use the BS forces for distribution were too dangerous, he told London, and he feared
that using the traditional drop-zones would make them 'useless
for other purposes'. He demanded that 'in order to co-ordinate
necessary measures' the Confidential Councillors must be
informed before action was taken. Next day the one-page pamphlets which were all that were left of the official Dutch press
printed – along with the news that street-fighting was going on in
Berlin, and that the price of bread would be increased by three
cents – a statement by Seyss-Inquart. It began: 'The Anglo-
Americans announce the dropping of small quantities of food, to
give the impression that they bring help against the hunger.
These quantities will never in reality be able to make up the
existing shortages . . . the measures announced by the Anglo-
Americans are nothing but a propaganda trick.' Instead, so
Seyss-Inquart revealed, the Germans had proposed to the Allies
that they should send ships and food transports from Brabant.
That alone would be acceptable to the Germans. 'All other
efforts . . . are but hollow propaganda with hidden military intentions against the German defences.'

It looked as if the Dutch had hoped too soon. Ike cabled to the
Combined Chiefs of Staff that he had received Seyss-Inquart's
telegram in which he rejected the food drops. 'As a result of this
message no free drops have been carried out.' But, as the Dutch
and the Allies soon discovered, the Nazi authorities were not as
negative as they seemed. When Louwes, Dr Hirschfeld and Van
der Vlugt met the State Commissioner again on 26 April, they

were given a friendly welcome with the words: 'So the blessing comes from above.'

The three Dutchmen told him that, now the population knew there was talk about food from the sky, they were not sure that the Dutch could be controlled if it failed to arrive. 'We have to find an arrangement that will make the drops possible,' Van der Vlugt argued. Louwes thought that it would be possible to drop the foodstuffs on four airports, and received the unexpected support of General Blaskowitz. The German commander had some days earlier remarked that he might have to surrender to the Allies on the day that all food supplies ran out, and possibly he hoped – with the unwitting help of the Allies – to delay that moment. Hirschfeld put more pressure on the State Commissioner by remonstrating that he was responsible for the well-being of 4.5 million people, that there was no food left and that he must sacrifice the stocks of the German Army – sufficient for four months – for the Dutch population.

Seyss-Inquart finally gave way to all these arguments, Blaskowitz made up a flight schedule and in the afternoon a telegram was sent to London, in which the Duindigt racecourse near The Hague, and Ypenburg, Valkenburg and Waalhaven (near Rotterdam) airports were designated as drop-zones. The operation could start on 27 April and would continue daily from eight o'clock in the morning till seven o'clock in the evening; the places would be marked with a white cross, and green and red lights would signal when the drops could start.

The BBC, who had just announced that the drops were cancelled, hastily withdrew the news-item, and on the British airfields enormous activity started. Operation Manna, as the British had christened it, was on its way. More than six hundred tons of food had to be loaded into the 253 Lancaster bombers which the RAF had provided. And on the night of 26 April twenty-seven volunteers worked in hail and snow to hoist the food, packed in bags normally used for cement, into specially designed straps in the bays where the bombs were usually suspended. Even crews just back from bombing missions over Germany lent a hand to stuff the planes. Each of them carried 3280 man-rations for one day in packs of twenty-three pounds each – containing flour, chocolate, egg powder, tea and even salt and pepper.

Communications between The Hague, London and Reims, in

the meantime, continued in order to settle the last details. Colonel Koot warned Ike to drop only inside the designated areas: 'German soldiers have been ordered to shoot at any aircraft outside the target zone' – and Van der Vlugt cabled him not to use Waalhaven as it was still mined, but to go to the Kralingse Lake instead.

By the late evening of 27 April everything was ready to go, and Eisenhower sent Seyss-Inquart a message that the air drops would start the next day. He reported at the same time to George Marshall in Washington that he had also told the Nazi official that 'if he attempted to interfere I would treat every officer and man responsible for such interference as violators of the laws of war'. He was bitterly angered by all the squabbles and told Marshall: 'While I have held my hand in fear of intensifying the Dutch suffering, if the German doesn't play the game absolutely, I intend to really punish him when I can. . . .'

The isolated Dutch in Occupied Holland waited impatiently while all these problems were sorted out at a higher level. Thursday, Friday and Saturday passed and nothing happened. It had only been a dream, which was now turning into a nightmare. They listened as much as possible to the radio, but the only news of importance was the death of Mussolini, executed by Italian partisans, and the fact that on 26 April the Americans and Russians had made their first contact on the Elbe. No news about the food-drops at all. Everybody talked about it, discussing the pros and cons; and, although some thought it a stupid plan because it could lead to chaos and fighting, most saw it as a sign that the war was almost over. And nobody knew that it was only the terrible weather that forced the planes to return to base six times after taking off. On one airfield the RAF crews got so irritated about the constant delays that they marched to their commander's office, shouting: 'The Dutch must get this food – the Dutch *will* get this food.'

At last on Sunday, 29 April, the first Lancasters were able to take off successfully, in spite of a freak blizzard which forced them down as low as 150 metres at times as they flew across the North Sea.

Amongst the commanders of the Lancasters was one Dutchman, H. P. J. Heukensfeldt-Jansen, and among the crews charged with unloading was the journalist H. George Franks. 'We

252

crossed the sea on our mission shortly after midday and approached The Hague at a very low level,' he reported. 'Our target area, the Ypenburg civil airport, was clearly visible. It had been marked out by Pathfinders with green flares and in the centre was a white cross surmounted by a red light.' A reporter from the *News Chronicle* in another plane, shaken by the storm, told his English readers: 'We had thought that the rain would have kept the Dutch inside, but they were waving sheets and tablecloths from the roofs. An old man on a bike waved so passionately that he almost fell off. There were hundreds of children in the street.'

'From the moment we crossed the Dutch coast, people in the fields and on the roads waved frantically,' Franks remembered. 'But it was not until we were actually flying over The Hague that we saw what this Manna from Heaven really meant for the Dutch.' The same inhabitants who eight weeks earlier had fled from the RAF bombs on their city were all out in the street, and it was a great moment for Franks when at a signal from the commander he pushed out the first parcels, which tumbled through the sky 'like confetti from a giant hand'. It was, he wrote, as if 'the grocer called on the people of The Hague – for the first time in years'.

One Englishman, the commander of a Flying Fortress, remembered even years later the joy and enthusiasm which he could see on the upturned faces as his plane skimmed the streets. 'We were eating roast-beef sandwiches in the plane and we felt it as an improper luxury. One of my men was so carried away that he threw his own tin of cigarettes down and others followed his example.' For those who participated in Operation Manna it was an unforgettable moment, but for us down there even more.

It was half-past one in the afternoon when the first planes approached their four drop-zones and in every house in western Holland a moment of tense silence fell. 'We stared at each other,' Raatgever in The Hague wrote. 'Bombers on Sunday? I looked outside and there I suddenly saw over the roofs two bombers, which roared like heavy cockchafers to the west. My youngest daughter began to cry and asked anxiously: "They won't do us any harm?" But we understood suddenly: those are the Allied planes that bring us food. We left our meal, raced outside, waved with hats, shawls, flags, sheets, with anything, to the planes which by now were thundering over our streets in an interminable stream. In a flash our whole quiet street was filled with a cheering, waving crowd and the elated people were even dancing on their roofs. . . . Many had tears in their eyes, others could not utter more than a few inarticulate cries. . . .'

Their emotions were too much for many. 'They shouted, cheered, cried and sang,' someone remembered, and even the writer Bert Voeten, who had been sceptical at first about the idea of the food-drops, changed his mind. 'They've been,' he wrote enthusiastically. 'They flew low past my window. The whole town was shaking. People ran like mad into the streets. It was beautiful. How could I ever have written that it was nonsense? Perhaps it is true, but the gesture alone does so much good.' A little girl told her mother: 'I was trembling when they came, but it was not because of the cold.' Van der Vlugt, whose efforts to get an agreement with the Nazi authorities had put him in danger of being kidnapped by the Underground, watched the scene from the roof of his house together with Louwes, and felt that it had all been worth while. He was deeply moved and immensely grateful.

When the planes arrived over Hilversum a few days later – the Germans had extended the drop-zones to ten – the same scenes were repeated. I remember very vividly this most moving moment of the war when forty heavily loaded planes flew low over the town and dropped their goods on the heath at Crailo. Our lane, so sad since the oak trees had disappeared that winter, and so shabby with its neglected houses, was full of waving and shouting people, while the green- and brown-coloured food-bombs, standing out sharply against the pale blue sky, came hurtling down. It gave me goose-pimples, and nobody cared about the tears that were running down all our faces.

An IKB report stated: 'Never will Holland forget the spectacle of the endless stream of planes which "bombarded" our terrorised cities with goods of which we had forgotten the existence.' Another official reported: 'The air-drop was psychologically a great success. The emotion and enthusiasm were so tremendous that one forgot one's hunger.' And a third commented in stilted, but heartfelt, words: 'If any emotions could still stir our hurt and blunted feelings, it was only these generous gifts of those who were recognised as our friends in the moment of our greatest distress.'

But the most moving expression of our feelings was in a poem from Yge Foppema.

> Pilots who came to us while waging
> The bloodiest war that ever yet befell
> Mankind, and that for five years had been raging
> Around and o'er us making life hell
> Lo, how we wave at you, now all is well.
> Look how we raise our children on our shoulders,
> And they will tell
> Their children's children when they're old and wise
> How man, like God, dropped Manna from the skies.

Princess Juliana celebrated her thirty-sixth birthday on Monday, 30 April. Still in London, she received a telegram that touched her profoundly. It was from 383 Dutchmen who had recently been liberated from the concentration-camp of Buchenwald. 'The Dutch in Buchenwald wish your Royal Highness, HM The Queen, the Prince of the Netherlands and the royal family a happy birthday and express the hope that it is given to you to return soon to a liberated Netherlands.' The Princess answered: 'I send you my deeply moved thanks for your message, on behalf of my mother and us all. We are longing to be able to welcome you soon in the Fatherland.'

But at Spelderholt, the headquarters of Prince Bernhard near Apeldoorn, the Prince's staff – and the Prince himself – forgot for once the birthday of the Princess. The organisation of the food-drops took all their attention. On that second day of Operation Manna there were still some problems to sort out to make it run more smoothly. Some of the Allied planes, for instance, had been shot at by the Germans. In a telegram from the Supreme Command, the Prince was asked to convey to Seyss-Inquart a request for an immediate ceasefire.

Another problem was Rotterdam. The telegram giving instructions to switch the flights to the Kralingse Lake had arrived too late, and the parcels had as a result been dropped in the mined Waalhaven, while others had landed in the water. Hungry citizens had not hesitated to run the risk of being blown up and had stormed the fields to seize some of the food 'bombs'. Part of the consignment had fallen into streets, killing one person, and on to houses, but there the public in general had behaved in a very disciplined way.

In one street, where a parcel of chocolate had fallen, the children were formed into a neat queue before the sweets were distributed. In another street the food had been given to the sick, but in most cases the parcels had been handed over to the authorities.

In The Hague there had not been enough transport, and in spite of the help from 4000 people 'flour, tea, and so on, got left out in the rain', it was reported. 'The worst off were the parcels with margarine. The loose packets were smashed flat on the ground, so that the margarine covered the field in a thin layer, but they say that a lot can still be saved.'

One thing was sure: the Germans – apart from the few shooting incidents – had stuck to their agreement and kept far away from the food supplies. On the first Sunday they had encircled all the landing-grounds with anti-aircraft guns and troops, in case the drops were an Allied stratagem, and Gestapo and SD were present to see if arms were amongst the parcels. But on the second day no German was to be seen, and the guns had disappeared.

One problem was more difficult to solve. The drops had caused an enormous emotional upheaval among the Dutch, which could have its dangers. 'Strange stories started to circulate, which all had one theme: Fortress Holland is surrendering tomorrow,' Raatgever noticed on the evening of 29 April in The Hague. 'Everywhere there are excited people discussing the possibilities, and here and there they start to jig and sing.' Diemer in Rotterdam reported the same atmosphere. 'We had to be indoors at eight, but then there was suddenly news that the capitulation by the German troops was a fact everywhere and that the Canadians would arrive tonight.' According to some, Stalin would announce the end of the war when on 1 May, Tuesday next, he gave his traditional May Day speech.

But it was nowhere near the truth and, although the drops went on day by day – a total of 500 British and 300 American planes would unload during that week no less than 7458 tons of food – many of the Dutch began to feel restless again. A report from one

Underground group voiced these feelings, pointing out that the air drops gave the impression that the liberation of western Holland was to be delayed. Radio Oranje had foreseen this and told us on 29 April: 'The help which has started has to be seen separately from the course of the war. Some might have the impression that the Allies are bringing us bread instead of freedom. But', the speaker assured us, 'you can face the future with confidence.'

Most of the Dutch were immensely grateful, and were convinced that the end of the war was near. 'Fear was finished and death fled,' wrote an Amsterdammer in his diary, and Diemer noted: 'We are no longer isolated from the world. The Dutch prison door has been rammed open.'

One question, however, kept us all guessing. When would we receive this treasure? Thousands of people were involved in sorting the stuff but, as Colonel Koot mentioned in his telegram to the Government in London, the Dutch had to be patient.

Louwes was indeed faced with an enormous problem. 'After we had transported the goods with great care to the warehouses, we had to see what we could distribute,' he explained later.

Some parcels contained a pound of pepper, others seven kilograms of margarine, or twenty kilograms of flour, and the Dutch food authorities were anxious to give everybody a reasonably balanced diet, consisting of a quantity of carbohydrates, fats and protein. 'We had to be careful also', Louwes recalled, 'that the inhabitants of one part of town should find the same goods in the shops to prevent arguments.' Everything had to be weighed and sorted out. To everybody's amazement very little was lost – only five per cent ended up in the wrong hands – but the days of scrupulous and even fussy organisation made it an agonising delay for us. And when, at last, it was distributed ten days later the food arrived too late for many.

'The efforts that were made to divide the goods as conscientiously as possible had undeniably cost tens of people their lives,' one authority revealed later. 'This happened in a country where for ten days, in the literal sense of the word, people had had *nothing* to eat.' It was the dark side of 'the finest dropping of the war'.

CHAPTER TWENTY-FIVE

'A Great Moment'

ACHTERVELD is barely a pinprick on the map of Holland. It lies eight kilometres east of Amersfoort, not far from the Grebbe Line, and it had never made history until Saturday, 28 April 1945. That day, just before eleven o'clock, a column of jeeps and staff-cars raced through the streets, preceded by military police with screaming sirens and white flags. The procession came to a halt in front of the St Josef School, and a few Allied officers jumped energetically out of their vehicles and walked briskly into the building. Major-General Sir Francis de Guingand, Montgomery's Chief of Staff, tall and very British, had arrived with Major-General A. Galloway, the Canadian who was responsible for the relief of Holland. In their company was the plump figure of Colonel J. Zenkowitsch, the representative of the Russian Army.

The group had flown that morning from Brussels to Nijmegen, and travelled from there by road through devastated Arnhem to Achterveld, for the first meeting with delegates from State Commissioner Seyss-Inquart. Two officers of the Canadian Army that occupied the region were waiting for them, and the men went at once into conference to discuss their approach to the Germans. 'There was an atmosphere of subdued excitement,' De Guingand wrote later, 'for it was obvious to everyone that something of great moment was taking place.'

The whole show was watched by the villagers who, wondering about the ceasefire that had started three hours earlier, excitedly discussed the chances of peace. Their hopes were raised higher when suddenly another car approached, with four blindfolded German officers in it. They had been brought from Amersfoort via a long-winded detour and looked, according to De Guingand, 'a rather miserable and cold-looking collection'. They were Dr Schwebel, the representative of Seyss-Inquart, and Dr Friedrich

Plutzar, the spokesman for General Blaskowitz, with two accompanying officers.

'I had arranged that the head civilian and the head soldier should be brought into the conference room to see me before the remainder was allowed in,' De Guingand wrote. 'The door opened and the two Germans stepped in.' After saluting, the Englishman saw with amazement that the two were extending their hands in greeting, but he ignored them and simply returned the salute. Their credentials were checked and the others were asked to come in and join them at two long tables in the bare classroom.

De Guingand started with a little speech in which he explained the situation as the Allies saw it: Germany had failed in its duty as occupying power and the Dutch population was seriously short of food. 'I said that I understood that the German High Command were now willing to allow us to send food in order to save the Dutch nation from starvation and General Eisenhower was prepared to help on the condition that the food would reach the Dutch and should not be taken by the Germans.'

While he was talking he studied Schwebel with distaste. Never had he seen such a repulsive man in his life. 'A plump, sweating German', he described him, 'who possessed the largest red nose I have ever seen, the end of which was like several ripe strawberries sewn together.' Schwebel, unaware of these thoughts, explained that he could make no definite commitments until Seyss-Inquart had seen the exact proposals, but he admitted that the situation was as the General had stated. The two teams now settled down to discuss the Allied relief plan, which was very extensive.

In the first place there were the food-drops – starting next day – which, as both parties agreed, were in fact the least practical but the fastest method; then relief by barges, loaded and ready to depart from southern Holland through the inland waterways, then by ship from Antwerp to Rotterdam, and finally by road and by rail. The Germans approved the whole scheme in principle, and it was decided that experts would meet on Sunday to arrange the details.

The proposed meeting between Seyss-Inquart and General Eisenhower's Chief of Staff, Bedell Smith, was the next point. De Guingand saw such a meeting as a necessity in order to formalise the relief agreement, but he hoped that it might also lead to the possible neutralisation of western Holland. Schwebel hesitated, but finally agreed that a conference should take place two days later, on Monday, 30 April. He wished to hold it on the German side of the front line, but De Guingand refused, 'pointing out that as we were undertaking a commitment which by all rules of war should have been theirs, therefore they should conform to our wishes'. The school in Achterveld was once more chosen as the meeting-place and, at the request of Schwebel, the Englishman promised that Seyss-Inquart could come without a blindfold. It didn't matter what he would see, he told the German, they had lost the war anyway.

It was time for lunch, and after some sandwiches De Guingand tried to get Schwebel on one side by himself, but the German was suspicious and insisted on keeping Dr Plutzar with him. They sat down in another classroom and, although De Guingand now knew very well that Schwebel had no authority to make decisions, he just wanted to see his reaction when he mentioned the word 'truce'. 'Having stressed the fact that they were now isolated from Germany, and that resistance in that country appeared to be collapsing, I pointed out how difficult feeding the Dutch would be if hostilities continued. For our part we were prepared to hold fast on the line of the Grebbe and Eem rivers.'

Schwebel, who never mentioned a word of this conversation in his official report to Seyss-Inquart, looked uncomfortable and, 'glancing repeatedly at the soldier next to him', said he was not empowered to discuss such matters. He promised to convey the remarks of De Guingand to his chief, and after the obligatory documents had been signed the Germans left for Occupied Holland. The hamlet returned to its usual quiet and peace.

While the conference was going on in Achterveld, astonishing news had reached The Hague: Himmler had offered Unconditional Surrender to the United States and Great Britain. The Confidential Councillors at once got in touch with Van der Vlugt, and the overworked mediator went to see Seyss-Inquart in the hope of finding out more.

The State Commissioner was too busy to receive Van der Vlugt, but two of his assistants told the Dutchman that they knew of nothing. If, however, there was truth in the rumour, they undertook to act as quickly as possible to prevent difficulties in the

Netherlands, in particular with the Dutch SS and the Landwacht, which might become troublesome. Van der Vlugt feared most for the lives of the prisoners, who might – as had happened in Vught, Zutphen and elsewhere – be massacred at the last moment, and the Germans thought that in that case 'the façade of German authority' must be maintained as long as possible, while behind it the handover of power was organised.

Next day, while the first planes dropped their food parcels over Holland, and the German troops in Italian Tyrol surrendered to the Allies, Schwebel told Van der Vlugt that there was no question of capitulation. 'Even Truman has published a denial,' he wrote. Obviously he knew nothing of the proposals from Himmler, passed on by Count Folke Bernadotte, the President of the Swedish Red Cross, of capitulation to the Western Allies, which both the United States and Britain had rejected as it was against the principle of Unconditional Surrender to all Allies, Russia included.

Van der Vlugt used that Sunday to compose a lengthy memorandum to Schwebel about a series of incidents. In many parts of Occupied Holland the Nazis had lost heart, he wrote. Some had offered to hand over their weapons to the Resistance and in one province the whole SD had wanted to surrender. At the same time flooding and destruction were going on contrary to all promises, and even executions still took place. It was obvious that the German authorities no longer had any control over their people and that quick action was required. He therefore demanded on behalf of the Dutch authorities that political prisoners should be at once released, the Dutch SS and Landwacht disarmed, and all explosives removed.

In Apeldoorn the same questions were discussed that day at the headquarters of Prince Bernhard. Van der Gaag and Neher, both back from London, were briefing the Prince, who had temporarily abandoned the food-drops because he had been invited, as Commander of the Dutch Army, to join the conference with Seyss-Inquart next day. Together they produced a programme of fourteen points to lay before the German authorities, exacting – apart from the usual demands of no executions, inundations or destruction – the release of female political prisoners, the handing over of the Nazified Dutch Red Cross to the Confidential Councillors, the replacement of Dutch SS by German troops, and a stop to the requisitioning of people, transport and telephones.

The Dutch in Occupied western Holland were initially completely ignorant of all that was happening, but suddenly that weekend a strange rumour flew round. 'It was so fantastic it was almost impossible to believe,' Raatgever wrote. According to the rumour, Prince Bernhard, together with American, British and Russian officers, had organised a meeting with the Nazi authorities somewhere near Amersfoort.

For once, the rumour was true. Early in the morning of Monday, 30 April, Seyss-Inquart left The Hague with Schwebel and Lieutenant-General P. Reichelt, the Chief of Staff of Blaskowitz, on his way to Achterveld. About the same time Louwes departed for the same destination with a Dutch team of six men in a car propelled by a gas generator. Louwes had been invited by the Germans to drive over with them, but had refused, afraid of being compromised. The evening before, however, he had received a telegram from Gerbrandy, who appealed to him to come, giving him a guarantee that he personally would safeguard his reputation. Louwes had none the less insisted on his own transport to underline his personal policy, and it had been accepted by the Germans.

Arriving at eleven o'clock at Amersfoort, the Dutch convoy joined the Germans and together they drove to Hoevelaken, where they had to stop. The Nazi authorities and the Dutch delegation, surrounded by soldiers with white flags, walked through the German line of fire to the main road, jumping over ditches and barbed wire. Some of the farms they passed were still inhabited, and people rushed out to ask the Dutchmen if all this meant peace or surrender, but the answer was noncommittal. At the crossing on the railway line from Amersfoort to Apeldoorn Canadian soldiers were waiting with a white flag to take over the guard from the Germans. It was a solemn moment, remembered by Dr Dols, Louwes' second-in-command. 'After a warm greeting for us, we took our place in jeeps and drove through the first lines of the Allied Front.' They then changed to limousines and, escorted by motorised police with white flags, drove to Achterveld.

The Dutch representatives were surprised to see red, white and blue flags waving everywhere and remembered suddenly that it was the birthday of Princess Juliana. At half-past twelve they arrived at the school in Achterveld. Prince Bernhard was waiting for them, taking photographs and leaning against an enormous Mercedes with the number-plate RKI (Reichskommissar 1). He had found the car in Apeldoorn and had been unable to resist the temptation to drive it to Achterveld. Seyss-Inquart was visibly shocked when he saw his own car again, but looked away coldly.

Shortly before, the excited villagers had cheered the arrival of General Bedell Smith and his team, which coincided with that of the Russian representative, Major-General Ivan Susloparov, from Paris, but now all eyes were on the Germans, 'the central figures in this drama'. A Canadian official reported: 'Leading the procession, limping along slightly in advance and looking straight in front of him, moved the hated Seyss-Inquart. . . .' They went into the school and, once they were inside, the Allied officers followed through another door.

While the Germans were kept under armed guard and without any refreshment in one classroom, in another the greetings and introductions took place over real Dutch refreshments. Especially for the Dutch from Occupied Holland it was a moving occasion. When the Prince's Chief of Staff, Charles van Houten, came into the room one of the Dutchmen rushed up to him and began to speak in English. Van Houten answered in Dutch, and for a moment the man stared at him before bursting into tears. Deeply moved, the officer had to answer hundreds of questions while some of his compatriots felt compelled to touch him.

The Prince, who at his arrival in Achterveld had been welcomed enthusiastically by the villagers with shouts like 'How is the Princess?' and 'Give our love to Juliana', was also surrounded at once by the Dutch team. Chatting with them, he gave them the first real cigarettes they had smoked in years. But the conference had to begin, and at exactly one o'clock the two enemies faced each other: Seyss-Inquart was furious at his reception, and even more so when Prince Bernhard refused to rise when he came into the room, but he listened attentively to the introduction, which dealt with the food situation.

In cold, matter-of-fact language De Guingand opened the discussion, repeating what had been proposed two days earlier. 'Bedell Smith asked Seyss-Inquart if the plan in outline was agreed to and, if so, could the detailed examination commence?' De Guingand noted: 'The German appeared to be satisfied and so the meeting broke up and various study groups were formed to examine each particular problem.' There was a naval group to deal with the shipping, an air group for the food-drops and so on, each composed of a British, Dutch and German representative.

'Watching this scene I found it difficult to believe I wasn't dreaming,' De Guingand remembered. 'For all intents and purposes it reminded me of a staff-college exercise with the study-groups arguing amongst themselves as to the best way to solve the particular problem.' It was, he thought, particularly 'a delight' to watch the Dutch, and 'their pleasure at having contact with the Allies and the outside world after all this time'. It was obvious to him that they now knew that the end of their sufferings was very near, and he noticed with satisfaction 'they could not believe that we were prepared to help to such a large extent'. Louwes was very impressed indeed and found the result of all the deliberations most encouraging. It looked as if food could start coming in the next day.

Bedell Smith did not take part in the talks. He had decided he could use the time to find out what Seyss-Inquart thought about the surrender of the German forces in Holland. In the presence of Prince Bernhard and some others, and over stiff gins, this serious business was tackled. Bedell Smith explained first that Eisenhower was very disturbed at the plight of the Dutch and that he was holding the Germans responsible for any disasters. 'He then went on to describe the general situation,' De Guingand reported. 'He said that it was only a matter of weeks, or perhaps days, before Germany must admit complete and absolute defeat.' Seyss-Inquart reacted with the surprising words 'I entirely agree', and Bedell Smith at once asked him why he should not surrender now.

Seyss-Inquart had received an anxious phone call from Blaskowitz in Hilversum the night before, warning him that their superiors in Berlin had got wind of the talks, and he answered now that he had received no orders which would allow him to take such action and that it was the task of the Commander-in-Chief, Blaskowitz, to decide. Bedell Smith shrugged. 'But surely, Reichskommissar, it is the politicians who dictate the policy to the soldiers, and in any case our information points to the fact that no real Supreme Command exists any more in Germany today.'

The argument visibly made a deep impression on Seyss-Inquart, but he asked stubbornly: 'But what would future generations of Germans say about me if I complied with your suggestion – what would history say about my conduct?' Bedell Smith decided to get tough. 'Now look here, Reichs-Marshal' – as he called him by mistake – 'General Eisenhower has instructed me to say that he will hold you directly responsible for any further useless bloodshed. You have lost the war and you know it. And if through pig-headedness, you cause more loss of life to Allied troops or Dutch civilians, you will have to pay the penalty. And you know what that means – the wall and the firing squad.'

Seyss-Inquart seemed to have lost his voice and stared with watery eyes behind his glasses at Bedell Smith, before whispering: 'I am not afraid – I am a German.' Bedell Smith gave up. 'I wonder if you realise I am giving you your last chance?' he asked sharply. The German nodded. 'Yes, I realise that.' 'You know the feelings of the Dutch people towards you?' Smith asked again. 'You know you will probably be shot?' Seyss-Inquart hesitated a moment and then said softly: 'That leaves me cold.' For Bedell Smith the only and obvious answer was: 'It usually does.'

The deliberations about the relief programme had in the meantime been finalised: sixteen hundred tons of food would be sent in daily to the distressed area, seven hundred by rail from Den Bosch to Ede, three hundred by road to Amersfoort and six hundred by barge to Renkum. The trucks would go through a special corridor between Wageningen and Rhenen, and the port of Rotterdam would be opened at the end of the week for the arrival of three ships with two thousand tons. The historic conference had come to an end, but before the parties dispersed it was decided to meet again on 2 May at Wageningen. When someone remarked that there was no bridge over the river, Galloway laughed and answered: 'We will take care of that.'

Seyss-Inquart stepped into the waiting car, but Schwebel pulled at his sleeve: 'We have refused to capitulate,' the delegate told him, 'and rightly so, but I have the impression that we are the only Germans to have had a serious talk with the enemy. Let us, before we leave, ask General Bedell Smith to give you a safe-conduct to Berlin to ask their permission to begin talks about a general surrender.'

Schwebel had just come from the American Chief of Staff,

where he had pleaded for one last effort to come to some arrangement. It was nothing to him personally, he told Bedell Smith. He had lost his wife and sons and he cared nothing for his own future, but, as Bedell Smith wrote in his memoirs, 'he felt that many lives might be saved by resuming the conversation'. Schwebel, who had discovered that Bedell Smith was the grandson of a German officer, thought – as he wrote rather optimistically in his report of the meeting – that the American general understood that Seyss-Inquart refused to leave his country in the lurch. It might therefore be possible to try to find a solution from a different angle, he reasoned, and Bedell Smith had agreed to try once more.

But he had not expected what now followed. Seyss-Inquart, taking Schwebel's advice and still dreaming of an international role in politics, turned back to him with the new idea of asking for a pass to go to Berlin. It was vetoed at once. Holland alone was his affair, Bedell Smith told the State Commissioner, and he reported later to Eisenhower that he had refused permission to Seyss-Inquart to go to Berlin 'on the grounds that if he wished to surrender Holland he could do so forthwith'. He explained to the Nazi at the same time that 'the methods of approach to the Supreme Commander, recognised by the customs of war, remained available to the German military commanders'.

Seyss-Inquart must have misunderstood him. In his report Schwebel stated that Bedell Smith had reacted positively, and had said that under the circumstances a safe-conduct would be possible. According to Schwebel the American had told Seyss-Inquart that the decision was up to Eisenhower, to whom 'he would give the official request from the State Commissioner'.

The Germans left 'in much better spirits' than they had arrived, Prince Bernhard later heard. Returning into Occupied territory Seyss-Inquart even had the nerve to tell Louwes that it had been 'a magnificent reception'. How the Dutch felt about being back in Occupied Holland he did not ask and they left him in a hurry to celebrate the birthday of one of them, and the fact that help was on its way. Eisenhower, in his report to Gerbrandy in London and the British Chiefs of Staff, wrote: 'The conferences were . . . completely successful in respect of the introduction of food into western Holland, but otherwise results were entirely negative.'

Seyss-Inquart, according to Bedell Smith, had 'lost his last chance to show the slightest magnanimity of heart or concern for useless suffering'. He would pay dearly for it.

CHAPTER TWENTY-SIX

The Game Is Over

'IT IS reported from the Führer's Headquarters that our Führer, Adolf Hitler, has fallen this afternoon at his command post in the Reich Chancellery fighting to the last breath against Bolshevism and for Germany,' announced Hamburg Radio, the only radio station still in German hands, on Tuesday, 1 May, at half-past ten in the evening. 'On Monday the Führer appointed Admiral Doenitz as his successor.'

In western Holland, where the hungry Dutch were waiting with growing impatience for the distribution of the Allied 'food bombs', and even more eagerly for their liberation, the news of the death of 'the scourge of the earth and the idol of the Germans' was very calmly received. Nobody knew how he had died, but that he had 'heroically fallen in the war', as one paper wrote, nobody believed. Some refused even to believe that he had died at all. 'I tell you,' an Amsterdammer wrote in his diary, 'they will make him rise from his grave just like Jesus Christ, perhaps in three days, perhaps in a year, whenever the Nazi gang thinks it fit.' Only much later did it become known that Hitler, after marrying his mistress Eva Braun, had committed suicide in his bunker in the heart of Berlin.

The only people who mourned his death in Holland were the few NSB members still left. *Volk en Vaderland*, the Nazi weekly, dedicated its last ever issue to a eulogy in which Hitler was described as 'not only Germany's greatest son, but the greatest European who had ever lived'. History – 'always right' – would judge Hitler, the editor Jan Hollander stated, 'but it is already now beyond a doubt that the nameless soldier from the First World War will live on in history when all his contemporary rivals are forgotten'. Edzard Modderman, editor of the SS weekly *Storm*, was convinced that a 'future without the Führer does not exist. His heroic death is not the end, it is the beginning. Adolf Hitler, our Führer, is and remains for us and for always the security for the future,' he rambled on, 'even for the Dutch nation.'

Seyss-Inquart, in a statement which he did not bother to translate into Dutch, said: 'German soldiers, German men and women, German youth in Fortress Holland. I call you, listen and understand with a strong heart: our Führer has fallen in the battle, his visible work has ended. . . . His spirit will never disappear. . . . Don't cover his picture, but bring flowers to him, who has made our lives proud and worth living.'

By the time it was published, the State Commissioner was already in a speedboat on the North Sea on his way to Germany, where Admiral Doenitz waited for him at his Navy headquarters at Plon in Schleswig-Holstein. In his will Hitler had at last offered his 'Governor' in the Netherlands what he had wished for so desperately: the post of Foreign Minister. It would, Seyss-Inquart thought, give him a better chance to play his role in history and to discuss his ideas of negotiations with the Western Allies.

For the Dutch, the end of the war now seemed a matter of days, but they were very long days. 'If it comes soon,' Dr Mees recorded on 2 May, 'it will be just in time to save us from a terrible and immense disaster (although it will be too late for many). It is awful, the hunger. . . . Everything and everybody is so poorly and shabbily dressed. Close friends are hardly recognisable, they are so thin, hollow-eyed with pale colour and with clothes which are much too large.' The food-drops, however, continued and were still greeted as enthusiastically as in the beginning. 'This morning four hundred American Flying Fortresses delivered 800,000 kilograms of food,' the Rotterdam doctor wrote, 'and this afternoon many Lancasters. We have now received a total of 3.5 million kilograms.'

Even more efficient help had now started. At seven o'clock on 2 May Lieutenant-Colonel E. A. de Geer had given the starting signal for Operation Faustus and the first three-ton trucks began their journey through no-man's-land to a food depot at Rhenen. 'It is the intention to deliver twenty-five hundred tons daily,' Radio Oranje told us, which meant that every Dutchman would receive seventeen hundred calories a day. The first day the load consisted mainly of fats and on Thursday, 3 May, the trucks brought tinned meat, biscuits and sugar. From that day on, the operation was in full swing, and for the next week every half-hour a convoy of thirty vehicles crossed the truce line. The Canadians had 750 trucks available, while the Dutch food authorities had selected 200 Dutch drivers, who had first to be instructed on how to handle the trucks as most of them were no longer used to driving petrol-engined vehicles. Radio Oranje reported how delighted they had been to receive some cigarettes, 'because the only people who smoked were the supervising SS men, who had enormous cigars'.

How the first convoys were greeted is not difficult to guess. When the first hundred and twenty trucks rolled into Utrecht with three hundred tons of food, the whole city was in uproar. Women embraced the drivers, who, after unloading, turned back in a hurry to collect a new load.

The BBC reporter, Robert Dunnett, followed one of the transports and cabled: 'All was silent as we passed through the deserted wreckage of the little town of Wageningen and with a rather naked feeling we passed through our forward infantry positions, along a dead straight, cobbled main road, lined with tall trees running between the green fields and orchards in late blossom. We passed through a roadblock the Germans had built and broken up again to allow food convoys through.' About four hundred yards farther on he saw an astonishing sight: crates and barrels of food for about two miles. Two SS men were cycling up and down, while a British dispatch rider passed them unhindered. Dutch police in their black uniforms stood chatting to Canadian and British officers. At the bottom of the road was a stout wooden barrier with smoke rising from the houses beyond it: the German positions.

A Dutchman told Dunnett how urgently the help was needed. 'People in big Dutch towns had been keeping more and more to their houses. Some had notices on their doors saying: "Any food left here will be welcomed", but they had not the strength to go out looking for it. The death-rate is still rising, and they are unable to bury the dead.'

The men who were let through by the Germans to drive the trucks looked 'sallow or pale and pinched', and an officer told Dunnett that they were tremendously willing to work, but got tired very quickly. As one lorry was being unloaded a little sugar was sprinkled on to the road. 'To the Dutchmen who scooped it up, it was one of the biggest treats of their lives.' When he returned to the Canadian front, a Dutchman came up to him and asked in broken English, 'You coming soon?' but he added sadly: 'It is no good – all floods and Germans.'

It was only too true: despite their promises, the Germans were continuing to flood vast tracts of Dutch farmland, and placing explosives at strategic points. Prince Bernhard warned both the Supreme Command and Gerbrandy in London that the Germans had taken away from their meeting with Bedell Smith the unfortunate impression that the Allies were a soft proposition – 'much easier to talk to . . . than those demanding and aggressive Dutch in The Hague' – and that the reality of surrender might still be weeks away.

Angrily, Bedell Smith dispatched curt messages to Seyss-Inquart and Blaskowitz. 'I am informed that the German Occupation forces are carrying out raids, and shooting and flooding has not ceased,' said the telegram to the German army commander. 'I have informed the Reichskommissar that I will hold him personally responsible. . . .' And he wired to the anxious and indignant Gerbrandy: ' A strong message has been sent to Seyss-Inquart telling him he will be held responsible for misdeeds, shootings included.'

Prince Bernhard seized the opportunity to tackle Dr Schwebel on the same subject when the two men met on 2 May to discuss relief questions. What was being done, asked the Prince, to stop the executions and inundations? Schwebel, embarrassed, admitted that no orders had been given to stop them since the Nazis were waiting to know the outcome of the negotiations. In an angry outburst, the Prince told him that this was no way to deal with the Allies, and demanded that the Landwacht and the Dutch SS be disarmed at once, and that the other conditions be observed – demands which Schwebel undertook to pass on to Blaskowitz.

The Prince's rage produced results. The relieved Dutch noticed that the German soldiers suddenly disappeared from the street. 'They have a curfew,' Diemer reported. Only the SS and SD were still roaming around, and capable of anything. It was a strange time. 'We're sitting between coercion and freedom,' Diemer said. Radio Oranje constantly warned listeners not to take any hasty action, and to remain vigilant. But the feeling roused by the approach of Liberation could no longer be suppressed. 'All flags had been taken out of their boxes,' he wrote on Thursday, 3 May, 'and the orange ribbons are ready. The radio-sets have been taken out of attics and sheds, and put back in their old place in the living-room, clean and ready for use.'

This time, expectations were no longer based on false hopes, and on that day negotiations for a real truce were opened between Lieutenant-General Charles Foulkes, the commander of the Canadian troops in the Netherlands, and General Blaskowitz. It was the first time that a German and an Allied commander met in Holland without the presence of a Nazi official and, when Blaskowitz returned on Friday, Foulkes decided to try to open the eyes of this stubborn German with the froglike face. He told him of the capitulation of the German army in Italy and, pointing to a map on the wall, showed him what was left of Germany. The General paled and looked disturbed, but his German military mentality made it impossible for him to disobey orders, and he would agree only to a total truce during the food transports. In the afternoon British and German field telephonists met together in no-man's-land to lay a 'hot line' connecting Blaskowitz's headquarters with that of Foulkes.

The same afternoon, an even more unusual meeting took place. In a villa in Laren near Hilversum, leaders of the Dutch Resistance were received by Lieutenant-General Reichelt, Chief of Staff of the Wehrmacht in Fortress Holland. Never before had the two enemies been willing to get together, but through a middleman, a former director of Philips, Walterscheid, the German officer had made it known that he would appreciate a discussion with those partisans. One problem had to be solved before the talks could start. The Wehrmacht General only wanted to meet someone of the same rank, and with some difficulty Colonel Koot, who thought this beneath his military honour, was persuaded to pretend he was a general, too – a fiction made fact later in the day by Prince Bernhard.

At first, the main subject of the discussions seemed to be the German preparations for destruction and inundation which the Resistance wished to have halted. Reichelt promised to do his best, but then suddenly switched to his real reason for wishing to see the Dutchmen. Turning to Koot, he asked abruptly: 'Are your troops recognised?'

Koot answered briefly: 'Yes, General.'

'By whom?' the German wanted to know.

'By our Queen.'

'May I ask you where your Queen is?'

'In Anneville near Breda.'

'I suppose that you can get in touch with the Queen?'

The answer was a short 'yes'. Reichelt thought briefly.

'I would like to ask you something,' he began hesitantly. 'Are you willing to ask your Queen if for an honest German general and his honest German soldiers – and I don't count the Gestapo, SS, the Green Police, the Dutch Landwacht and other scum – there is any possibility of receiving in advance a guarantee that they will not be handed over to the Russians?' The truth had come out, if with some difficulty.

Koot, slightly taken aback, could only say one thing. He told the General that German soldiers had obeyed the Führer and had committed acts against the laws of war. This was all too well known to the Allies. He would nevertheless inform the Queen of the request.

'And if you don't do that,' concluded Reichelt, 'then we will fight on to the bitter end.'

During the conversation Reichelt had made it very clear that Seyss-Inquart no longer counted for anything. The State Commissioner was in fact still absent in Schleswig-Holstein, preparing for his great role as mediator. On 3 May he had reported his talks with Bedell Smith to Doenitz and, although he had no great hope of splitting the Allies and persuading the Americans and British to accept Germany's capitulation, he felt that it was worth the effort to try.

He wanted to return at once to Holland to get in touch with the Allied Supreme Command, but a violent storm prevented his boat leaving the harbour at Plon and instead he telephoned to Schwebel in The Hague. That afternoon a surprised Van der Vlugt received a visit from the German delegate, who told him excitedly that Seyss-Inquart had been appointed as the contact man with the Allies. 'But he is unable to return,' he told Van der Vlugt, begging him to be so kind as to ask the Allies for a safe-conduct for Seyss-Inquart to Holland 'so that he can start the peace negotiations from here'. Van der Vlugt was not very much impressed and, showing Schwebel the door, told him that there was only one thing left for the Germans: Unconditional Surrender – adding 'and for that they have no need of Seyss-Inquart. Let him stay with Doenitz.'

Whether Schwebel reported this remark to Seyss-Inquart is unknown, but the State Commissioner next day made another effort to return to Holland, this time overland. He got no farther than Hamburg, where his car, mingling with the Allied military traffic, could not remain unnoticed. A British military policeman stopped him, and when Seyss-Inquart showed him his papers with the words 'I'm going to Montgomery' the policeman agreed laconically: 'You bloody well are.'

Together with his three companions the State Commissioner was taken to the Atlantik Hotel, where a Dutch captain, just leaving the hotel, could not believe his eyes and exclaimed: 'But that is Six-and-a-Quarter.' For Seyss-Inquart, the game was over.

All the other Germans had to wait a few hours longer for the end, but that evening the German troops in north-west Germany, Denmark, the Friesian Islands and in Holland surrendered to Montgomery. The *Vliegende Hollander* ('Flying Dutchman') – the popular little pamphlet, produced in London by Radio Oranje man Louis de Jong and during those last months regularly dropped over Holland, bringing us the latest news – wrote in its last issue that the signing of the capitulation was one of the most dramatic moments in the war. 'Montgomery treated the Germans coldly and ruthlessly,' the reporter wrote. 'He showed them his maps to prove that their position was hopeless, and on Friday, 4 May 1945, at ten-past eight the Germans understood it.' On that rainy cold evening Admiral Hans von Friedeburg and General Eberhard Kinzel, with three other Germans, entered Monty's tent on the Lüneburg Heath.

The Field-Marshal followed them and, turning to the waiting journalists, said smilingly: Gentlemen, this is the moment.' They took their seats at a simple wooden table covered with a blue cloth, and Montgomery read out slowly the conditions for capitulation. The five Germans listened without a flicker of an eyelid, and signed without a word. Montgomery was last. The whole ceremony had taken five minutes: one million German soldiers surrendered unconditionally.

Montgomery at once informed Eisenhower, who issued a statement to the press and radio, announcing the disintegration of the German forces on the Western Front. He added a warning: 'Any further losses the Germans incur on this front are due to their failure instantly to quit. They know they are beaten and any hesitation is due either to their own stupidity or that of the German Government. On land, sea and air the Germans are thoroughly whipped. Their only recourse is to surrender.' Churchill sent an elated telegram to Anthony Eden in San Francisco, bringing him the news of the 'tremendous surrender' with the understatement: 'This is quite a satisfactory incident in our military history.'

Louis de Jong in London got the news from a BBC colleague just when he had concluded his news broadcast on Radio Oranje – with the laconic excuse: 'Sorry, old chap, we just forgot.' But Radio Rising Netherlands did better and was the first to break the news – two minutes earlier than the BBC. Broadcaster Henk van den Broek was still working in his office in Eindhoven, when at 8.45 p.m. the telephone rang and an excited editor told him that the press agencies were talking about a capitulation of the German army in the western sector. What to do? Was Holland included?

One telephone call to an Allied official was sufficient to confirm that Fortress Holland had fallen, too. 'Half a minute to let it penetrate,' Van den Broek wrote later. 'The Germans have capitulated. . . . Five years of waiting and longing are rewarded.'

A few minutes later he was breathlessly sitting behind the microphone. Without a text, stuttering, and in half-formed sentences Van den Broek told his Dutch listeners at two minutes before nine o'clock that their country was free again. It was the highlight of his career. Five minutes later he was back with more information: for Holland the capitulation would be in force from Saturday, 5 May, at eight o'clock in the morning. 'Long live the Queen, long live victory.'

CHAPTER TWENTY-SEVEN

The Capitulation

ON FRIDAY, 4 May, at nine o'clock in the evening, Hilversum was very quiet. The eight o'clock curfew kept people indoors and, apart from a few patrolling German soldiers and Dutch police-men, the streets were deserted. It was still daylight and I was lying in bed, dozing off. Suddenly I heard the slamming of doors and excited voices in the lane. Jumping out of bed I peered outside. Everywhere people were talking, laughing, shaking hands as if congratulating each other, slapping each other on the back and kissing. I raced downstairs, where in the little room my parents were looking at each other in bewilderment. 'The Germans have capitulated,' my father said, and nobody stopped me when I rushed upstairs again, got dressed and went outside.

Eleven years old, I was still too small to be noticed, but I listened eagerly to the grown-ups, emaciated and sallow, but so relieved, happy as I had never seen them before. Montgomery had done it, and the Canadians would come tomorrow. Here and there in spite of the radio's warning – 'the Germans are still around' – a flag appeared. In the middle of a little group I discovered a Jewish girl I had known years ago, but whose existence I and all the others had forgotten. She had spent three years in an attic room of our neighbour's and nobody had known it. She was deathly pale, but her eyes glittered and she just could not stop talking. A little farther on a group of young men were looking around them as if dazed. Years of 'diving' indoors had given them the same paleness and the same stiffness of movement as the girl.

Suddenly a radio in a window blared the Wilhelmus, our national anthem. A silence fell, and some began with trembling voices to sing; others followed. Not the six stanzas the Germans had allowed during the war; this time it was the forbidden first verse – 'Wilhelmus of Orange, am I of Dutch blood; true to the fatherland am I till death'. It was composed in the sixteenth century, when the Dutch fought for eighty years their War of Liberation against the Spanish tyrant, and it expressed the longing for freedom that our forefathers had felt. The feeling hadn't changed over all those centuries – we were free.

In the lane around the corner the sound of a gramophone: 'When the Saints Go Marching In'. That's how we felt about the Allies; and I, who had never heard it before, listened spell-bound while some people began to dance. Someone had found a bottle of Genever, saved for this occasion, and did the rounds; someone else gave cigars away, and everybody laughed and cried and shouted and danced. Five frightful years of oppression, eight terrible months of hunger, were over. A new world was about to begin.

I had hardly been six years old when I saw the first proud German soldiers march into Hilversum, silently watched by the Dutch. For five long years I had only been able to sniff longingly at a pot which had once contained peanut butter, but had never lost the smell of it – now I would taste it again. I would eat bananas, oranges, chocolate – but no more rye cakes, sugarbeet or skimmed milk. For eight long months I had tried to read and do my homework by the light of a candle or a little wick in a bowl filled with oil – soon we would be able to switch on the lights again. No more fear at the sound of jackboots; of the Landwacht who might confiscate my load of collected wood; of bombs. Real shoes, instead of crude wooden pattens. Perhaps even a bike, and certainly train rides again.

Although I, as a young boy, had suffered very little compared to so many, even I felt the excitement, the joy, and the sadness for those who had not survived, and I simply watched, sitting on the stump of a tree long since disappeared into someone's stove, while dusk fell and the people danced and sang. We'd woken up from a nightmare.

It was the same everywhere. 'Those who had heard the news rushed into the streets and shouted it to each other,' wrote a Rotterdammer. Another remembered: 'We didn't know any more what to do. We went to friends, but met them halfway. . . . I saw people dancing in the street, they were jumping up and down. Honourable burghers who would never lose their composure, and certainly would never run, were now racing around

277

like boys, hugging each other, throwing their hats in the air. . . . It must be a silly sight, but what does it matter? Nothing matters, we all have a feeling that fills us till we burst – and only shouting and wild movements can release us.'

Douwenga, the evacuee from Wageningen, still in Naarden and thin and exhausted, heard the news from a neighbour. 'It is finished. We're dancing in the room, then suddenly silence. Someone opened the piano; we're choking with emotion and then we sing with all our heart our beautiful Wilhelmus. . . . At last we are free, no war, no hunger, no terror, no danger. . . . We can speak without fear, we can breathe freely.'

The 'diver' Maurits Dekker in Amsterdam left his hiding-place: 'There were more people in the streets like us, singing, with a head full of joy and an empty stomach.' In The Hague a school-teacher who had also been hiding walked around in a daze. 'I meet my neighbours and see them close-up. It gives me a shock. Some are so thin that I hardly recognise them. . . . It is terrible; pale emaciated faces, but the joy shines in all the eyes, the happiness for our new-born freedom.' Some people were too weak to come outside, but one did it nevertheless: 'He is leaning against the doorposts and tears are rolling down his cheek.'

*A Jewish girl, after five years of total isolation and fear, is sobbing over her diaries. 'I feel strange, glad and sad, at the same time, sad because we, Jews, lost the war. My first reaction is a crying fit. I think of the thousands and ten thousands who have been taken away and are unable to celebrate this great, unforgettable moment.'

In the prison in the Weteringschans in Amsterdam the journalist A. H. van Namen, arrested in January by the SD, peeped through the bars of his cell windows. A man was standing on the roof of the neighbouring Park Hotel, with a flagpole. 'What is he doing? He puts it up and fastens it. . . . If there were only a Dutch flag waving from it, I thought in my silly optimism. . . . And three minutes later a large orange flag is blowing in the wind on the roof. I can't believe it. It cannot be true. I pace the cell as I have done before. Six paces one way, six back. Peace? Capitulation? When will I be sure? Oh, God, give me the certainty. I cannot stand it any longer.'

Only a few yards away a German soldier recorded his feelings. The telephone in his office, the German headquarters on the

Museumplein, had fallen silent. 'The guards were doing their duty as always. The dispatch drivers were bored, hanging around in a corner. Soldiers go up and down these stairs, as before. The secretaries are sitting behind their desks and staring out of their windows. On the roofs, on top of the Rijksmuseum the Dutch flags are waving, English planes are glittering in the sunlight on their way to the south. Some of us show their powerless fury with an occasional curse, then they fall silent again, waiting without a word for the unknown, as we have learned in those long years of soldiering.'

The most moving expression of what the free Dutch felt that evening was perhaps the demonstration at Anneville near Breda. Queen Wilhelmina, together with Princess Juliana, had settled there after returning to her country on 26 April. She had planned her homecoming without informing the Government until the last moment, only telling General Kruls, the Chief of the Dutch Military Authority, what her intentions were during a visit to London. The General, taken by surprise, rushed back to Breda to discover that Anneville, the little castle chosen for Wilhelmina as her temporary residence, and only just vacated by the Dutch Army Command, had no furniture whatsoever, no stores of food and no guards.

With the help of neighbours, he scraped some necessities together and, when a message came from London that the Queen was ready to leave, the house was habitable, if rather primitively equipped.

'I left Laneswood with the same little suitcase I had carried when I arrived in Harwich five years before,' the Queen wrote in her memoirs. Accompanied by Princess Juliana and England-vaarders Erik Hazelhoff Roelfzema and Peter Tazelaar she drove to the RAF airfield nearby, where a DC3 was waiting to take her to Gilze-Rijen near Breda. Take-off was slightly delayed since her two aides, taking a quick cup of coffee, were watching the wrong runway. When they finally discovered their mistake, they found a few furious Dutch dignitaries waiting, but the Queen smiled. 'I understand it very well,' she remarked to the embarrassed young men. 'You were having a drink to celebrate our going home.'

At Gilze-Rijen the two men were the first to leave the plane, and then the Queen appeared. 'She breathed in the air with great pleasure,' Roelfzema wrote later, 'and looked down the steps.

279

They were steep, and there was but one railing at the left side, where Peter was standing. I stretched out my hand to help her, but she paid no attention at all. The first step on the soil of the fatherland after five years of exile, and helped by somebody? No question of it.'

In the windy airport a small crowd of Dutchmen were waiting – and trying hard to recover from a shock received a few minutes earlier. One of the planes of the Queen's convoy had made a crash landing and disappeared in a cloud of dust and smoke. Firemen rushed to help, followed by an anxious Prince Bernhard, but it turned out that it was not the Queen's plane, and, just as she landed, formality had returned. The RAF Guard of Honour was standing rigidly at attention, while Prince Bernhard, still slightly shaken, embraced his mother-in-law and his wife.

There were no speeches or other official ceremonies and the Queen drove straight to Anneville, where she with the Princess, her two aides and her secretary settled down at once to a frugal existence. She insisted on sticking to the official rations, and when she filled in a request for her ration-card she did this under the name 'Wilhelmina', profession 'Queen'.

'We had not yet recovered from the first emotions of our homecoming,' she remembered later, 'when on the fourth of May the news came that armistice had been signed. We had just finished dinner and I had returned to the drawing-room to do a little more work when Tazelaar came dashing into the room and nearly speechless with emotion only just managed to say: "The armistice has been signed; it's peace." What a sensation, what an indescribable burden was lifted off me at that moment. . . . We could live as normal people again. . . .' Tazelaar told Roelfzema, who had been absent at this historic moment, how the Queen and he had shaken each other's hand 'like mad'. 'I even believe that she was slapping my shoulder with the other hand.'

That day General Kruls paid the Queen a visit to discuss future plans and to ask her if she was satisfied with her accommodation. Far from accepting his apologies for the primitive circumstances Wilhelmina complained to him that the surroundings were too luxurious and once again she repeated her romantic wish to live in one of the small houses near the church in Ulvenhout, or to knock on the door of a farmhouse and ask for shelter. The General left her for a conversation with Juliana, and it was then that the good news reached the Queen through Tazelaar.

Radiant, she came out of her room to tell Juliana and the General, and in his memoirs the ambitious Kruls mentioned proudly, but wrongly, that he was the first to congratulate her – Tazelaar had beaten him to it.

He was quickly followed by the other members of the Queen's staff, who came rushing into the castle. The Queen proposed a toast, realising at the same time, however, that there was no alcohol in Anneville. Fortunately her aides had not exactly obeyed her orders to keep alcohol out of the house, and now confessed this. For once Queen Wilhelmina smiled indulgently, and the bottles were allowed to appear.

A proposal by Princess Juliana that they should go to Breda was rejected by the Queen, who feared that it would lead to too great an excitement for the people there. The population of Breda, anyhow, had a much better idea. Spontaneously a procession was formed in the town, and set out for Anneville. A policeman saw the crowd approaching and went to the castle to alert the Queen. In a hurry all the lights were switched on, while the headlights of a car were directed to the terrace before the house, where Wilhelmina and her daughter took their place. The gates were opened, and the singing and waving crowd was let in to salute this little dumpy lady who for all those years had been for them the symbol of freedom.

It was the warmest welcome Queen Wilhelmina could have wished. It was her real homecoming, and Roelfzema felt, as he wrote, that 'something happened between people and Queen which escaped us'. The march went on for hours, and only a rainstorm at midnight could at last cool the enthusiasm of Queen and people.

Peter Tazelaar had been sent to invite Prince Bernhard to come to Anneville and join the celebrations, but he met with an accident and was taken into hospital, where he was discovered only a few days later. It was, anyhow, doubtful if the Prince would have had time to leave his headquarters in Spelderholt. He had preoccupations of his own.

Bernhard had heard the news of the capitulation from a cyclist who yelled 'The surrender is signed' to him, just as he was leaving a telephone box – which in this case was a transformer-station from where the lines to the Underground in Occupied country ran. The conversation he had had with the BS commander, Colonel Koot, had deeply disturbed him. The Colonel had told him that he feared he would be unable to control his men any longer and asked the Prince if he could arrange for the surrender of the Germans to his troops. The Prince had promised to do his best and, hearing now of the capitulation, rushed to General Foulkes, who confirmed that the documents had been signed. 'The Germans are to hand over their arms to us,' he announced, 'and your people in Occupied Territory are not to bear arms for at least three days.' Deeply upset by this blow, the Prince rang Henri Koot again, who promised to try to do his best to keep his men in check.

Coming home to Spelderholt, the Prince found his staff celebrating and for a moment he relaxed. With a glass of champagne, left behind by Seyss-Inquart, he made a little speech warning them that 'the worst was over, but the real peace had still to be won'. He left his 180 men and women at their party, and disappeared to think about a speech he intended to make to his Forces of the Interior the next day in which he would have to explain why, after so many years of waiting and preparations, they were not now needed. That night he did not sleep.

He was not the only one. 'It is Saturday morning, a quarter-past three,' a schoolteacher in Delft jotted down in his diary. 'I still cannot fall asleep. The events of the last hours have moved me so much that I cannot relax in spite of my tiredness. Hundreds of thoughts thunder like wild horses through my brain.' Like everybody else he was waiting tensely for eight o'clock in the morning when the capitulation was to become effective, and when at last the moment came he looked out of his window. 'In the street a few people. They are silent. . . . The clock strikes eight. Now the war is really over.'

In Wageningen, ruined and deserted since September 1944, on Saturday, 5 May, the last preparations were made for the ceremony at which General Blaskowitz would surrender his 120,000 men to General Foulkes. In the heavily damaged De Wereld Hotel some trestle tables were carried into the dining-room, and kitchen chairs placed round them. The wallpaper was torn, and through the glassless windows and the cracks in the walls the wind blew in freely. But the sun was shining.

The thoughts of at least one former inhabitant of Wageningen, Douwenga, went back to the same month of May, five years ago, when that same place had been the scene of triumph for the Germans. 'The German officers sat there after the destruction of our town, well fed and polished under the blossoming chestnut trees in the garden of the hotel.' The Dutch Army had just capitulated. 'A stream of homeless refugees trailed past through the ruins of the destroyed houses.' Douwenga had been waiting for a pass to be able to enter the town. 'Suddenly one of the women of our group of three families, which shared joys and sorrows in those terrible days, burst out in tears and wanted to attack the usurpers. . . .' Now this same stage, he thought with delight, 'is being used for the humiliation of the once so powerful Third Reich'.

Prince Bernhard was ready to go early that morning. The Canadians had invited him not only as Commander of the Dutch Army, but also because he knew the German mentality. 'It is for us of great value', a Canadian officer had remarked, 'that he could intervene and put the Germans in their own manner in their place if they would be too arrogant.' What the Prince thought about this reference to his German origin nobody knows, but on Saturday, 5 May, he travelled with a few members of his staff from Apeldoorn in two German Mercedes, the RK1, and the recently discovered RK2, left behind by Seyss-Inquart in Groningen. His secretary, Marie Brave Maks, had not wanted to miss this historic moment and came as a stowaway, hidden under rolls of paper. When the Prince discovered her, he gave her permission to come if she would keep an eye on his little white dog, Martin. 'He doesn't like that German General,' he warned.

Arriving at the hotel they found some Canadian officers and thirty-odd journalists, and five minutes later the Prince was joined by Foulkes, soon followed by the German convoy. A pale and obviously exhausted Blaskowitz got out and saluted. The waiting Dutch were surprised to see a rather dishevelled-looking citizen in a raincoat follow the German General out of the car, and be embraced by the other Dutchmen in their Allied uniforms. It was J. J. F. Borghouts, alias Peter Zuid, a Commander of the Forces of the Interior who had been dropped into Occupied territory in March to help instruct the Resistance fighters, and who now returned to the free world, thin and pale, but still with the same dirty little hat he had always worn.

The Prince's staff were delighted to see their friend safely back, and Marie Brave Maks was so excited that she forgot the little dog, who at once tried to bite Blaskowitz in his shiny boots.

The delegation quickly disappeared into the hotel, where they took their seats in the improvised conference room and where an unperturbed Foulkes was soon facing a nervous Blaskowitz. It was a businesslike gathering, and any atmosphere of victors and defeated was lacking. In a clear voice the Canadian Commander told the Germans that Montgomery had asked him to read the terms of surrender. 'Is the General prepared to accept my reading this and prepared to negotiate for turning his troops over to me?' The answer was a short 'Jawohl'. The Canadian told the German General what he had to do: keep his troops where they were till Canadian troops arrived and were able to assemble the Germans in certain places, from where they would be transported to Germany. They were allowed to keep their arms. He demanded, too, that explosives should be removed from sites which could endanger public installations.

The points were typed out on different slips of paper and Foulkes asked the interpreter to explain to Blaskowitz that he would not ask him to sign these separately, 'because I want it all on one piece of paper'. Blaskowitz agreed and asked for some time to consider the proposals. It was difficult for him to decide, he said, because so much was going through his head. He worried mainly about the difficulty of contacting his troops in time, which might lead to trouble if the Canadians came too soon. Foulkes understood him. 'That is all right. The General can take this away with him and study it, and I just require a receipt that he has received it. That's all.'

The Prince, who in a way felt sorry for the German General – 'a military man of the old sort' – opened the discussion in the role of Commander of his Forces of the Interior, and it led to the only incident during this conference. When the German General spoke of the Resistance fighters as 'Schweinhunde' (pigs) the Prince jumped up and bit back: 'And it's *you* who said that – you who deal with the SS.' Calming down, he asked Blaskowitz to make a serious effort to disarm the SS and the Landwacht, but the General admitted: 'I cannot lock them up, I have not the power, but I'll agree to concentrate them all in one place.'

At half-past four the talks were over. Blaskowitz signed a receipt for the conditions, and the surrender of his army was in effect. Those waiting outside saw the door of the De Wereld Hotel open again, and the German General, looking considerably less arrogant, reappeared. The Prince had a few last words with him, a Dutchman handed him some documents and the German drove off. Nobody moved or jeered.

It was time for the Prince to inform his Dutch soldiers in western Holland about their role, or, rather, about the fact that there was no role for them. He drove to Eindhoven, where on Radio Rising Netherlands he delivered a speech which he hoped would prevent disorder and violence. After praising the strength and perseverance of the Dutch in general, he asked particularly that the Forces of the Interior should not take any 'rash actions'. It was known to them by now that they were to stay unarmed for at least another three days, and the Prince begged them to comply with the directions of SHAEF. 'I expect that you will observe these orders both in your own interest and in the interest of peace and order,' he stated, ending with the reminder that 'a difficult but gratifying task awaits our people. . . . Know and accept your responsibilities.'

He had never expected his appeal to be effective, and it was certainly very hard for the Resistance fighters. One leader of a little group wrote in his diary how he had tried desperately to change the mind of his local commander. 'But he can't do it. I tell him of our disappointment, that we wanted to be present in these historic days. It was promised to us and we had practised for it. But it doesn't help.' And to the enormous relief of their Commander, Prince Bernhard, he, like all the others in western Holland, obeyed his orders.

Later that day Prime Minister Gerbrandy, still in London, confirmed the signing of the capitulation. 'The German Reich with its criminal rulers . . . is beaten. . . . Drink the cup of joy to the bottom, but don't forget the suffering that's mixed in it,' he told the Dutch. His words, however, were received that evening with some irritation in Holland. The day had brought disappointment and disillusionment. Impatient as they were, the Dutch had expected that the Allied armies would roll in at once. Thousands of them had been waiting outside the cities on the main roads, but no one came and one Rotterdammer wondered irritably: 'Do I feel free? We still have to be inside, and when we put out the flag we are shot at. The Huns are everywhere.'

It was for many very difficult to imagine that they were free, and even harder to understand what freedom meant. Someone summed it all up: 'There will be food again; gas, light and water; trains and trams will be running; our men will come back from forced labour in Germany; our prisoners of war and students will return; I will be able to go out whenever I want; I can remove the blackout paper; I don't have to be afraid when a car comes into the street; nor when the doorbell rings at night; there will be papers, cinemas, dancing and cafés; families will be reunited if torture has not been fatal; there will be no Westerbork, Amersfoort and Vught built by the Huns; I can ride my bike without fear of confiscation, and I can listen to any radio station I choose; school and office hours will be normal again, and after the defeat of Japan humanity will find a means to banish war once and for all.'

But even this summary made it impossible to grasp it all, and his last lines reflected the feelings of hundreds and thousands of Dutch people, who after the first enthusiasm of the night before felt lost – as if they were living in an unreal dream, in an emptiness: 'I had thought that the end would mean a relief, something like taking off a leaden suit. But it is different. I just cannot get used to the thought of being really free.'

CHAPTER TWENTY-EIGHT

'Welcome, Boys'

'AT LAST we are master of our own land, in our own houses. Beaten is the enemy, from east to west, from north to south, gone are the firing squad, the prison and the torture-camps, over the nameless pressure, the thought of prosecution, ended is the tale of famine.' For Queen Wilhelmina, on Saturday, 5 May, in the studios of Radio Rising Netherlands in Eindhoven, it was more than a dramatic moment. That evening she spoke for the first time in her liberated kingdom to a free nation, and as she said: 'Our language knows no words for what goes on in our hearts in this, our hour of liberation.' The few days she had spent in Anneville had not destroyed her ideals of a new society, a chastened nation. On the contrary, it had strengthened them, and she said so: 'Under the usurper's pressure we have rediscovered ourselves, our national force has been reawakened. We will give proof of this . . . let's join hands, driven by our inner force, and not loiter on the road down which they, whom we honour so much, have preceded us, as they have testified with their blood.'

If it had been up to her, she would have rushed to the north-west, but it was still considered too dangerous. Instead she sent Erik Hazelhoff Roelfzema, 'the Soldier of Orange', with a wreath to Amsterdam, to lay it for her on the spot where, shortly before the surrender, twenty Amsterdammers had been executed. Roelfzema's car, however, broke down, and he had to hitch-hike his way to the capital, where he arrived on Sunday, 6 May, sitting on a load of dirty linen and carrying the royal wreath around his neck.

That Sunday, rainy and stormy, was a very strange day. Although the capitulation was signed, nobody yet knew when the Canadians would appear. The Germans were still roaming around, here and there shooting incidents were reported, in most places the flags had been taken down and the dancing had stopped. Commanders of the BS urged the citizens in pamphlets to be careful. The pent-up tension exploded here and there in attacks on NSB men – although it never came to the threatened 'Hatchet Day' – and, in particular, girls who had fraternised with the German soldiers had a rough time. They were dragged out of their houses and their heads shaved.

'I saw this sort of popular judgement four times,' one Dutchman wrote, but he felt little pity. 'They've got what they deserved.' He watched while the men shaved them with pocket scissors or even pocket knives, letting the girls finally go 'like plucked chickens'. Another witnessed an attack on an NSB headquarters. 'The windows have been smashed to pieces and now they're emptying the building. I see two beautiful Delft-blue vases fly through the air, books, papers, everything has to go. . . . The portrait of Hitler sails through the window and is trampled on by onlookers.'

The uncertainty of what exactly was going to happen was nerve-racking, especially when a declaration from Seyss-Inquart's deputy was nailed up on the few trees left in the big cities, announcing that there was no question of capitulation in Holland. Authority was still in the hands of the German Occupying Forces. 'Keep order and quiet. We will take action against demonstrations, if necessary with weapons.' 'It was the last lie of the Germans,' Dr Mees remarked, but it created an atmosphere of fear, and not without reason. The writer Walter Maass was present when a German raiding party discovered a hand grenade that Sunday in the cupboard of a sixteen-year-old boy. It was just an empty souvenir, but the commanding sergeant, slightly drunk, ordered the summary execution of the boy. One of the German soldiers found out that the weapon was harmless, and prevented the murder at the last minute.

In Rotterdam the situation was the most incomprehensible. When Diemer in all innocence went out for a stroll with an orange ribbon in his buttonhole, a passer-by warned him, 'Be careful, they are still shooting to kill', and only then did he hear that the German Commander of Rotterdam was refusing to surrender. Mayor Pieter Oud, who had already taken back his seat from his NSB predecessor, Mussert's deputy, Müller, found it wiser to disappear again to wait and see what was going to happen.

Initially it was the intention of the German Commander to turn a certain part of north Rotterdam into a citadel and fight on to the last man, but late on Sunday some Underground leaders received an invitation to come and meet the Commander in his office.

A newspaper, the *Vrije-Pers* ('Free Press'), reported the bizarre reception of the small group, who after arriving at the German headquarters had to wait for a while. 'We did not understand why,' one of them told the reporter, 'but we were soon wiser, because suddenly a number of barbarians, armed to the teeth, appeared from the cellar and encircled us, Sten guns at the ready and prepared with the well-known German grimness to attack if ordered.' The Dutchmen protested, but a German officer told them that this was the normal procedure and that they had nothing to fear. 'In the middle of this dispute another group of those heavily armed and dangerous-looking men surfaced, and we snarled at the SS officers that we were leaving at once.' One German, fat but fast, raced upstairs to warn the Commander, who appeared within seconds. 'He shouted from upstairs a few commands, giving his men a piece of his mind in such foul language that they scrambled in panic and fright down the stairs back into the cellar.' The meeting continued in a politer tone, and after one hour's negotiations the Germans gave in and promised to hand Rotterdam over to the Canadians as soon as they arrived.

A day earlier, another conference about the transfer of power had taken place in the Javastraat in The Hague, where the Confidential Councillors met in an atmosphere of confusion and uncertainty. The representatives of the Dutch Government were faced with a situation they had never foreseen. Although it was officially announced that the capitulation was a fact, the Germans were still masters. Van der Vlugt was running from pillar to post to persuade Schwebel and other German authorities to get the Army and German police off the streets, and to hand over to the Dutch police or the BS. But none of them wanted to go that far. Should the Councillors now try to stage a coup as in Italy? The Socialist leader Willem Drees found the comparison unrealistic. In Italy the partisans had risen while the war was still going on, he pointed out, and, besides, the BS in The Hague, for example, had only 250 to 300 able men, 'completely insufficient to consider an armed rising'. The consequence would be a bloodbath while Liberation was near.

On the other hand, chaos would follow if they did not act at all.

Reports came in of incidents in Rotterdam, Gouda, Leiden, Utrecht and Alkmaar, where the BS had either arrested the mayor or captured the town hall. In some cases BS men had disarmed German soldiers and were themselves arrested when the German police came to the aid of their compatriots. It was very difficult for the Councillors to decide what to do, and in the end they made only one gesture, and not a very impressive one. A telegram was sent to London in which they warned that the Germans were refusing to accept the capitulation, and were keeping their police force on the streets. The message went on: 'Here and there clashes because of jeering, destruction and other excesses. . . . First victims have fallen and situation gets more dangerous. . . . Demand fast execution of capitulation.' And with this lame cry for help the meeting was adjourned until next day.

The minutes of the Councillors' Sunday meeting were, however, considerably shorter. The Germans had conceded defeat in The Hague and at twelve o'clock Mayor S. J. R. de Monchy, reinstated after having been sacked by the Germans in 1940 during the pro-Orange demonstration on Prince Bernhard's birthday, came into the conference room to invite the Councillors to witness the hoisting of the flag on the St Jacobs Tower. 'It was decided to accept the invitation,' so the minutes stated.

For the first time the men who had worked so hard and long for this moment appeared from behind the scenes to show themselves to the public, now flocking to watch the hoisting of the flag – the signal for every citizen of The Hague that they were free to celebrate. The chairman, Bosch van Rosenthal, who had just heard that his brother had been executed in April, read the proclamation that he and the other Councillors had composed months ago: 'The Netherlands have regained their freedom. The tyranny that pierced our hearts has been driven away.' The crowd cheered and a little Jewish girl, with the yellow star still on her coat, advanced and handed Mayor De Monchy a bunch of flowers. With a gentle hand he removed the star.

Delft followed four hours later with the booming chime of the heavy bell in its old tower, 'Oude Jan'. 'I cannot see the flag on the New Church, but my neighbour shouted to me that it is waving,' one citizen wrote. He hurried to the market-place. 'It is overcrowded. . . . Near the statue of Hugo Grotius is commotion and when I look carefully I see the reason; two "Hun-girls" are being shaved. They are the first of a long and shameful list.' A movement on the balcony took his attention away from the incident: 'A large number of people appeared, amongst whom I recognise our former mayor with his wife. He is surrounded by the BS, the Resistance, which has surfaced at last. They make a somewhat amateurish impression in their overalls and with their helmets.' Their automatic weapons looked good, he thought: but he could not help worrying if they knew how to handle them. The mayor asked for silence. . . . 'I notice that he is shouting aloud, but of the whole proclamation I hear only the words "citizens" and a little later "we are free". . . . Finally we all sing, moved, the good old Wilhelmus.'

In Rotterdam that evening Diemer listened enviously to the stories of his son and daughter, who had come from The Hague on their bikes. There, they were free, while in Rotterdam Germans and BS were still confronting each other, although – as he had heard by now – the Germans had at least promised to hand over the command to the Allied troops when they arrived.

In Amsterdam at eight o'clock in the evening A. H. van Namen, still in the prison on the Weteringschaus and under threat of being taken to the notorious prison in Scheveningen, was at last allowed to pack. 'Sie können nach Hause' – 'You can go home.' But, when he was on the point of leaving, the 'worst torture of my life' followed. The Commander called him back and said that someone in the SD wished to have a word with him. 'Two hours long I paced through the prison. Nobody came. . . . I tried to kill time by talking to the guards, SS men who all had their excuses: "We are not responsible for what has happened here. Orders are orders." ' He walked past the cells, still occupied by five men, and heard one of them saying: 'But tomorrow we will be free!' He would never know what happened to them, only that on Ascension Day they still had not been found. . . . 'At ten o'clock the Commander shook my hand with a happy face.' The SD man had not turned up, and he could really go. 'Floating, I walked out of the prison and fell in the arms of those with whom I shared joy and sorrow for three, four years.' It was unbelievable to him. 'I have the freedom, a new freedom, they have given me a new life back. . . .'

On the morning of Monday, 7 May, at seven o'clock, the first

Allied soldiers entered western Holland. After a grey weekend
the sun was shining as a reconnaissance platoon of Yorkshiremen
from the 49th British Division drove up to Utrecht as its first
liberators. Radio Oranje reported that the inhabitants had welcomed the men with incredible enthusiasm, even more so than in
Paris, while the bells of Holland's highest tower, the Dom, were
pealing. The same broadcast gave us the news of Germany's total
unconditional surrender. The order from Admiral Doenitz, the
German President, was given early in the morning from Flens-
burg and, while 550 bombers from the RAF were busy dropping
another 1250 tons of peace-bombs full of food over Holland,
Field-Marshal Alfred Jodl and Admiral von Friedeburg came to
Eisenhower's headquarters at Reims to sign the documents of
surrender at 2.40 p.m.

Ike himself was not present at the ceremony, but when he
received the two Germans afterwards he asked them severely if
they understood the conditions and if they were able to implement them. They were, the two men said, and Jodl asked if he
could say a word. He got permission and with a halting voice he
stated that from the moment of this signature 'the German nation
and the German Armies were at the mercy of the conquerors'.
The German Foreign Minister, Schwerin von Krosigk, told the
Germans on the radio: 'After almost six years of incomparable
hardship Germany has given way to the overwhelming Allied
forces.' The Third Reich of a Thousand Years had come to an
end after only twelve.

In The Hague the NSB leader Anton Mussert waited re-
signedly in the office of his so-called State Secretariat on the
Korte Vijverberg. Three days earlier he had been discharged
from hospital, where he had been admitted with concussion after
a car accident. There was no fighting spirit left in him, and when
the Canadians came to arrest him he followed without protest.
'The man who one week ago still said he would fight till death
gave himself up quietly,' sneered the radio for the last time.

In Amsterdam's German headquarters the telephone rang that
day only once, and the conversation that followed lasted an hour.
When Amsterdam's Commander, Major Körner, finally hung
up, everybody waited tensely. At last he spoke: Germany had
surrendered, and all explosives placed in the town were to be
removed. There was some confusion about what to do with them,

292

and one officer proposed they should be thrown in one of the canals, but Körner thought it better to store them in a place which could be guarded against 'terrorists'.

While his men went to work, Körner began to dictate his last orders. 'He was no longer able to concentrate. He dictated haltingly and with many errors,' one of his staff recalled. 'The secretary had to repeat the text constantly. . . . His eyes were sunken, his face was blotched, his voice tired, and he ended his work with the words: "We never thought it would come to this." '

Amsterdam itself had to live through one more tragedy. Gathering together on Monday morning on the Dam – where the grim grey baroque palace, built in Holland's golden seventeenth century, was as always the centre for any national celebration – the Amsterdammers were waiting. Nobody knew for what. The Queen? The Canadian liberators?

The mood was gay, and people danced and sang round a barrel organ, when suddenly shots rang out. Mr Gijsbert van Hall, later mayor of Amsterdam, had come from nearby Blaricum to the capital on his bicycle to meet some friends, and he witnessed the scene from the Industrial Club on the corner of Dam and Rokin. The first shots were followed by a hail of bullets, fired by a bunch of drunken German naval officers in the Grote Club – the 'big club' – on the corner of the Kalverstraat. 'It was a ghastly sight,' he wrote later. 'The people ran away in panic . . . and in a few seconds the Dam was empty, except for dozens of dying and wounded persons.' After a few minutes a boy in a Boy Scout uniform arrived on a carrier cycle with a white flag. He pushed it on to the square where he lifted one or two hurt people on to his cycle. 'We held our breath,' Van Hall remembered, 'but fortunately the Germans did not shoot anymore.'

A little later a car came racing down the Rokin in which sat some German 'Green' policemen, rigidly disciplined in rows of four, guns between their legs. 'It was obvious that they had come to make an end to the massacre,' Van Hall recorded, but some BS members didn't grasp the situation and aimed at the car. The Germans tumbled over each other, and one fell into the street. The driver stamped on his accelerator and disappeared in a hurry. In the meantime the Germans in the Grote Club had kept quiet. They had received a telephoned order to stop shooting which came from the Ortskommandant, the German Military commander – at least, so they thought. It was in fact an Austrian who had spoken to them, Dr H. A. R. Trampusch, who, having left his country after the *Anschluss* in 1938, had joined the Resistance in Holland during the war. On 7 May he was on the Dam, with some of his men, but when they wanted to shoot back with bazookas at the Germans in the Club he stopped them. He went to the telephone office behind the palace to telephone the drunken men, and his impeccable German was sufficient to change their minds – orders are orders. But for nineteen people it was too late. They had been killed, while another hundred and seventeen had been wounded.

When the Dutch entered the Grote Club later that day they discovered thousands of hand-grenades in the big hall. 'One can hardly imagine what would have happened if the BS had shot back with a bazooka,' Mr van Hall reflected.

While Amsterdam was mourning and The Hague celebrating, Rotterdam began at last to relax, if cautiously. The citizens, seeing the first BS men marching by, hesitantly hoisted some flags again and put the orange badges back on their coats. The street signs which had names of members of the royal family were reinstated, and the NSB mayor Müller was arrested. Diemer, celebrating the liberation with some friends, heard a loud booing at ten o'clock that night, and looking outside discovered that the first followers of Mussert, who had not fled on Mad Tuesday, were being taken away from their houses and arrested by the BS. On his way back he stopped for a moment in the Hoflaan, where twenty candles burned for the twenty men executed there a few weeks earlier.

Next day the first Canadian, a dispatch rider, reached the city. 'In front of the Town Hall an enormous cheering crowd,' a Rotterdammer remembered. In the middle of the crowd he discovered a little man in khaki who was almost crushed in the excitement. 'Carried by the people, covered with flowers, he was taken into the Town Hall.' He followed and inside met two British reporters who preceded the arrival of the troops. They told him that on entering Rotterdam they at first thought they had never seen such a beautiful garden town . . . 'till we learned it was all demolition. It is worse than Liverpool.' Not far from Rotterdam, in Ridderkerk, the war's last massacre took place in the meantime. It happened when the mayor of the little town ordered some BS men to arrest a number of 'Hun-girls'. Led by policeman J. van den Berg, five men dressed in their blue overalls and with the orange armbands went ahead. At nine o'clock in the evening, while they were standing with three of their prisoners in front of the house of the local doctor, C. Berger, a German officer passed in a truck, together with his Dutch girlfriend. The BS men stopped them and ordered her to get out, but at a signal from the officer a German sergeant stormed out of a nearby house and threw two grenades – without effect. The ten drunken soldiers who had followed him, however, opened fire on the BS men, who fled with some bystanders inside the doctor's house. After firing at it for a while, the Germans stormed the house, dragged women and children outside, put the eleven men present against the wall and shot them down, one by one. Before they returned to their drinking bout, they executed a wounded man, who tried to hide himself behind a sofa but gave himself away by his moans.

When, a few minutes later, a BS command of twenty men came to the rescue, eight men were dead, including Dr Berger. The others, who had pretended to be shot, survived.

Tuesday, 8 May, had been proclaimed by Winston Churchill as VE-Day, Victory in Europe Day. 'What a shame that Roosevelt will not be with us this day,' Dr Mees wrote, but most people had no time to think about those things. Although Prince Bernhard had by now stopped the celebrations at Spelderholt, most Dutch people were preparing themselves for the climax of their liberation.

Radio Rising Netherlands had announced that the Allied troops were on their way. 'They have a long march behind them,' the broadcaster said. 'They've come from Egypt and Tunisia, they have the dust of Sicily and the mud of Cassino on their boots. They have fought in Normandy, at the Scheldt, at Arnhem – and now they will come to Amsterdam, Rotterdam, The Hague and Utrecht, to Hook of Holland and Den Helder, to Alkmaar and Hilversum. . . .'

There, in Hilversum, I was waiting on 8 May, tense and excited, very early in the morning on the Groest, one of the main thoroughfares in the town. I was standing at the foot of the impressive St Vitus Church, opposite the once so glamorous Gooiland Hotel, its shiny white-tiled façade now covered with grime, and many of its windows replaced by cardboard. A huge red, white and blue flag tried to hide the damage and a long banner shouted 'Welcome, Liberators'.

The trees on the Groest, too big and heavy to be hacked down, were in full green, and orange ribbons spanned the road. Hundred of flags flapped in the gentle spring breeze, and they gave the town an atmosphere of gaiety I'd never known. Children in orange skirts and shirts, women in what was left of their Sunday best, young men in suits that had become too large, they all pattered around on their wooden or cork soles and their clogs, with flags in their hands and orange ribbons in their hair, badges on their lapels or sashes around their shoulders – and smiling happily.

A feast of colour was lining the street. A barrel-organ played the Wilhelmus, followed by Holland's wartime hit, 'Ouwe Taaie' ('Old Tough'), or the good old 'We're Going to Hang Out the Washing on the Siegfried Line'. People joined the music, and now and then slogans such as 'Long Live Orange' and 'Hooray for the Tommies' rose from the crowd like a wave, while we waited for the magic moment.

Suddenly a cry – 'There they come' – a heavy rumble . . . and around the bend the first tanks appeared. The Canadian soldiers, healthy-looking big chaps with broad grins, were hardly visible. On the tanks and trucks scores of skinny children and girls were seated triumphantly, even on the turrets and the guns, almost hiding our heroes. Good-humouredly they were pulled down by others who wanted to have a festive ride or to hug the soldiers. Chewing-gum and cigarettes flew through the air, and flowers were thrown back, while the parade moved very slowly, rattling along the Groest. People shouted themselves hoarse, some cried without shame, others laughed almost hysterically.

Everybody waved and waved and cheered – 'Welcome, boys'. The soldiers, who must have seen some enthusiastic receptions before, got carried away nevertheless, and one of them, a happy smiling girl around his neck, shouted: 'We're here to stay.' Another cheer went up. They were here to stay; freedom was here to stay. The proof had arrived – five years minus two days after the Germans had marched into the Netherlands.

CHAPTER TWENTY-NINE

An Empty Country

THE MAY days of 1945 were a happy time for most Dutch people. In Hilversum the Canadians set up camp in what was left of the Korversbos, not far from where I lived. They were daily invaded by us little boys and girls, and we all chewed gum as if we'd never done anything else. Those bronze, sturdily built young men were warm-hearted, and so different from the grim and humourless Germans. They were generous with their tins of food, their beer and their cigarettes, and readily shared their rations with the bony creatures we were. Hundreds of young Dutchmen lost their girlfriends – at least, for a time – to the attractions of a pair of nylon stockings; and, while children and girls had a good time, the young Dutchmen – thin, pale and weak compared to the healthy, tanned and virile liberators – were soon less happy and certainly less lucky. One of them remembered that, when meeting a Canadian soldier, he was cut short even before he began a conversation with the ironical remark: 'Yes, yes, I know, welcome to Holland, got a smoke?'

Their green jeeps and trucks replaced the grey generator-propelled cars of the Germans, and hated German street-signs such as 'Zum Rathaus' gave way to more civilised signposts that said 'Town Hall'. Life was messy, unsettled, full of goodwill, and, not surprisingly, we were celebrating every night. Every self-respecting neighbourhood organised a street-party and the fraternisation was general. I made local history at one street fête by running full tilt into a metal wire, stretched across the road at the level of my neck. I came to lying on the divan at home, with worried faces peering down at me. I later heard proudly that I had stopped the party for a while, but the slight concussion the doctor said I had was not enough to stop me participating in next day's egg-and-spoon and sack races in another street, or watching an open-air performance of another Mickey Mouse cartoon. 'Give Me Five Minutes More' and 'Don't Fence Me In' were the new hit songs, and the deep-throated voice of Zarah Leander had made way for Bing Crosby and the Andrews Sisters. 'Meat and vegetables' out of brown army tins, and omelettes from dried egg-powder had replaced the soup from the central kitchens.

But all the festivities and celebrations those first days – how did we recover our strength so soon? – had for many Dutch people a disastrous effect. Dr Mees, cautious as always, mentioned it as early as 8 May. He was worried that the enthusiastic welcome would give the Canadians the wrong impression. 'They don't see the thousands who are too weak and underfed to come out, and who have to stay in bed.' He was right. Jack Drummond, leader of the specially equipped Nutrition Committee which entered the Western Provinces (the B2 area), first reported on 8 May: 'Treatment began in Rotterdam, The Hague and Amsterdam, on Thursday last. Position in these towns and Utrecht far better than anticipated. People in the streets thin but not starved.' The report ended with the remark: 'General impression of preliminary survey is that the situation is infinitely better than expected.'

General de Guingand, Montgomery's Chief of Staff, was, according to his book, *Operation Victory*, convinced that the situation in Holland was not all that bad. He thought that the Dutch Government in London was the origin of all the disaster stories, adding soothingly: 'You could not blame them, for naturally they were extremely anxious to ensure that everything possible was being done for their country . . . but', he believed, 'I think they were rather inclined to exaggerate the condition of starvation.'

But what the Allies saw was only a façade, behind which enormous misery was hidden, and they realised it soon enough. The head of the Netherlands District HQ, General Galloway, reported after a few days: 'On first appearance the condition of the people has proved unfortunately very deceptive. In the advent of Allied troops, the soldiers were greeted with cheers and bunting, and made a progress through a smiling countryside. But it was deceptive because men and women who are slowly dying of starvation in their beds unfortunately cannot walk gaily about the street waving flags.' He went on: 'It is an empty country, inhabited by a hungry and, in the towns, a semi-starved population.'

Louwes, who had been re-appointed as Commissioner for

Food Supply by the Chief of the Netherlands Military Authority, General Kruls, told English observers that if he had not held back some tons of potatoes and flour – sufficient to carry on till 5 May – the supplies would have given out on 15 April. And as Galloway noticed: 'The existing food supplies are practically nil. A day's ration consists of a very small cup of nasty "ersatz" soup, a very small piece of an unappetising and sticky substance called bread and a wafer of sugarbeet. It is hardly surprising that the large proportion of the population who were unable to buy on the black market have lost, on average, forty-five pounds in weight.'

Research had been done, he wrote. 'Out of a hundred people taken at random in the streets (and these are the people that are seen walking about every day and does not include those that are so weak that they remain indoors) fifteen per cent showed signs of malnutrition, fifty per cent were definitely under-nourished and thirty-five per cent were more or less normal. It is', he added, 'of interest to note that there were five times as many males suffering from starvation as females.'

Jack Drummond, who with his main assistant, Dr Beattie, and a team of experts had by now done his homework, too, wrote to London: 'Reports of the large number of deaths in the western Dutch towns from starvation are quite correct. We saw hundreds of people of both sexes and all ages as emaciated from starvation as any we had seen at Belsen concentration camp.'

To his disappointment the Dutch, no matter how starving they were, refused the special predigested proteins and vitamins which the English had developed. Most of the 70,000 doses the British factories had produced had to be thrown away, as after two days even the worst cases were fed up with its revoltingly sweet taste, and demanded potatoes, beans, bacon and bread.

Allied and Dutch teams went round the streets of Holland's big cities to try to discover the silently dying, and were stunned. They were followed by observers like the two journalists from Limburg, liberated eight months earlier, who came to Amsterdam on 21 May to see how 'the other half lived'. Hardly arrived at the Krasnapolsky Hotel on the Dam, they were besieged by sixty hungry people who queued for the leftovers from the hotel and begged the two men for food. 'When we gave one of them a slice of our white Limburg bread, they all came running to us and in a trice we had given away what was brought as our provisions for five days.' A doctor told them next day that all over Amsterdam at least 30,000 people were dying. In the hope of saving them, twenty-two special clinics had been opened.

M. B. Knowles, a representative of the British Ministry of Food at the Embassy in The Hague, travelling through Holland between 13 and 17 May, had long conversations with Drummond, who told him that in The Hague alone there were some 20,000 cases of extreme starvation – five per cent of the population. 'And if this figure should prove applicable to the other large towns as well,' Knowles reported to London, 'there might be anything up to 150,000 cases in the whole area.' He had been taken to a hospital and was deeply shocked. 'To the layman it was incredible that these people should still be living.'

Knowles visited a special kitchen, too, where 1200 daily meals, consisting of a soup of about 300 calories, were distributed. 'The applicants were mostly poor people and a large number of them were very emaciated, with the typical swollen ankles of the hunger oedema.' Worse still, every day they discovered other horrible cases, Drummond told Knowles, and he gave him two examples – 'one of an orphanage run by a pro-Nazi and the other a lunatic asylum in both of which the patients were on the "Belsen" level'. Knowles urged London to pour food into Holland 'with the greatest speed'.

His companion on the trip, Anthony Lousada, sent over by the British Ministry of Production, had his own observations to add. He was most shocked by a visit to a working-class home in Amsterdam. 'It was, as usual in Holland, very clean. During the winter they had been reduced to using doors and furniture for heating. Many trees in the streets have also been used. The house is occupied by an elderly woman and her daughter-in-law, aged 40, and two children. The daughter is in a very bad way, having had her ration card stolen. The mother-in-law could not feed her as all of the food was required by the children. The daughter-in-law was terrified when it was suggested she go into hospital. She was Jewish, and in her mind departure in an ambulance could only have one meaning.'

A visit to a soup-kitchen, run by the Catholic Church and feeding 600 children daily, revealed that thirty per cent of the children were ten to fifteen per cent under normal weight, and thirty per cent to an even greater degree, and he noticed that it was young children, in particular, between five and twelve years, young men from eighteen to thirty years old, and old women who seemed to be the worst sufferers.

Some of the statistics published in the middle of May by the Dutch Salvation Army spoke for themselves. Their people in The Hague made what might best be described as house-to-house searches, and their reports were heartbreaking.

Paulus Potterstraat: No. 82 – this family is in a serious state of semi-starvation; the father has already died of starvation. 33 – this is a very old lady who has been ill since September as a result of hunger. Her son is also in need of treatment; 70 – the baby has eczema; 43 – just returned from Germany; 40 – this is a very needy family. The mother is paralysed all down the side as a result of air-raid shock. . . . The family is neglected. She has a baby of 18 months who is very under-sized and in need of special feeding, the father is unemployed; 415 – small boy, has eaten nothing for fourteen days. Yesterday broke out in a rash. Father has badly blistered feet, having walked home from Germany. This family is unattended as their doctor has been arrested. 359 – father has lost 50 pounds in weight in three months; 400 – family in terrible condition. All floorboards have been taken up for fuel. Children aged 8, 7, 5 and 3 in very weak condition. Mother starving. Father just returned from Germany. Sleeping on the floor.

Another report dated 20 May reported that the Salvation Army in The Hague had dealt with 1171 cases in one relief section alone, of which 1127 were cases of malnutrition and 44 of semi-starvation.

In Rotterdam, according to Galloway, the situation was even worse, and the female volunteers who went around in that city found the first week after liberation no less than 33,000 cases of hunger oedema, which number had increased a week later to 55,000. 'The death-rate has risen day by day,' a doctor wrote. In certain parts, especially where wooden emergency houses had been erected after the heavy bombardments in 1940 and the destruction of autumn 1944, the situation was deplorable. 'In some of these houses we found such cases of misery and pollution that we had to evacuate the inhabitants, wash them, give them new clothes and shelter elsewhere.'

301

Circumstances gradually improved, thanks to aid from Sweden, Switzerland, England and the southern provinces where the population sacrificed part of their own meagre rations, but only very slowly, reported Sir Neville Bland, the British Ambassador to the Netherlands, to Churchill on 6 June.

Sir Neville had the opportunity to see it for himself, returning to Holland on Friday, 25 May, on board HMS *Garth*, to take up again the post he had been forced to leave five years earlier. His arrival in Rotterdam was an emotional affair and his old chauffeur's welcome was particularly touching – 'tears running down his cheeks'. The car was still the same as he had used when fleeing from the Nazis to the Hook of Holland on 13 May 1940. The Embassy in The Hague was full of flowers and messages like 'Welcome to our Liberators'.

Next day he visited the Secretary-General of Foreign Affairs, M. Snouck Hurgronje, but 'political conversation with Mr Snouck was out of the question', Sir Neville wrote to Churchill. 'He was too eager to talk, and enquire about old friends . . . the only thing of general interest he told me was that he, and everybody else who could afford it, had bought unashamedly in the black market, but for which he would never have survived.'

The Ambassador and his wife set out almost at once to discover how bad the situation was, and on Monday, 27 May, they visited a children's and a general hospital in The Hague, in the company of Drummond's assistant, Dr Beattie. Sir Neville left it to his wife to report to the British Prime Minister.

'The babies were tragic,' she began, 'they looked like old men – or else they lay in a semi-conscious state. But Dr Beattie said most of the ones that managed to get into hospital would be saved, though the mortality of the ones in the houses was terribly high. Most of the cases we saw had very distended stomachs, but no fat at all on their arms and legs; many of them were bleeding at the feet as the bones were barely covered with skin.' The babies were being kept alive on plasma and vitamins, but some of them would not put on weight and it would take a long time before they would be back to normal, the doctor told the Ambassador and his wife.

Next visit was to a feeding centre where, as Lady Bland reported, Dr Beattie found most of his hospital cases. At half-past twelve the first customers turned up, and the couple looked on in horror while they walked with great difficulty to their seats, but they were even more shocked when Dr Beattie told them that it often happened that people dropped dead while talking to him. A visit to a school was equally depressing. Nearly all the children were lice-ridden and had conjunctivitis. 'They are too apathetic to do much lessons and all have pale, grave faces with huge eyes and many have bad teeth.'

Finally they went to see the general hospital, which was over-crowded. But Dr Beattie had better news. 'He says the majority will recover and the difference after one week's nursing is amazing,' Lady Bland wrote. How great their hunger had been was shown by the habit many patients had of hiding their food – 'they cannot believe the rations will continue'. In the women's ward the patients looked terribly worn and thin, but Dr Beattie told her that the women had much better resistance than the men. 'All the cases had hunger oedema with immensely swollen legs, and sores on their bodies.'

The Ambassador added his own comment: 'There is no possible doubt that under-nourishment is universal and starvation and semi-starvation lamentably widespread.' He was more than upset. 'Most children had no socks or stockings, many had no shoes either . . . there are far fewer people about the streets than in normal times. Many people are riding bicycles without tyres, making a hideous noise on the cobbles. The streets are dirty and untidy . . . clothing is miscellaneous and uncouth . . . there is electric light in some districts . . . the water supply is functioning, but the pressure is low. The canals and squares are still caked with garbage . . . telephoning is impossible, except between the various army and naval authorities.' There was a terrible shortage of nurses and other medical personnel, mainly due to the fact that the Dutch authorities had maintained that they did not need the teams of British nurses who were ready to come out – an error the Dutch Prime Minister admitted only when it was too late.

But in spite of Sir Neville's gloomy report the worst was over. The Dutch authorities, together with the Red Cross and a great number of other volunteer organisations, had the situation almost completely under control by the end of May. With great enthusiasm and persistence they saved thousands and thousands of lives, treating in May alone more than 245,000 people in hospitals and special clinics, and distributing 185,000 rations daily to outside patients.

They could not, however, prevent the death from hunger in these first months of 1945 of three times the number of babies as in the same period of 1944, and twice that of children between one and five years old. The number of women that succumbed increased by 72 per cent and that of men by 168 per cent. To mention one more statistic: 15.03 persons in every thousand died in the Hunger Winter – against ten in 1944. A total of 18,000 people simply starved to death.

CHAPTER THIRTY

'The Old Things'

THE 18,000 Dutch men, women and children who starved to death during the Hunger Winter were only a small percentage of all those who died in the Second World War fighting in and for the Netherlands. The Liberation of the country cost the lives of more than 50,000 Allied soldiers – Americans, Canadian, British, Belgians, French and Polish – and their bodies were either sent home or laid to rest in Dutch soil. The thousands of little white crosses in the military cemeteries form an eternal memorial, as do the graves of the 4500 Dutch soldiers who fell for their own country, and the 258 prisoners of war who perished in German camps. More than 1500 Dutch sailors found a grave at sea.

The 18,000 victims of the Hunger Winter were also only a fraction of the Dutch citizens killed by the Nazi violence which swept like a savage wave over Holland during the five years of war. Of the 120,000 Jews who were dragged away to extermination-camps, 104,000 did not survive; 23,000 Dutchmen died in air raids; more than 5000 succumbed in prisons and concentration-camps; and of the 550,000 Dutch men who were forced to work in the Third Reich or for the Nazis in Holland – 16 per cent of the male population – 30,000 never returned.

Executions, most of them summary, claimed 2800 victims, 1560 of these during the Hunger Winter, 19 of them women. And statistics suggest that 50,000 Dutchmen died during the war simply because medical help was inadequate. A gruesome total of 237,300 Netherlanders – excluding the 10,000 who were killed fighting for the Germans – lost their lives, out of a population of 8.8 million.

These are just figures, but they represent much more. They reflect the suffering of millions who lost those they loved, their friends and their colleagues, and whose families were torn apart.

They represent also the millions of Dutchmen who survived the Nazi terror in a totally devastated country. 'Neither the nation itself during Occupation nor I in England could imagine what would be left of our country and people after the war,' Queen Wilhelmina wrote in the last pages of her memoirs. 'We could not have suspected how widespread the destruction would be at the end of the struggle and how tired and physically weakened, and in what psychological condition our people would return to freedom.'

The Queen had returned to The Hague at the end of May to take up residence in a simple house in Scheveningen; General Kruls, Chief of the Military Authority, had taken over from the Confidential Councillors in a cool but polite ceremony; and the Resistance fighter Willem Schermerhorn had succeeded Gerbrandy as Prime Minister on 14 May. The three were faced with what seemed an impossible task.

More than 400,000 people, driven from their homes, had to be brought back and often rehoused; more than 260,000 men straggled back from Germany and they had to be taken care of. Anthony Lousada of the British Ministry of Production witnessed their miserable homecoming in May. 'The long roads of Holland are a sad sight,' he wrote to London, 'everywhere there are knots of people asking for lifts.' He saw a large band of Dutch men, most of them just schoolboys, tramping back home. 'They were tired and limping, but many miles lay in front of them. Even when these people do reach their homes they may well find their houses destroyed or their families deported.' Not to speak of the land that they would find flooded – eight per cent of the whole country, one-third of that by sea water.

The inundation and destruction of the Netherlands had been carried out, like the looting, with German efficiency, amplified by Nazi viciousness. Reich Marshal Hermann Goering first formulated the principle of plunder in a speech to the State Commissioners in 1940, when he told them that they were not appointed to promote the wellbeing of the Occupied peoples, but to exploit them. And they never forgot it.

To begin with, the Dutch had to pay Seyss-Inquart three million guilders monthly for his 'keep', which did not include the military costs paid directly by the Dutch Ministry of Finance. On top of that he regularly imposed fines on towns guilty of trespassing against German rules. Amsterdam, for instance, had to pay 15 million guilders after the February strike of 1941, and Hilversum was fined 2.5 million guilders at the same time.

After the Russian campaign started in June 1941, Berlin demanded a 'voluntary' monthly contribution of 50 million guilders, and the total amount of money that disappeared into Nazi pockets during those years was about 15 billion guilders against the value of 1938 (more than 90 billion in today's terms).

That was only the cash. The Dutch Government tried to make an inventory of the capital goods that were stolen, and it amounted to 50,000 items from manufacturing and industries. Among them were 13,786 metal-working machines, 681 for woodwork, 2729 from the textile industry, 18,098 electric motors and 358 printing presses.

Large enterprises like the oil refineries at Pernis near Rotterdam and the steelworks at Ijmuiden were partly dismantled and shipped wholesale to Germany, and 406 large and small ships confiscated. Of the 19,000 barges Holland possessed at the beginning of the war, 8000 had been lost by the end, and of the dredgers, so important to the Dutch lowlands and their polders and canals, thirty-one were stolen and twenty-two sunk.

What had been, until September 1944, a reasonably well-organised programme of exploitation turned into sheer looting in the Hunger Winter. The railway strike gave the Germans an excuse – if they needed one – to take away 54 per cent of the locomotives, 79 per cent of the electric rolling stock, 65 per cent of the passenger carriages and 96 per cent of the freight trucks. In addition, 90,000 lengths of rail and 1.6 million sleepers were lifted and transported across the border. It made the State Railways, until September 1944 the obedient executive of German orders, the hardest-hit enterprise in the Netherlands.

Of the 100,000 motor-cars in Holland in 1940 no more than 34,000 were left to the Dutch, and of the 53,000 trucks only 14,000. They kept only 700 of their 4500 buses – like the cars and trucks mainly hidden away – and 25,000 of their 65,000 motorbikes, while the number of pedal bicycles was halved to two million. Church bells were taken down, historic guns removed, copperware had to be handed in, together with radio sets, clothing, blankets and whatever took the fancy of the Nazis; and, finally, 154,647 kilograms of refined gold disappeared into the safes of Berlin. Holland's livestock were not safe, either: 320,000 cows and 472,036 pigs ended up in Germany, together with 114,220 of the 325,000 horses.

How thoroughly this plunder was carried out was once again demonstrated in September 1944 when it was reported to Reichsminister Albert Speer, responsible for war production, that Holland could still contribute 'considerable stocks of meat and vegetables in tins'. The official had already given orders to dismantle all Dutch industrial installations for transport to Germany, but thought that the Dutch consumer should certainly not have what was lacking in the Third Reich. He proposed, therefore, that a convoy of trucks should be sent to pick up the food.

With the help of a special squad – and of some Dutch who received five per cent of the food for their treason – he ransacked the destitute country and with satisfaction discovered amongst other good things 12,000 kilograms of sugar, six freight trucks full of textiles, five carriages of pots and pans, 2259 bottles of spirit, 315 alarm clocks and 20,333 cigarette cases. As a present, he sent his boss in Berlin 10 kilograms of butter and 35 bars of chocolate.

A special case was the theft of Dutch works of art, and that of paintings in particular. The Netherlands, with its famous masters of the golden seventeenth century, was a paradise for German art-lovers and collectors, and already in 1943 Himmler was scheming to bring Dutch treasures to Berlin. When it was pointed out to him that moving them would only demonstrate that the Germans felt vulnerable in the west, Himmler dropped the idea.

In the autumn of 1944, however, Joseph Goebbels suddenly took an interest in the collection of the famous Amsterdam Rijksmuseum, including the priceless 'Nightwatch' by Rembrandt, sheltering in the caves of the St Pietersberg in Zuid-Limburg. This time it was Seyss-Inquart who refused to act. 'I had reliable guards placed at the shelter,' he said later at his trial in Nuremburg, 'and also sent an official from the Dutch Government who was authorised to hand over the pictures to the approaching enemy troops.' And so it happened.

It did not stop the Germans from stealing at least 346 seventeenth-century masterworks – among them 27 by Rembrandt, 12 by Frans Hals, 47 by Jan Steen and 40 by Rubens. Of the more modern paintings, 13 by Vincent van Gogh disappeared into German collections, later to be returned with the others.

It is difficult to estimate the cost of the material damage done to the Netherlands, but experts have calculated that it must have been around 12 billion guilders (180 billion at today's rate). Added to this was a debt of 4.5 billion guilders for goods delivered to Germany, but never paid, and finally the reconstruction and repairs which cost the Dutch at least another 12 billion guilders (180 billion).

Seventy per cent of all the damage had been done during the Hunger Winter, after September 1944 when Operation Market Garden failed and the railway strike had started. How far were these two events responsible for the disaster that overtook Holland that winter?

Victory at Arnhem would almost certainly have liberated the whole of the Netherlands in the autumn of 1944. The battle was bravely fought, and lost. Although the Germans at that time had been thoroughly demoralised, Arnhem restored their self-confidence with astonishing speed and any effort by the Allies to liberate north-western Holland after September 1944 without sufficient troops would probably have inflicted even worse horrors on the Dutch.

If defeat in Market Garden prolonged the sufferings of the Dutch, the railway strike undeniably added to the hardships of the Hunger Winter since it froze the transport of food supplies throughout Holland. The strike had been ordered by Professor Gerbrandy at the request of the Allies, and he felt it had to go on as it was the greatest contribution the Dutch could make to the Allied cause. His decision certainly had far-reaching consequences.

Up to the beginning of the railway strike the Dutch had been a people like any other, trying to live a normal life in spite of the Nazi Occupation. There were heroes and there were cowards, but most of the Dutch were ordinary law-abiding and hard-working people who simply longed for a peaceful and quiet life. Only 78,000 were brave – or, according to some, foolish – enough to join the Resistance part- or full-time, while the Dutch Nazi movement at its height counted almost the same number – 80,000 members.

The railway strike in September 1944 changed all this. It was the grand gesture against Nazism that the Dutch needed to restore their national pride – and many followed the example of the 30,000 railway workers. Those who had worked for the Resistance since the beginning of the war spoke condescendingly of 'September Warriors', but many of those felt sincerely that now Liberation was approaching they wished to contribute something positive. The terror the Germans exercised that winter, added to the general disgust at the Nazi system, strengthened Dutch opposition to it, and reinforced national unity. Most of the Dutch wanted to survive the war in honour; they wanted to show the world that they had been beaten, but not defeated, in spite of all their hardship. For once they were united in their refusal to work for or help the Nazi tyrants.

The end of the war, however, also brought this unity to an end. The country had to be rebuilt, and that was the first consideration for the sober-minded and solid burghers. The task kept them together for a while, but underneath this semblance of united reconstruction the old habits came back, and the renewal of the basic fabric of the political system, the creation of a new society of which Queen Wilhelmina, amongst others, had dreamed, soon took second place, to fade finally into oblivion.

Those who had hoped for a 'political adventure' and expected a thorough change in Dutch politics were disappointed. Democracy with all its failing was too deeply ingrained in the Dutch character to allow the more autocratic system that some had wished. But also those were betrayed who had planned for a less divided political world and who had dreamed of a greater unity amongst the Dutch. The saying that one Dutchman is a religion, two a church and three a schism was true of politics, too, and the first elections at the end of 1946 brought most of the old parties back into Parliament.

What many around her had foreseen and feared happened: Queen Wilhelmina, who with her strength and perseverance had been the nation's rallying-point during the war, was deeply disillusioned. 'We had not been able to reckon on the desolate reality,' she wrote sadly in her memoirs. 'Does this not make it understandable that much disappointment was in store for us? That many things did not go as hoped and expected? That promising plans were not carried out? And that many of the old things came back?' Worst of all for her: although Holland was resurrected, 'it was not that better country that the Resistance heroes had seen in their mind's eye when they went to meet their death'.

If it was not a better society, it was at least a free country that came out of the war, where an enormous amount of work had to be done. The Dutch realised this very soon, and in June the celebrations came to an end. The flags were folded away, the street parties were over, and the daily preoccupations returned.

Hilversum slowly began to look like its normal self again. Everything was still very scarce, but here and there the cardboard in broken windows was replaced by glass, the roots of the trees that had disappeared into our stoves were dug out and replaced by saplings, the camouflage net over the Town Hall tower was taken away, and my school re-opened after a thorough clean-up. But between lessons we still had to queue for our food and mess around with ration-coupons, shoes were not to be had and clothing was as rare, and the army tins of beans in tomato sauce, the egg powder and the 'meat and vegetables' were our staple diet for a long time to come.

Fear, however, had disappeared and, even if one worried about problems of food and clothing, a footstep in the street or a knock on the door was no longer a reason for dread. And when on the evening of 6 June, exactly one year after D-Day, someone rang the doorbell of our house in the Potgieterlaan I opened the door without a beating heart. Before me stood a sturdy boy who looked at me from behind his glasses. I asked him what he wanted and he laughed. 'I'm your brother.'

After an absence of two and a half months Wim had returned on his bike from Friesland, unrecognisable to me who was still used to thin and rather underfed people, and was now confronted with someone who looked 'normal', even if I called it fat. Another family, split up by the war, was reunited. We had survived the Hunger Winter.

Bibliography

BOOKS

Aalbers, P. G., *Slag om Arnhem* (Zutphen, 1975). Bibliography of printed sources.
Adriani Engels, M. J. and Wallagh, G. H., *Nacht over Nederland* (Amsterdam, 1946).
Albregts, R., *Van huis en haard verdreven* (Middelharnis, 1945).
Angus, Tom, *Men of Arnhem* (London, 1976).
B., Tj. de, *De Slag om Zutphen* (Zutphen, 1945).
Baardman, C., *Modder is gevaarlijk* (The Hague, n.d.).
—, *Wat de griend verborg* (The Hague, n.d.).
Baarle, W. H. van, *Slag om B2* (1945).
Bergh, Joris van den, *De post in de Vloeiweide* (Breda, 1945).
Besgen, Achim, *Der Stille Befehl* (Munich, 1960).
Beus, J. G. de, *De Wedergeboorte van het Koninkrijk* (London, 1942).
Bishop, Jim, *FDR's Last Year* (London, 1974).
Blokzijl, Max, *Ik zei tot ons volk . . .* (Utrecht, 1943).
Boer, J. F. M. de and Duparc, S., *Kroniek van Amsterdam over de jaren 1940–1945* (Amsterdam, 1948).
Boeree, Th. A., *Kroniek van Ede gedurende de bezettingstijd* (Ede, n.d.).
Boerema, I. (ed.), *Medische ervaringen in Nederland tijdens de Bezetting* (Groningen, 1947).
Bok, J., *De kliniek der hongerziekte* (Leiden, 1949).
Boom, Tine, *Zo was het: fourageren in Drente* (Zaandam, 1945).
Boorder, R. Tj. de and Kruiderink, W., *Rovers plunderen Arnhem* (Arnhem, 1945).
Bout, D. C. A. (ed.), *In de strijd om ons volksbestaan* (The Hague, 1947).
Boven, Adriaan van, *Jan Jansen in bezet gebied* (Kampen, 1946).
Brave Maks, Marie, *Prins Bernhard in oorlogstijd* (Amsterdam, 1962).
Broek, H. J. van den, *Hier Radio Oranje* (Amsterdam, n.d.).
Butcher, Harry Cecil, *Three Years with Eisenhower* (New York, 1946).
Buytendijk, F. J. J. and others, *De reactie van ons volk op de bevrijding* (Groningen, 1946).
Campen, S. I. P. van, *The Quest for Security* (The Hague, 1956).
Carlgren, W. M., *Swedish Foreign Policy during the Second World War* (London, 1977).

Churchill, Winston S., *The Second World War*, vol. VI (London, 1954).

Clerq, G. de, *Amsterdam tijdens de hongerperiode* (Amsterdam, 1945).

Cohen, Elie Aron, *Het Duitse Concentratiekamp* (Amsterdam, 1952).

Coles, Harry L. and Weinberg, Albert K., *Civil Affairs: soldiers become governors* (Washington, DC, 1964).

Cookridge, E. H., *Inside SOE* (London, 1966).

Davids, Henriette, *Mijn levenslied* (Gouda, 1948).

Dekker, C. and others, *1940–1945, een analyse van het verzet* (Amsterdam, 1945).

Dekker, Maurits, *Jozef duikt* (Utrecht, 1961).

Delft, A. J. A. C. van, *Zwarte Handel* (Amsterdam, 1945).

Dell, Joh. C. C., *Zutphen in dagen van spanning* (Zutphen, n.d.).

Diemer, H., *Op den rand van leven en dood* (Utrecht, 1946).

Doelman, C., *Arnhem, stad der berzitlozen* (Arnhem, 1945).

Donnison, F. S. V., *Civil Affairs and Military Government in North-West Europe, 1944–46* (London, 1961).

Doolaard, A. den, *Europa tegen de Moffen* (Amsterdam, 1946).

Douwenga, J., *Vlucht* (Wageningen, 1946).

Drees, Willem, *Neerslag van een werkzaam leven* (Assen, 1972).

—, *Van Mei tot Mei* (Assen, 1958).

Driel, B. van, *Commandogroep Biesbosch* (Helmond, 1945).

Drummond, Sir Jack, *Malnutrition and Starvation in Western Netherlands* (The Hague, 1948).

Eisenhower, Dwight D., *Crusade in Europe* (London, 1949).

—, *Papers*, vol. IV (London, 1970).

Ellis, L. F. and others, *Victory in the West*, 2 vols (London, 1962).

Epstein, M. (ed.), *The Annual Register 1944, 1945* (London, 1946).

Essame, Hubert, *The Battle for Germany* (London, 1969).

F., J. W., *Ons laatste halfjaar oorlog achter Arnhem's front* (Doetinchem, 1946).

Farrar-Hockley, Anthony, *Arnhem, Parachutisten vallen uit de hemel* (Utrecht, 1972).

Feldkamp, C., *De begrafenis-moeilijkheden in 1945 te Amsterdam* (Amsterdam, n.d.).

Frederiks, K. J., *Op de bres, 1940–1944* (The Hague, 1945).

Frequin, Louis and others, *Arnhems kruisweg* (Amsterdam, 1946).

Friedman-van der Heide, Reine, *Drie processen* (Amsterdam, 1946).

Gerbrandy, Pieter S., *Eenige hoofdpunten van het regeringsbeleid in Londen gedurende de oorlogsjaren 1940–45* (The Hague, 1946).

Gerritsen, J. and others, *Burgers in bezettingstijd* (Nijkerk, 1945).

Goudriaan, J., *Vriend en vijand* (Amsterdam, 1961).

Graaf, F. A. de, *Op leven en dood* (Rotterdam, 1946).

Groen, Koos and Maanen, Willem G. van, *Putten op de Veluwe* (Zutphen, 1977).

Groot, Norbert A. de, *Als sterren van de hemel* (Bussum, 1977).

Groskamp-ten Have, Amy, *Daar wordt gebeld . . .* (Amsterdam, 1945).

Guingand, Sir Francis Wilfred de, *Operation Victory* (London, 1947).
Hackett, Gen. Sir John W., *I Was a Stranger* (London, 1977).
Hall, G. van, *Ervaringen van een Amsterdammer* (Amsterdam, 1976).
Hatch, Alden, *HRH Prince Bernhard of the Netherlands* (London, 1962).
Hawes, Stephen and White, Ralph (eds), *Resistance in Europe 1939–45* (London, 1975).
Hawkins, D. and Boyd, D. (eds), *War Report* (London, 1946).
Hazelhoff Roelfzema, Erik, *Soldaat van Oranje 1940–45* (Baarn, n.d.).
Heaps, Leo, *The Grey Goose of Arnhem* (London, 1976).
Heukelom, W. H. J., *Kleine klompjes* (Panningen, 1945).
Heule, T. van, *Nederland en het werelddrama* (Meppel, 1945).
Heydecker, J. J. and Leeb, J., *Opmars naar de galg – het proces van Neurenberg* (Amsterdam, 1961).
Hibbert, Christopher, *The Battle of Arnhem* (London, 1962).
Hijmans, A., *Wat allereerst nodig is* (Alten, 1946).
Hilten, D. A. van, *Van Capitulatie tot Capitulatie* (Leiden, 1949).
Hirschfeld, H. M., *Herinneringen uit de bezettingstijd* (Amsterdam, 1960).
't Hoen, I. J. and Witte, J. C., *Zet en Tegenzet* (Zaandijk, 1976).
Hoets, Pieter Hans, *Vrijgevaren* (Rotterdam, 1976).
Hofland, H. J. A. and others, *Vastberaden, maar soepel en met mate* (Amsterdam, 1976).
Hoogh, H. P. de and Flines, G. de, *Onder het Hakenkuis* (Deventer, 1945).
Horrocks, Sir Brian, *Corps Commander* (London, 1977).
Iddekinge, P. R. A. van, *Arnhem September 1944* (Arnhem, 1969).
Jacobsen, Hans A. and Dollinger, Hans (eds), *Der Zweite Weltkrieg in Bildern und Dokumenten*, vols IX–X (Munich, 1968).
Jong, Louis de, *De Bezetting* (Amsterdam, 1973).
—, *Het Koninkrijk der Nederlanden in de Tweede Wereldoorlog*, 8 vols (The Hague, 1969–78).
—, *Je maintiendrai . . .* (London, 1945).
—, *Tussentijds, Historische Studies* (Amsterdam, 1977).
Jong, Louis de and Stoppelman, Joseph W. F., *The Lion Rampant* (New York, 1943).
Jong, Salomon de, *Joodse oorlogsherinneringen* (Franeker, 1975).
Jonge, A. A. de, *Het Nationaal-Socialisme in Nederland* (The Hague, 1968).
Kammeyer, J. H. D., *Vijf jaar onder Duitschen druk* (n.d.).
Kersten, Felix, *Klerk en beul, Himmler van nabij* (Amsterdam, 1948).
—, *Memoirs, 1940–1945* (London, 1956).
Kessel, Lipmann, *Surgeon at Arms* (London, 1976).
Kleffens, E. N. van, *The Rape of the Netherlands* (London, n.d.).
Klein, W. C. and Grient Dreux, C. P. de (eds), *Pittige verhalen uit onveilige tijden* (The Hague, 1947).
Knepflé, G. A., *In naam der waarheid* (Amsterdam, 1946).
Konijnenburg, Emiel van, *Roof-restitutie en reparatie* (The Hague, 1947).
Koning, B., *Bevrijding van Nederland 1944–1945* (Nijkerk, 1960).
Kortweg, A., *Oorlog aan de Scheldemond* (Middelburg, 1948).

Koster, M., *Honger in Rotterdam* (Rotterdam, 1945).

Kruijer, G. J., *Hongertochten: Amsterdam tijdens de Hongerwinter* (Meppel, 1951).

Kruls, H. J., *Generaal in Nederland* (Bussum, 1975).

Lammers, J., *Moeder des vaderlands* (1972).

Lammerts van Bueren, A., *De verwoesting van een oude keizerstad* (Nijmegen, n.d.).

Loewenheim, Francis L. and others (eds), *Roosevelt and Churchill: their secret wartime correspondence* (London, 1975).

Lunshof, Henk A., *Als dieven in de nacht* (Amsterdam, 1948).

Maass, Walter B., *The Netherlands at War, 1940–1945* (London, 1970).

Marley, David (ed.), *The Daily Telegraph Story of the War, 1944, 1945*, 2 vols (London, 1945–6).

Martens, Allard and Dunlop, Daphne, *The Silent War* (London, 1961).

Mees, H., *Mijn oorlogsdagboek* (Rotterdam, 1945).

Merriam, Robert E., *The Battle of the Ardennes* (London, 1958).

Meulenbelt, J., *De Duitse tijd* (Utrecht, 1955).

Montgomery of Alamein, Viscount, *The Memoirs of Field-Marshal Montgomery* (London, 1958).

Mulder, Frans, *Ontvoering en ontvluchting* (Utrecht, 1945).

Mussert, Anton, *Het proces* (The Hague, 1948).

—, *Vijf nota's van Mussert aan Hitler* (The Hague, 1947).

Neuman, H. J., *Arthur Seyss-Inquart* (Utrecht, 1967).

Neve, Ed de, *NRXH* (The Hague, 1945).

Nierop, Is. van and Coster, Louis, *Westerbork* (The Hague, 1945).

North, John, *North-West Europe, 1944–45* (London, 1953).

Ojen, G. J. van, *De Binnenlandse strijdkrachten*, 2 vols (The Hague, 1972).

—, *Leven en werken van Henri Koot* (The Hague, 1978).

Penning, J. H., *Op dood spoor* (Amsterdam, 1945).

Pinto, Oresta, *Spycatcher* (London, 1955).

Pogue, Forrest C., *The Supreme Command* (Washington, DC, 1954).

Pompe, W. P. J., *Bevrijding* (Amsterdam, 1945).

Presser, J., *De nacht der Girondijnen* (1957).

—, *Ondergang, de vervolging en verdelging van het Nederlandse Jodendom (1940–1945)* (The Hague, 1965).

Presser, Sem, *Dat gebeurde hier* (1944).

Puchinger, G. (ed.), *Het dagboek van Mevrouw Colijn* (Kampen, 1960).

Raatgever, J. G., *Van Dolle Dinsdag tot de Bevrijding* (Amsterdam, n.d.).

Randwijk, H. M. van, *In de schaduw van gisteren, kroniek van het verzet* (Amsterdam, 1967).

Rauter, Hanns Albin, *Het proces* (The Hague, 1952).

Roosevelt, Elliot (ed.), *The Letters of Franklin D. Roosevelt*, vol. III (London, 1952).

Roosnek, K., *Hoe het was . . . November 1944–Augustus 1945* (Delft, 1973).

Rüter, A. J. C., *Rijden en staken, de Nederlandse Spoorwegen in oorlogstijd* (The Hague, 1960).

Rutten, Gerard, *Mijn papieren camera* (Bussum, 1976).
—, *Ontmoetingen met koningin Wilhelmina* (Utrecht, 1962).
Ryan, Cornelius, *A Bridge Too Far* (New York and London, 1974).
—, *The Last Battle* (New York and London, 1966).
Sandberg, H. W., *Witboek over de geschiedenis van het georganiseerde verzet* (Amsterdam, 1950).
Sanders, P., *Het Nationale Steunfonds* (The Hague, 1946).
Saunders, Hilary St George, *The Green Beret* (London, 1949).
Schnabel, Ernst, *The Footsteps of Anne Frank* (London, 1976).
Shulman, Milton, *Defeat in the West* (London, 1974).
Sijes, Benjamin Aaron, *Arbeidsinzet* (The Hague, 1966).
—, *De razzia van Rotterdam, 10–11 November 1944* (The Hague, 1951).
Sjenitzer-van Leening, T. M. (ed.), *Dagboekfragmenten 1940–1945* (The Hague, 1952).
Smedts, Mathieu, *Den Vaderland getrouwe . . .* (Amsterdam, 1962).
Smedts, Mathieu and Troost, C., *De lange nacht* (Amsterdam, 1965).
Smith, Walter Bedell, *Eisenhower's Six Great Decisions* (London, 1956).
Snoep, J., *Nederland in de branding* (Groningen, 1946).
Somer, J. M., *Zij sprongen in de nacht* (Assen, n.d.).
Speer, Albert, *Inside the Third Reich* (London, 1975).
Stacey, Charles Perry, *The Victory Campaign*, vol. III (Ottawa, 1960).
Stein, Zena and others, *Famine and Human Development: the Dutch Hunger Winter of 1944–45* (New York, 1975).
Stikker, Dirk U., *Memoires* (Rotterdam and The Hague, 1966).
Stokman, S. (ed.), *Het Verzet van de Nederlandsche Bisschoppen* (Utrecht, 1945).
Strijbos, Jan P., *De Noorvaarders* (Amsterdam, n.d.).
Sweers, B. M., *Vrije meningen in een vrij land* (Amsterdam, n.d.).
Swiecicki, Marek, *With the Red Devils at Arnhem* (London, 1945).
Tempel, J. van der, *Nederland in Londen* (Haarlem, 1947).
Thompson, R. W., *The 85 Days* (London, 1960).
Touw, H. C., *Het verzet der Hervormde Kerk*, 2 vols (The Hague, 1946).
Trevor-Roper, H. R., *De laatste dagen van Hitler* (The Hague, 1960), trans. of *The Last Days of Hitler*.
Trip de Beaufort, Agathe Henriette Laman, *Wilhelmina, 1880–1962* (The Hague, 1965).
Tromp, Th. P., *Verwoesting en wederopbouw* (Amsterdam, 1946).
Urquhart, R. E., *Arnhem* (London, 1960).
van der Heide, G., *Onder de handen van de rovers vandaan* (Arnhem, 1946).
van der Plas, Michel, *Mooie Vrede, een documentaire over Nederland in de jaren 1945–1955* (Utrecht, 1966).
van der Vlis, J. A., *Tragedie op Texel* (1957).
van der Vlist, Hendrika, *Die dag in September* (Bussum, 1975).
van der Woude, Johan, *Arnhem, betwiste stad* (Amsterdam, n.d.).
van der Zee, Sytze, *Voor Führer, Volk en Vaderland sneuvelde* (The Hague, 1975).

van der Zwan, Jaap, *De dag dat het Manna viel* (The Hague, n.d.).
Veld, E. in't, *De SS in Nederland*, 2 vols (The Hague, 1976).
Visser, J. G., *PTT 1940–1945* (The Hague, 1968).
Voeten, Bert, *Doortocht, een oorlogsdagboek 1940–1945* (Amsterdam, n.d.).
Vries, Leonard and Groot, J. de, *De Wervelwind, de Vliegende Hollander en andere uit de lucht verspreide vlugschriften* (Laren, 1974).
Vries, Leonard and others, *De jaren '40–'45, een documentaire* (Amsterdam, 1973).
Warmbrunn, Werner, *The Dutch under the German Occupation, 1940–45* (London, 1963).
Warrack, Graeme M., *Travel by Dark after Arnhem* (London, 1963).
Werkman, Evert (ed.), *Ik neem het niet* (Leiden, 1965).
Whiting, Charles and Trees, Wolfgang, *Van Dolle Dinsdag tot Bevrijding* (Haarlem, 1977).
Wilhelmina, Queen of the Netherlands, *Lonely but not Alone* (London, 1960).
Winkel, Lydia E., *De Ondergrondse Pers* (The Hague, 1954).
—, *Toen . . .* (The Hague, 1960).
Winkelman, P. H., *Heusden, geteisterd en bevrijd* (The Hague, 1950).
Wouters, Tj. (ed.), *Het drama van Putten* (Laren, 1948).
Zimmerman-Wolf, R. S. (ed.), *Het woord als wapen* (The Hague, 1952).
Zoetmulder, S. H. A. M. (ed.), *Nederland in den oorlog* (Utrecht, n.d.).

ARTICLES

Dols, prof. dr. ir. M. J. L., 'Enkele persoonlijke herinneringen aan het einde van de Hongerwinter '45', in *Voeding*, jaargang 16, no. 5, Mei 1955, pp.406–10.
Dols, prof. dr. ir. M. J. L. and Arcken, D. J. A. M. van, 'Food Supply and Nutrition in the Netherlands during and immediately after World War II', in *The Milbank Memorial Fund Quarterly* (New York), vol. XXIV, no. 4, October 1946, pp. 319–58; in Dutch in *Voeding*, jaargang 6, no. 7, Juli 1946, pp. 193–207.
Fock, C. L. W., 'De Nederlandse regering in Londen en de Spoorwegstaking', in *De Gids*, no. 12, December 1955, pp. 348–56.
Herweijer, A. W., 'Ziekteverschijneelen ten gevolge van ondervoeding, waargenomen gedurende de winter van 1944–45', in *Nederlandsch Tijdschrift voor Geneeskunde*, jaargang 90, no. 7/8, Februari 1946, pp. 123–6.
Sellin, Thorsten (ed.), 'The Netherlands during the Occupation', in *Annals of the American Academy of Political and Social Science*, vol. 245 (Philadelphia, Pa, 1946).

DOCUMENTS AND PAMPHLETS

Amersfoort, *Menschen trokken voorbij* (Utrecht, n.d.).

Amsterdam, *Amsterdam tussen invasie en bevrijding, juni 1944–mei 1945* (Amsterdam, n.d.).

—, *De eilanden en de Hongersnood* (Amsterdam, 1945).

—, *Geneeskundige en Gezondheidsdienst, 1944* (Amsterdam, n.d.).

—, *Maatschappelijk werk in de hoofdstad tijdens de Hongerwinter en na de bevrijding, Januari 1945–December 1946* (Amsterdam, 1947).

—, *Statistisch Jaarboek der Gemeente. 'Amsterdam gedurende de Tweede Wereldoorlog'* (Amsterdam, 1949).

—, *Weekrapport Contact-Commissie van het Rijksbureau voor de voedselvoorziening in Oorlogstijd* (Amsterdam, n.d.).

Baarn, *Kroniek van Baarn in de oorlogsjaren, 1940–1945* (Baarn, 1945).

Boskoop, *Winter 1944–1945 in Boskoop* (Boskoop, 1945).

Den Helder, *De Mannen van overste Wastenecker. De geschiedenis van de BS in N. Hollands Noorderkwartier* (Den Helder, 1947).

Eemland, *Verslag Werdeelcommissie van het Eemland-IKO Comite, 1944–1945* (Amersfoort, 1945).

Haarlem, *Winter 1944–1945* (Haarlem: Verslag Centraal Bureau voor Kindervoeding, n.d.).

Hall, Walraven van, *A Memoriam* (privately printed, n.d.).

Hilversum, *Gemeenteverslag over de jaren 1939–1949* (Hilversum, 1951).

Interkerkelijk Bureau voor Noodvoedselvoorziening (IKB), *Hongerend Volk, 1945 – en wat deed het IKB* (The Hague, 1945).

—, *Plaatselijk Interkerkelijk Bureau Verslag Eerste kwartaal 1945* (The Hague, 1945).

—, *Toelichting ter verstrekkingen op medische basis* (The Hague, 1945).

Koog-Zaandijk, *Rapport over de Nood-organisatie* (Zaandijk, 1945).

Laren, . . . *O Dat wintertje '45* (Laren, 1945).

Militair Gezag, *Hoe zit dat?* (Sectie voorlichting MG, 1945).

—, *Onderzoek naar sociale en hygiënische toestanden in het westen des lands,* sectie XIII (n.d.).

—, *Overzicht der werkzaamheden van het Militair Gezag gedurende de bijzondere staat van beleg* (n.d.).

Moordrecht, *Een lichtpunt in een donkeren tijd* (Moordrecht, 1945).

The Hague, *Commissie voorziening s'Gravenhage, Verslag der werkzaamheden in het tijdvak 11 April 1944–1 Augustus 1945* (n.d.).

—, *Het Duitsche aanbod tot een beeindiging fer feitelijke viajandelijkheden in het nog bezette Nederlandsche gebied van april 1945* (The Hague, 1946).

—, *Het onderwijs in Nederland. Verslag over de jaren 1944, 1945 en 1946* (The Hague, 1949).

—, *Regeringsbeleid 1940–1945(Enquêtecommissie)*, vols 4a, b, c, 5a, b, c, 7a, b (The Hague, 1950–5).

—, *Verslag over de jaren 1944 en 1945 van de geneeskundige hoofdinspecteur van de Volksgezondheid* (The Hague, 1949).

Verordnungsblatt für die bestetzten Niederlandische Gebiete, 5 vols (1940–5).

Vertrouwensmannen, *Verslag van de werkzaamheden van de Vertrouwens-mannen der regeering* (The Hague, 1946).

Watergraafsmeer, *Een jaar nood-comité, tuindorp Watergraafsmeer* (1946).

Index